WHAT ELSE IS PASTORAL?

What Else Is Pastoral?

*Renaissance Literature
and the Environment*

Ken Hiltner

Cornell University Press
Ithaca and London

First published 2011 by Cornell University Press
Printed in the United States of America

Library of Congress Cataloging-in-Publication Data

Hiltner, Ken.
    What else is pastoral? : Renaissance literature and the environment /
Ken Hiltner.
        p. cm.
    Includes bibliographical references and index.
    ISBN 978-0-8014-4940-6 (cloth : alk. paper)
    1. English literature—Early modern, 1500–1700—History and criticism.
2. Pastoral literature, English—History and criticism.   3. Nature in
literature.   4. Ecology in literature.   I. Title.
    PR418.P3H55 2011
    820.9'358209734—dc22   2010044420

Cornell University Press strives to use environmentally responsible
suppliers and materials to the fullest extent possible in the publishing of
its books. Such materials include vegetable-based, low-VOC inks and
acid-free papers that are recycled, totally chlorine-free, or partly composed
of nonwood fibers. For further information, visit our website at www.
cornellpress.cornell.edu.

Cloth printing   10 9 8 7 6 5 4 3 2 1

For Talya

Contents

Acknowledgments

I owe so many debts of thanks that it is difficult to know where to begin, other than to acknowledge that such generosity can never be adequately repaid. First, special thanks are due Barbara Lewalski. Without her kind, patient, and generous support and guidance, which involved reading seemingly endless revisions of this material, this book would never have come into being. I owe a similar debt to Gordon Teskey, who helped me work through the theoretical underpinnings of my approach, often during long and pleasant bike rides, and to Stephen Greenblatt, who patiently and repeatedly offered invaluable help and support along the way. I also owe thanks to many members of the faculty at Harvard University. Among them, Elaine Scarry, Jim Engel, and Marge Garber certainly deserve special note. The book also benefited enormously from suggestions made by Rob Watson, Angus Fletcher, John Rumrich, and Peter Potter.

I also want to thank my mother Caroline and my brother Harry, as my fascination with the environment began many years ago on our family's farm. Finally, my wife, Talya Meyers, who read a second round of seemingly endless revisions of this book, carefully line editing each, while generously offering suggestions and support at every turn, deserves my deepest gratitude.

Portions of my fifth chapter (as well as a few tidbits from other sections) have appeared, in somewhat different form, in three essays: "Early Modern Ecology," in *A Companion to English Renaissance Literature and Culture* (Blackwell, 2010); "Renaissance Literature and Our Contemporary Attitude Toward Global Warming," in *Interdisciplinary Studies in Literature and the Environment* 16.3 (summer 2009); and "'Belch'd fire and rowling smoke': Air Pollution in *Paradise Lost,*" in *Milton, Rights and Liberties* (Essays from the Eighth International Milton Conference, Peter Lang, 2006). A few paragraphs of material from chapter 1 appear in my entry on "Nature," in *The Princeton Encyclopedia of Poetry and Poetics* (Princeton University Press, 2011), and in the essay "Ripeness: Thoreau's Critique of Technological Modernity," in *The Concord Saunterer,* Special *Walden* Sesquicentennial Issue, ed. Richard J. Schneider (The Walden Society, 2004).

INTRODUCTION

This book argues that Renaissance pastoral poetry is more often a form of nature writing than one might think. This claim may seem puzzling to casual readers, who might even imagine pastoral to be the most common form of Renaissance nature writing, but it will likely be received with skepticism by the broad swath of literary critics who question whether early modern pastoral is generally concerned with the countryside at all. While acknowledging that pastoral literature begins to deal with literal landscapes starting in the eighteenth century, these critics, led by Paul Alpers and Annabel Patterson, argue that Renaissance pastoral is a highly figurative mode of writing that has little to do with the countryside—and everything to do with culture and politics. Understood this way, pastoral poetry is a mode of veiled writing that conceals biting critiques of contemporary politics behind pleasant tales of shepherds and their flocks. If there is an essential opposition in Renaissance pastoral, in this view it is not between rural countryside and city, but rather between country and court, with the former serving as foil to reveal corruption at the latter.

Focusing on politics, this approach unabashedly marginalizes the role of the environment.

Further adding to the suspicion that Renaissance pastoral is not a true form of nature writing is the seemingly prima-facie case that, to be deserving of the moniker "nature writing," such works should describe the natural world. While early modern pastoral literature sometimes provides images of the environment, it must be admitted that these descriptions, when present at all, are usually kept to a minimum. By contrast, what we generally think of as nature writing, such as that penned by Wordsworth or Thoreau, is replete with descriptions of the natural world. Why then is this not the case with Renaissance pastoral? Expressed more generally, if, as we are often told, mimesis is central to the working of literature, why then does Renaissance pastoral poetry, if indeed a form of nature writing, not offer detailed representations of the environment?

Setting aside these essentially literary questions, another issue quickly emerges. In this book, I argue that our current environmental crisis clearly has its roots in the Renaissance, a claim that may also be met with skepticism. Of course, certain environmental issues, such as deforestation, were timely ones in the early modern period. Studies such as Robert Pogue Harrison's *Forests: The Shadow of Civilization* make this point irrefutable.[1] However, Harrison makes equally clear that deforestation is by no means an early modern phenomenon, but rather has shadowed human civilizations for thousands of years. Because environmental changes resulting from technological modernity, such as widespread urban air pollution due to the burning of fossil fuels, seemingly had yet to emerge in Renaissance England, it is often assumed that the era of Wordsworth and Dickens differs fundamentally from that of Spenser and Milton. Even if a case could be made that a handful of Renaissance writers touch on truly modern environmental issues, it could be argued this is an anomaly, as environmental consciousness had not yet made a mass appearance in early modern England. By contrast, when such awareness indisputably came on the scene in the second half of the twentieth century in America and England, it was signaled by public demonstrations, carefully constructed arguments in its defense (often taking the form of environmental protest

---

1. See Robert Pogue Harrison, *Forests: The Shadow of Civilization* (Chicago: University of Chicago Press, 1992).

literature), legislative changes, and a general rise in environmental consciousness. Where is the evidence that any of this took place in Renaissance England?

The foregoing issue raises the concern of presentism. I have noticed a surprisingly common response, from both scholars and laypeople, when they learn that I approach Renaissance literature from an environmental perspective: most suspect that I am primarily interested in contemporary environmental issues. This is somewhat unusual in Renaissance studies. We do not, for example, expect Milton to have anything particularly useful to tell us about divorce today, even though he wrote important tracts on the subject, as the practice of divorce *then* was altogether unlike it is *now*. But with environmental issues, there is often the expectation that literature from the past should help us understand, perhaps even manage, our present environmental crisis. This expectation mirrors a major shift in ecocritical studies in the past decade. In the 1980s and 1990s, when environmental criticism emerged as an influential movement, there was often a preoccupation with nature writing, wilderness, and texts celebrating pristine environments (or at least those imagined as pristine), such as Thoreau's *Walden*. However, because concern over our present environmental crisis and issues like global warming is now fueling ecocritical interests, second-wave environmental critics often see texts that romanticize untouched environments as offering little insight into our present crisis. Consequently, eschewing fetishized accounts of pristine "nature," twenty-first-century ecocritics are often concerned with a variety of landscapes, including places like suburbs and cities, frequently directing themselves to sites of environmental devastation and texts that do the same.

However, as conventional wisdom holds that our present environmental crisis emerged alongside technological modernity and the so-called Industrial Revolution, ecocritics and casual readers alike are often doubtful when second-wave ecocritical approaches, such as my own, push back into the Renaissance, as these appear to be presentist projects that mistakenly see, as we say, *nunc pro tunc* ("now for then"), when then seems very different than now environmentally.

Complicating matters—and seemingly in a way that further cuts off scholars working in earlier periods from contemporary ecocritical debates— is the fact that twenty-first-century environmental criticism has been profoundly influenced by the environmental justice movement, which takes into account issues such as gender, class, race, and colonialism. In many respects, this movement did for ecocriticism what second-wave feminist critics, such as Gayatri Spivak, did in their field in the 1980s. Just as Spivak warned that it was both naïve and potentially dangerous to consider issues relating to gender without also taking into account a range of additional factors, such as class and race, the environmental justice movement made clear that ecocritics also need to consider these and other factors, including gender. As one might imagine, this complicates—and greatly enriches— the practice of environmental criticism. However, because truly modern environmental problems appear to postdate the Renaissance, it would in turn suggest that the cultural fallout from them, which is of special interest to the many ecocritics influenced by the environmental justice movement, would also come after the period.

Given the above concerns, I expect resistance to a green reading of Renaissance pastoral. Nonetheless, this book argues that (1) Renaissance pastoral, in addition to sometimes being a figurative mode masking political controversies, is also frequently concerned with literal landscapes, even though it does little to describe them, and (2) early modern England was indeed in the throes of what can only be described as a "modern" environmental crisis, which engendered a number of contemporary debates, some of which address issues of environmental justice that informed (and were informed by) both canonical and noncanonical literature of the period.

In order to begin building this case, I consider in chapter 1 what a surprising number of ecocritics have managed to avoid: nature. At first glance this may seem counterintuitive. After all, aren't ecocritics by definition necessarily concerned, at least to some extent, with nature? Perhaps, but the issue is enormously complicated, as Raymond Williams noted a generation ago, by the fact that "nature" may well be the most complex word, signifying the most difficult concept, in the English language.[2] To throw light on this complicated situation, my approach is to return to the ancient, though still profoundly illuminating, debate over nature and its representation recorded in Plato's *Cratylus*.

According to Aristotle, even at the end of his life Plato doubted whether we could ever be truly successful in our efforts to represent, by way of

---

2. Raymond Williams, *Keywords: A Vocabulary of Culture and Society,* rev. ed. (New York: Oxford University Press, 1983), 219.

language (or in any other way, for that matter), the physical environment revealed through sensory experience. The difficulty is that nature (*physis*), which pre-Socratic Greeks generally understood as endlessly varied and wildly in flux, shifts so quickly that, no sooner have we uttered a word (or produced some other sign) in an effort to signal it, than that which was to be signified has already changed and slipped away. True, Plato argued that not only can ethical concepts like Beauty and Justice be successfully represented by means of language, they form the basis of representation itself. In order to do so, he posited an immutable realm securely "beyond nature" (*meta-physikē*), and its relentless flux, where he imagined such Ideas as having actual existence. However, with respect to the environment revealed by our senses, the problem is that, without stable referents that are by definition metaphysical (which, as we shall see, cannot avoid being in tension with *physis*), such an environment can perhaps never truly be successfully represented. This issue is at once epistemological and cultural, as it raises both the question of what we know, as well as how we share it, by way of language. While a range of poststructural thinkers in the second half of the twentieth century made clear that this issue was never fully resolved, as Robert Watson compellingly argues in his *Back to Nature: The Green and the Real in the Late Renaissance* (although on a somewhat different register),[3] the question of whether nature could be successfully represented was very much open in the Renaissance.

My argument regarding this important question is simple: faced with this anxiety, some Renaissance poets and artists, including those that produced pastoral works, sidestep this issue by largely avoiding mimesis and representation. As we shall see repeatedly throughout this book, when confronted with an environment wildly in flux, these artists sometimes turn away from representation and its challenges, choosing instead to gesture to what lies outside of the work. Consequently, Renaissance nature writing, which is frequently in the pastoral mode, often works best when it neither mimics nor represents anything.

In chapter 1, I suggest that the deployment of such a gestural strategy helps explain the general lack of lavish description in Renaissance pastoral. As Angus Fletcher perceptively argued in his study of environmental

---

3. Robert N. Watson, *Back to Nature: The Green and the Real in the Late Renaissance* (Philadelphia: University of Pennsylvania Press, 2006).

poetry, in the three centuries that separate us from the early modern period, nature writing became, for a variety of reasons, increasingly descriptive.[4] Because we tend to view literature from prior periods through the lens of this highly representational later poetry, we risk seeing earlier nature writing, with its sparse descriptions, as not only deficient, but perhaps not concerned with nature at all. Throughout this book I argue that this lens has indeed distorted our perception of Renaissance pastoral. Recalling Plato's anxiety over the challenges that come with the representation of nature, which was still very much alive in the Renaissance (as Watson makes clear), it should come as little surprise that early modern poets often avoid lavish descriptions of the environment. What should come as a surprise, however, is that literary theorists have often ignored the simple fact that nature writing, as well as works of art more generally, can function gesturally without significantly deploying mimesis.

As I suggested in my opening paragraph of this Introduction, when asked if the obvious preoccupation with landscape in Renaissance pastoral might have some environmental significance, most literary critics today, I suspect, would respond that the obligatory bucolic setting of pastoral is merely a convention inherited from Theocritus and Virgil, with no deeper meaning. To defend this position, readers like Paul Alpers and Annabel Patterson repeatedly turn to Virgil's first Eclogue. In order to reveal that their position fails to tell much of pastoral's story, it is to this eclogue that I turn in my second chapter.

Chapter 2 begins with an ecocritical reading of Virgil's first Eclogue in order to show the important role that cities, in this case Rome, have had in the development of pastoral literature. My argument is that, as Virgil's Rome sprawled into its surrounding environs, the endangered countryside began to appear as if for the first time to its citizens and artists, who as a consequence, developed an environmental consciousness. This chapter explores a number of works that similarly facilitate such an appearance of the countryside: Aemilia Lanyer's "The Description of Cooke-ham," John Stow's 1597 *Survey of London,* and early modern London itself. Drawing on the phenomenological thinking of Martin Heidegger, I suggest that being human all too often means that we fail to become thematically aware

---

4. Angus Fletcher, *A New Theory for American Poetry: Democracy, the Environment, and the Future of Imagination* (Cambridge, MA: Harvard University Press, 2004).

of the natural backdrop into which we are born and against which we live our lives. This can perhaps most easily be understood metaphorically by the way in which the backdrop of a play largely escapes the attention of its audience, who often understandably focus (like Alpers and Patterson) on the human action taking place center stage. However, when one backdrop replaces another, we at once become aware of both old and new backgrounds. Similarly, when a change occurs in the natural backdrop, such as its being endangered by the expansion of a city, our attention is often forcefully drawn not only to the city coming onto the scene, but to the backdrop it replaces, as the endangered countryside makes its belated emergence into appearance even as it disappears.

This phenomenon is at the heart of Virgil's first Eclogue, which is altogether ironic, as this text is now considered by many critics to be among Virgil's most allegorical, and hence least concerned with the countryside and environment, works. However, a careful look to the competing speeches of the Eclogue's two characters, Meliboeus and Tityrus, makes clear that Meliboeus is desperately trying to make his companion aware of the environment surrounding them, which has emerged into appearance for him as he learns he is to be exiled from it. Tityrus counters, however, by attempting to make Meliboeus aware of the political reality that brought about the exile. The larger argument, however, only emerges from the dialogue taken as a whole: we need to consider the impact that our political and cultural decisions have on the environment. Although Meliboeus and Tityrus may not have convinced each other of their respective arguments by the Eclogue's end, readers are ideally positioned to comprehend both, as well as how they are interrelated.

In chapter 3 I explore in detail how pastoral works often avoid mimesis by first considering how certain works of architecture make little attempt at presenting an image of their surrounding environments. Early modern London, for example, did not reveal its adjoining countryside by working like a painting, mimetically providing a portrait of its surroundings. Rather, because it made such a striking contrast to the countryside on which it encroached, London not only caused that countryside to emerge into appearance, it deeply impacted how the countryside appeared (looked) to individuals aesthetically engaged by what had appeared (emerged into awareness). Pointing away from themselves to the countryside, such works act gesturally, rather than representationally, in facilitating the appearance of the environment—and, in the bargain, fostering an environmental consciousness in those to whom it appears.

Ben Jonson takes up this phenomenon in "To Penshurst," exploring how a poem, like a work of architecture (in this case the home of his patron Sir Robert Sidney), can reveal much about its surrounding environment that had not been apparent before, yet in a way that is not principally representational. In "To Penshurst," Jonson considers whether it might be possible for a human dwelling to reveal, yet not endanger, the countryside. Unlike early modern London, such a dwelling would not reveal its surrounding environs by being something altogether other; quite the contrary, by being startlingly like its surroundings, it would prompt those viewing the house into seeing the countryside as if for the first time. Like Sidney's house (and indirectly like London), Jonson's poem offers few representations of the country estate it at first glance seems to describe; rather, the poem repeatedly gestures away from itself to the environment, the Sidney estate, emerging into appearance outside of the text. A look at his first Eclogue confirms that this was Virgil's strategy as well.

As many writers of Renaissance pastoral extensively used a gestural, rather than representational, strategy, I have continued in chapter 4 to investigate this nonmimetic quality by means of a range of English writers, including William Forrest, Thomas Lodge, John Beaumont, Giles Fletcher, John Dennys, Alexander Ross, William Drummond, Henry Vaughan, and Abraham Cowley. This chapter also examines seventeenth-century English translations of Greek and Latin texts, Petrarch's eclogues and letters, and the works of other continental writers, such as Justus Lipsius. Like "To Penshurst," these diverse texts not only operate without significantly employing mimesis, they also are very much concerned with facilitating for the reader the appearance (emergence) of the countryside outside of the text. This chapter also underscores the fact that Renaissance pastoral in England is largely a London phenomenon, as most artists contributing significantly to pastoral's development in the early modern period lived in or near London at some point. Whether named outright or simply referenced as the "City" or "Town," London looms large in Renaissance England's pastoral art.

Taken together, my first four chapters provide a foundation from which to consider the appearance of the countryside in English Renaissance literature as an epistemological emergence (which in turn gave rise to an environmental consciousness) that this art helped to facilitate. While these chapters lay out the theoretical underpinnings of a green reading of Renaissance literature and pastoral, the question still remains whether early modern England was actually in the throes of a "modern" environmental crisis. Renaissance London's suburban sprawl, and the pastoral poems it helped motivate, hardly proves that the island was experiencing such an event. The question also remains whether pastoral was the only form of Renaissance nature writing. Consequently, my final three chapters aim to make clear that (1) early modern England was indeed experiencing a number of strikingly modern environmental crises that influenced its literature, and (2) texts influenced by these crises came in a variety of forms and genres.

I realize that it may seem as if I am putting the cart before the horse by not making the case that there were modern environmental crises in early modern England before considering the change in consciousness, as well as artistic responses, that these crises engendered. Nonetheless, it is, I think, crucial to explore how we become aware of environmental change, as well as attempt to communicate such awareness, before focusing on what brings about such changes in consciousness. Failing to take these factors into account can significantly distort our impression of both the crises themselves and contemporary awareness of them. For example, because Renaissance poets sometimes employed a gestural strategy that resulted in their works not being replete with the sort of lush descriptions of the environment that we have come to expect from later writers (such as the Romantics), it may not only seem as if these early modern artists did not have the same sort of environmental awareness as their future counterparts, but also, as they failed to bequeath us extensive descriptions of environmental devastation, lead us to mistakenly conclude that the problems themselves were still a century or more in the future. In general, because this strategy often gestures away from the crises (for example, to London's surrounding countryside, rather than to the urban and suburban changes causing that landscape to emerge into appearance), it may point us in precisely the wrong direction—toward environments imagined as pristine, which may be anything but, and away from the very problems threatening them.

With an understanding of environmental consciousness in place, I consider in chapters 5 though 7 a particular environmental issue—urban air pollution, sweeping changes in land use, and the environmental implications of colonization—as well as three very different literary forms that were employed in framing a response to these crises. These chapters also address, respectively, three issues relating to environmental justice in Renaissance England: (1) urban air pollution's disproportionate impact on the poor, (2) the displacement of thousands of individuals across the island (as a concerted effort was made to drain watersheds, in the process relocating the human settlements there), and (3) wholesale efforts to disenfranchise the Irish population in order to implement sweeping changes in land use, especially as represented in *The Faerie Queene* and elsewhere in Spenser's writing.

In chapter 5, I consider one of the most important, though now nearly forgotten, environmental problems of the seventeenth century. While human beings have been burning fossil fuels for thousands of years, seventeenth-century Londoners, having deforested the area surrounding their city, were almost exclusively burning a particularly dangerous form of highly sulfurous coal that created in both scope and type a problem that had not been encountered before. As seventeenth-century England was mining and burning three to four times more coal than the rest of Europe (where wood was still relatively plentiful as a fuel) combined, with most of it being burned in London, this early modern city was the first on the planet to experience on a large scale the now ubiquitous and characteristically modern problem of urban air pollution. Perhaps not surprisingly, the first English work to take as its subject urban air pollution, John Evelyn's 1661 *Fumifugium,* established a model of environmental writing that reemerged in the twentieth century with works such as Rachel Carson's *Silent Spring.*

What is particularly interesting about this environmental situation is that early modern London's air-pollution crisis could very easily escape our notice if we relied solely on what have become canonical Renaissance literary texts, as air pollution rarely appears directly in such works. Part of the reason for this is that pastoral works, like "To Penshurst," are often too effective at holding a pastoral focus. In terms of our theatrical metaphor, these works are often exclusively concerned with drawing attention to, and facilitating the appearance of, the formerly "natural" backdrop being moved aside. Consequently, these works often give little or no consideration to the new backdrop, such as expanding London with its pollution-filled skies, emerging on the scene. Because our impression of Renaissance

England often comes from such texts, we risk remaining oblivious to early modern London's horrific air-pollution problem. This is, of course, ironic given that the very texts that provide evidence of an early modern environmental consciousness are sometimes the ones that, though motivated by environmental issues, nonetheless rarely address or mention these problems. Paradoxically, then, these milestone environmental texts often conceal the fact that they are the product of an environmentally decisive time.

However, if we look to the historical record, it becomes clear that by 1665, when Milton was writing *Paradise Lost,* it was already believed that respiratory illness caused by air pollution was second only to the Plague as the leading cause of death in London. It was also known to be responsible for a variety of additional environmental problems, such as widespread acid rain (which Charles I correctly believed had seriously damaged St. Paul's cathedral) and the extinction of entire species of local plants. One of my objectives in chapter 5 (and indeed in this book as a whole) is to provide historical evidence of what was happening in and outside of Renaissance England to indicate something of its true environmental situation. Once this context is restored, it quickly becomes apparent that, if we assume that Renaissance nature writing provides an accurate description of England's countryside as a whole, we not only risk misunderstanding how such texts often work (i.e., gesturally), but are in further danger of taking the countryside to which these texts gesture, which is often imagined in pastoral terms, as an accurate indicator of early modern England's overall environmental state. Because many literary critics make this assumption, this has unfortunately and ironically resulted in the widespread belief that Renaissance England was, for the most part, a bucolic country.

If we look, however, to a work that was enormously popular in the seventeenth century, Sir John Denham's *Cooper's Hill,* it becomes clear that not every poet of the period shied away from London's environmental crises. As chapter 5 makes clear, Denham rather accurately describes many of seventeenth-century England's environmental problems, including air pollution. Consequently, Denham's view from Cooper's Hill is hardly a green one. Had the poet wished to portray such a scene, he needed only to literally turn away from the emerging modernity of London and the Thames Valley before him to the rural English countryside coming into appearance at his back—and thus perform the signature turn of the Romantics. In parts of rural England, air pollution, acid rain, species loss, and many other environmental problems had yet to become significant issues even as the nineteenth century opened. But Denham refused to turn away, as many poets did after him, even those writing in the hill genre he created. So successful was this turn away from England's true environmental situation that the lens it has given us has long distorted how we view much of the poetry from the period. Part of my goal in the present work is to make this distortion, and the true state of England it has concealed, clear by drawing attention to previously ignored environmental crises in the early modern period. As we shall see in chapter 6, another such problem involved sweeping changes in land use.

Largely overlooked by critics, the radical groups known as Levellers and Diggers did not appear first in the mid seventeenth century, but rather, in 1607. Because these early Levellers and Diggers, as well as similar environmental protesters from the 1620s through the 1640s, were frequently concerned with changing patterns of land use (and not, like their midcentury counterparts, largely with rights of property), we find in the literature that came out of these protests a number of strikingly modern environmental arguments. These issues reappear in the works of some of the most influential writers of the day, including William Camden, Michael Drayton, Andrew Marvell, and John Milton. In both the original protest literature and these more canonical texts, the countryside across England appeared in strikingly new ways. Because environmentally questionable projects endangered these places (for example, extraordinarily ambitious efforts to drain early modern England's vast tracts of wetlands and fens in order to put the land to new use), such previously "marginal" countryside began emerging into appearance across the island.

From this seventeenth-century protest literature we see that these protesters were developing a number of very modern environmental positions by arguing the need for diversity (both in plant and animal life); suggesting that changes to local ecosystems can have regional, even national, consequences; proposing that human cultures should be built on customs that respond to the particular conditions of local habitats; resisting the introduction of agricultural monocultures; and so forth. However, while the protesters were articulating this environmental discourse, prospective developers of England's early modern countryside were countering with their own by systematically touting the benefits of introduced species and monocultures; arguing that the vagaries of certain local ecosystems were so great that destruction of these otherwise fertile places was justified; and suggesting that the benefit to the poor (through a system remarkably like that of "trickle-down" economics) would warrant the destruction of existing ecosystems. Far from being just a local issue, these debates (along with accompanying riots and lawsuits) came to play a surprising role in contributing to the causes that brought about the turbulent midcentury political scene and indeed England's Civil War itself, with both Oliver Cromwell and the Leveller John Lilburne coming to the environmental protesters' defense.

What is provocative about these early environmental protesters is that different groups at different times were protesting what other groups were desperately fighting to protect. For example, some fought against the conversion of arable land to pasture, while others protested pasture being converted into arable land. Although initially somewhat paradoxical, this is consistent with the manner by which countrysides emerge into appearance for local inhabitants. Because what is "natural" for human beings is often the backdrop into which we are born, arable land appeared as natural to some of the protesters as pasture appeared to those in other locales. Consequently, pasture was unnatural to the former, and arable land to the latter. In neither case was the nature in question anything like what we would today call "wilderness." Only when an absolute reference to someplace as free as possible of human habitation is sought does wilderness emerge into appearance. Until that time, as we shall see, "natural" in this context is something of a freely floating signifier that can be ascribed, or denied, to a variety of locales.

This point is sometimes lost on modern environmentalists. Even though there were few places in early modern England that would be considered wilderness in our modern sense (most of the island had been deforested by the eleventh century), this did not stop the emergence of environmental consciousness in those who inhabited local ecosystems. Once an endangered countryside made its emergence into appearance, whether as arable land, pasture, wilderness, or something else, it was often seen not only as natural, but as a nature worth fiercely fighting to preserve. Because various countrysides were appearing (ironically at the very moment they were disappearing) all across England during the sixteenth and seventeenth centuries, it is perhaps not surprising that these dizzying changes would in time lead some individuals to seek an absolute reference in places least changed by human beings. Because such a reference was often sought in places with little human habitation, and early modern England itself had few such locales (save the small number of regions that the Romantics would later fixate on), prospective colonies soon came to be seen in such terms. Taken together, my first six chapters consider how early modern England's emerging countryside was often viewed in environmentally positive ways: worth venturing outside of London to appreciate, even worth rioting to preserve. Although these ways of thinking also had their environmental downsides (for example, the development and endangerment of London's countryside by some of the very individuals who appreciated it), there is an even less pleasant side to this story that needs to be explored in my final chapter.

In the same way that Renaissance London directed individuals to the appearance of the city's surroundings (as did sweeping environmental changes in other places across England), some English colonial discourse did the same for the environment outside of the island, insofar as it encouraged its citizens to leave their homes to experience the colonies. However, in this case, such literature not only encouraged appreciation of environments imagined as pristine, but also the mass exploitation of these newly emerging environs. Consequently, these colonized countrysides appeared not as valuable and worth saving, but as ripe for exploitation.

Edmund Spenser's views on the state of Ireland are particularly illuminating with respect to this sort of exploitation. Many postcolonial critics seem to understand the "colonized" as either individuals forced to become economic subproletarians in order to make the colonizer's material life possible, or as epistemological subalterns who allow the colonizer to consolidate a sense of "self" at their expense. While both views are valid, they risk ignoring the simple fact that places as well as human beings can be colonized. In some extreme cases, the colonized human beings were considered so inconsequential or recalcitrant that their mass elimination was called for to facilitate the smooth exploitation of the colonized place. Perhaps because of the sheer horror of this genocidal practice, we risk losing sight of the fact that these projects were not at root motivated by a desire to exploit a people, but rather a place. Unfortunately, Spenser called for such genocide in order to exploit Ireland's natural resources.

In *The Faerie Queene* and elsewhere, Spenser developed and adapted the georgic mode of writing in order to facilitate the environmental exploitation of Ireland. While pastoral literature was initially instrumental in portraying colonies as desirable, Edenlike places, pastoral *otium* was clearly in conflict with the hard work required to colonize a place. As the georgic ethic readily lent itself to this type of project, georgic literature, such as Hesiod's *Works and Days* and Virgil's *Georgics,* grew in popularity throughout English Renaissance.

As the georgic ethic of land use rose to dominance, Spenser and others, increasingly seeing themselves as hardworking husbandmen, began to portray the Irish negatively as still living a pastoral life as sheepherders, a life characterized by *otium,* with no interest in developing the fertile land on which they lived. What is at once fascinating and horrific about this situation is that by Spenser's time the georgic, husbandman ethic had risen to such dominance that it could be used as a rationale for genocide of the Irish people. Having witnessed Ireland's Munster famine of 1581, Spenser concluded that it was the result of the Irish people's having not adequately provided for themselves by carefully tilling the land. Spenser had little sympathy for the Irish, as he felt they had reaped what they had sown, or to be more accurate, were unable to reap what they had failed to sow. In a stroke of questionable genius, Spenser realized that the portrayal of the Irish as a nongeorgic "other" had been so successful that it could be used to justify their elimination, paving the way for the English colonization of Ireland.

Renaissance England was in many respects in the same position that we presently find ourselves, as the island, like the entire planet today, had few areas free of human habitation. While early modern England had the questionable luxury of looking to new lands outside of its own to inhabit, it also had to consider, as we also now must, how best to manage already inhabited lands. While some individuals (influenced by pastoral literature) would see each such place as a *locus amoenus,* this did not preclude the application of a georgic ethic to the countryside in order to preserve it in that state. The reverse was also possible: the georgic ethic, in the form of Ireland's colonizers, could threaten the countryside. While in the 1970s many environmentalists became critical of the georgic ethic because it risked positioning human beings in an essentially adversarial relationship to the earth (as in my example of Ireland), the counterexample of "To Penshurst" makes equally clear that the georgic ethic was by no means always environmentally irresponsible.

Unless we take as our example wilderness untouched by human hands (something even rarer today than it was in Renaissance England), it is the case that something approximating a georgic ethic is necessary to ensure careful stewardship of our planet. Indeed, understood in the most general sense, all acts of environmental preservation are in some sense georgic, as they undertake the hard work of tending to the earth. This applies both to those individuals who do the literal georgic work of preserving the countryside and to the artists who encourage such stewardship. Throughout this book, I aim to show how an awareness of the emerging environment, at the moment of its endangerment, caused the early modern English to debate, as we must now, how we as a species might best tend to our planet.

Part I

Literary Issues

1

The Nature of Art

Here it is easy to run into that dead-end in philosophy, where one believes
that the difficulty of the task consists in our having to describe appearances
that are hard to get hold of, the present experience that is slipping away
quickly, or something of that kind.

Ludwig Wittgenstein, *Philosophical Investigations*

Prior to Socrates, Plato was profoundly influenced by the philosopher
Cratylus, who may in fact have been his teacher. Outside of his appearance in Plato's dialogue that bears his name, we know little about him
other than what we learn from the *Metaphysics,* where Aristotle groups
him with a number of thinkers who, because they "saw that all of nature
was in flux, and that no true statement can be made about that which is in
such flux, concluded that, of course, regarding what is everywhere and in
every way changing, nothing could be said" (my translation).[1] Perhaps not
surprisingly, Aristotle names Cratylus as one of the followers of Heraclitus; however, because he observed that everywhere everything is changing
so quickly, Cratylus "criticized Heraclitus for saying that one cannot step
twice into the same stream, for he himself thought it could not be done

---

1. The epigraph from Wittgenstein that begins this chapter is my translation. Aristotle's
Metaphysics (Cambridge, MA: Harvard University Press, 1933), IV.1010a.5–7. All references to
The Metaphysics are to this text with my translations.

even once."[2] Because he doubted that language could represent an environment so manifestly and wildly in flux, Cratylus "ended by thinking it not proper to say anything at all, but only moved his finger" to communicate by gesture.[3]

There is, of course, something comic about the image of the mute and gesturing Cratylus; however, to Plato, assuming he took Cratylus seriously (which we have little reason to doubt), this may have seemed a frightening end for a philosopher, perhaps even for philosophy itself. It certainly did not bode well for the power of language to represent our ever-changing surroundings. Fortunately for Plato, he found a new teacher, Socrates, who promised to save language from nature's relentless flux by imagining a fixed and immutable realm securely "beyond nature," which, he reasoned, is what language must be referencing, or at least should represent if written or uttered truthfully by a knowledgeable person. However, if we are to believe Aristotle (and compelling reasons to do so have recently been put forth),[4] Plato remained loyal to Cratylus and Heraclitean thinking throughout his life, never accepting that Socrates' solution, which posits a metaphysical realm where ethical Ideas like Beauty and Justice have existence, generally applied to the sense objects we encounter in the physical environment.[5]

> In his youth he [Plato] became acquainted with Cratylus and Heraclitean doctrines, that all objects perceived by sense are ever in flux and that it is hence impossible to have knowledge about them. He held these views even in his later years. Socrates, however, devoting himself to ethical matters while neglecting nature [*physis*] as a whole, sought the universal in ethical matters, and hence was the first person to fix thought by way of definitions. Plato accepted this teaching, but believed that this did not apply to sensible things, but to something else [i.e., ethical Ideas]. For this reason, Plato held that it was impossible for the common definition to be of any sensible things, as they were always adrift in flux.[6]

The fact that his most celebrated student doubted that Socrates' realm of Ideas provided referents for the physical environment not only underscores

---

2. Aristotle, *Metaphysics,* IV.1010a.14–15.

3. Ibid., 13.

4. See David Sedley's *Plato's Cratylus* (Cambridge: Cambridge University Press, 2003), 16–21.

5. However, as we shall see, in the case of certain human works, Plato believed such sense objects could represent Ideas.

6. *Metaphysics,* I.987a32–b7.

the challenges that theories of representation face, it also opens up the question of how successful we are in our representational enterprises. Not surprisingly, these issues were never fully resolved. This became apparent in the twentieth century when a range of poststructural thinkers became, like Plato, dubious of the claim, which in some sense begins with Socrates, that there is a firm linguistic link (i.e., a "structure") between what phenomenologists call the "things themselves" and the words we use to represent them.

As a great deal of ink has been spilled on the question of representation, I do not presume to have anything new to add. Recalling the silent, gesturing Cratylus (whom I, like Plato, take very seriously), my interest is not in the representational, but rather the gestural, the fact that, when faced with the representational quagmire that has given pause to thinkers from Plato through Derrida, some poets and artists, especially those directing themselves to their surrounding environment, pointed us there too, rather than attempting to capture it on canvas, or between the covers of a book. Of course, they often (and often unavoidably) did that as well, but it is the gesture, and the preference of the gesture over the representation, that interests me most. As perhaps it should us all; for well over two thousand years, we have largely neglected gesture while endlessly theorizing and making a fetish of representation.

In his *Back to Nature: The Green and the Real in the Late Renaissance,*[7] Robert Watson compellingly argues that in the Renaissance there was considerable anxiety over whether works of art, including literature, could successfully represent reality and, in the process, truly lead us "back to nature" (i.e., mimetically connect us to the "things themselves"). Regarding this important concern, my argument in this and the next three chapters is a simple one: faced with this anxiety, some poets and artists in the Renaissance, especially those producing pastoral works, preferred Cratylic gestures over attempts at representation.

While this may seem like an arcane study of why such Cratylic gestures were favored and employed (and in some ways I suppose that it is), there is quite a bit at stake here. As Angus Fletcher astutely observed in his study of environmental poetry, "We find an argument, never settled but only deferred, between Plato's mathematical intuition that his Ideas are 'eternal'

---

7. Robert N. Watson, *Back to Nature: The Green and the Real in the Late Renaissance* (Philadelphia: University of Pennsylvania Press, 2006).

and the poets' belief that whatever undergoes change (and indeed change itself) yields the only true idea."[8] In the closing of his *Republic,* Plato famously alluded to an "ancient quarrel between philosophy and poetry" over who should control representations of reality. Since he argued that, at least with respect to ethical Ideas, only philosophers have access to what is "real," Plato clearly felt that they alone, and certainly not errant poets, should be sanctioned by the State to represent reality. While this dispute is certainly real, Fletcher points to another, even more basic, and perhaps even more important, quarrel between philosophy and poetry, one that draws into question the success of the representational project itself. Fletcher rightly points out that Plato was concerned with metaphysical Ideas, which, the philosopher argued, not only can be successfully represented in language, but form the basis of representation itself. On the other hand, certain Renaissance poets, especially pastoral poets concerned with the environment, direct themselves to that which is so manifestly and wildly in flux that its successful representation is, as it was for Cratylus, drawn into question, requiring them to devise strategies to deal with the problem, which is often not even acknowledged as a difficulty by philosophers after Plato.

Fletcher persuasively argues that, while certain Renaissance poets (like Milton) wrestled with the problem of representing the physical environment, it is not until early in the eighteenth century that James Thomson's enormously influential poem *The Seasons* squarely took on the problem by attempting to work out the manner by which a highly representational and descriptive poetic treatment of an ever-changing environment could be effectively achieved. After considering the many challenges that such descriptive poetry faced in the next century, Fletcher moves to Walt Whitman, who, he argues, largely inaugurated a new species of poetry, the "environment-poem," which itself *"is* an environment...such a poem does not merely suggest or indicate an environment as part of its thematic meaning, but actually gets the reader to enter into the poem as if it were the reader's environment of living."[9] To achieve this startling end, which so successfully represents an environment between the covers of a book that

8. Angus Fletcher, *A New Theory for American Poetry: Democracy, the Environment, and the Future of Imagination* (Cambridge, MA: Harvard University Press, 2004), 28. Parenthetical comment by Fletcher.
    9. Ibid., 122. Fletcher's emphasis.

readers are encouraged to imaginatively enter into it, Fletcher argues that the poets who stretched from Thomson to Whitman developed a variety of strategies for representing their environments. Just a year after Fletcher published his theory, Lawrence Buell, perhaps the most respected ecocritic working in the field, not only supported the notion of the "environment-poem," but suspected that it could be "extended beyond poetry to include (at least some examples of) other genres," though he questioned, I think rightly, whether Fletcher would endorse the move.[10]

While I find fascinating Fletcher's account of how poets from Milton onward wrestled with the task of representing an environment wildly in flux, in this book my interest is in the Renaissance and earlier periods, when there was often a reluctance to even make the attempt. Because we tend to see these earlier periods through the lens of the highly representational eighteenth- and nineteenth-century literature that Fletcher considers, we risk not even acknowledging these earlier pastoral works as environmental poetry. After all, how can they be when, sparse in description, they hardly represent the environment at all? Clearly, they do not fit the mold of the "environment-poem" introduced by Fletcher and endorsed by Buell.

Nonetheless, they are environment poems, just of a different sort. This acknowledgement is of central importance in understanding Renaissance pastoral. One of the reasons that we have generally failed to recognize early modern pastoral as a form of nature writing is because, as Fletcher perceptively notes, for more than three centuries we have gradually come to expect nature writing to be more and more representational. However, as Plato made clear, and about which many Renaissance artists were well aware (as Watson has demonstrated), the challenges that come with representing nature are more than a little daunting. Consequently, certain Renaissance writers, made anxious by these challenges, employed gestural strategies to produce pastoral works that, while short on description, are nonetheless "environment poems." To understand how they are, it will be helpful to return to one of the West's earliest and most provocative discussions of this issue: Plato's *Cratylus*. In the process, we can take up a question of special consequence to environmental critics, which few address: What is nature?

---

10. Lawrence Buell, T*he Future of Environmental Criticism: Environmental Crisis and Literary Imagination* (Oxford: Blackwell, 2005) 51. Parenthetical comment by Buell.

In his *Cratylus,* which is likely one of his later works, or at least one of the later works of his middle period, Plato takes the opportunity to reflect on the philosopher Cratylus and underscore the profound innovations made by Socrates. In the dialogue, Socrates suggests that quite a few Greek names and words (*onomata*) are, as Cratylus also suspects, firmly linked to what they name, in contrast to another character, Hermogenes, who holds that names are only linked to what they name by social convention. To make his case, Socrates postulates that long ago there were "name-givers" (*nomothetēs*), wise human beings who created the Greek language by naming things in a way that described them. For example, the Greek word for "human being," *anthrōpos,* according to Socrates, etymologically derives from three words that the name-givers grouped to form a description of human beings: *anathrōn ha opōpe,* literally "one who reflects on what one has seen." Because to Socrates, and many thinkers since, what makes human beings human is that we are presumably the only animal that thinks, this name appears apt. In the course of the *Cratylus* Socrates offers dozens of similarly descriptive etymologies.

Because many of these etymologies are simply absurd, critics have been unsure just how to receive the *Cratylus,* suspecting that Plato may not have intended it to be taken seriously. But recent scholarship has made clear that, as etymology was hardly an exact science in classical Greece, many of Socrates' etymologies would not have been questioned in antiquity. In the case of *anthrōpos,* for example, a range of ancient writers believed Socrates' etymology correct, including Ammonius, Damascius, Eusebius, Proclus, Stobeus, and others.[11] As it is likely that Plato intended these etymologies to be taken seriously, their overarching theme is striking.

According to Socrates, an astonishing number of Greek names originally signaled flux. For example, the word for the earth (a body one might imagine to be manifestly stable) is *gē* or *gaia,* which Socrates suggests is related to *gignesthai,* "to be born," which in turn is related to *gignomenon,* Plato's word for "becoming." But more than suggesting that cosmological entities such as the earth (as well as the gods) were named in a way that described their instability, Socrates launches into an etymological tour de force of a range of words signaling less tangible concepts: intelligence

---

11. See Sedley's *Plato's Cratylus,* 37, n19.

(*phronēsis*), judgment (*gnōmē*), thought (*noēsis*), knowledge (*epistēmē*), understanding (*synesis*), wisdom (*sophia*), good (*agathon*), justice (*dikaiosynē*), courage (*andreia*), vice (*kakia*), virtue (*aretē*), bad (*kakon*), ugly (*aischron*), beautiful (*kalon*), and many, many more.[12] All of these, according to Socrates, were originally named as ideas in flux.

It is immediately apparent that this list includes the sort of ethical ideas, such as justice and beauty, as well as related human faculties like intelligence and understanding, that became central to Plato's Theory of Ideas. Written contemporaneously with, if not after, the great works developing that theory (*Republic, Thaetetus, Phaedrus,* and, *Parmenides*), the *Cratylus* triumphantly underscores Socrates' astonishing innovation. It is not merely that he corrected the many philosophers who held that moral values (i.e., Ideas) are in flux, but also that he challenged the very underpinnings of Greek culture, which he claimed still expressed, through the language it had inherited, the belief that everywhere everything is in flux. For example, *kalon* may have once signaled that beauty is always changing, but Socrates argued that it must reference something more, something immutable, if the word is to have stable meaning. In the *Cratylus,* Socrates accepts the ancient etymologies and the belief that moral ideas appear to be in flux; however, he argues that the name-givers found this flux so dizzying that they could not see that beyond shifting appearances lie solid, immutable Ideas. Hence, Socrates holds that names are indeed linked to what they represent, but suggests that the name-givers misunderstood what in fact was being named, believing that each of the aforementioned Ideas was in flux.

As eloquent as Socrates' argument was, not everyone in the room was convinced. Cratylus, who had been eagerly listening to Socrates' extraordinary etymologies, immediately became persuaded that all is indeed in flux. (Thus, in the chronology presented by the dialogue, which is very likely historically inaccurate, it is Socrates who first introduces Cratylus to what will become his doctrine of flux.) In so doing, Cratylus, of course, ignores the overarching point Socrates has been making, that moral Ideas are impervious to this flux. Consequently, in the *Cratylus* Plato explains what may have lead Cratylus to conclude that nature is indeed in flux; however, he makes clear that, at least with respect to moral Ideas, Socrates reversed this view.

---

12. Plato, *Cratylus* (Cambridge, MA: Harvard University Press, 1926), 411a–417b. My translations.

What is at stake here is the answer to a basic, though crucial question: What is nature? Through his many etymologies, which he connects with the word *physis* (nature) throughout the *Cratylus,* Socrates argues that *physis* has traditionally been understood as flux. Aristotle seconds this suggestion in his *Metaphysics,* where he tries his own hand at etymology, arguing that the word "*physis* means the birth of that which grows, which would be suggested by pronouncing the 'y' in *physis* as long,"[13] thereby (in a somewhat convoluted way that need not concern us here) relating *physis* to *genesis,* which in turn is related to *gignomenon,* Plato's preferred word for "becoming": the endless process of birth, growth, and passing away. Although somewhat surprising, given the state of classical etymology, Aristotle is correct regarding the origin of *physis.* In fact, our word "nature," which derives from the Latin *natura,* also began this way, as did the Middle English *kynde* (in Anglo Saxon *cyn*), our language's homegrown word for the concept of nature, which competed with *natura* after its introduction into English.

Physis, natura, and *kynde* all once had and eventually lost the same original meaning. Prior to their long and varied histories, each word signaled birth and growth.[14] However, each eventually lost this original sense[15] as

---

13. *Metaphysics,* V.1014b.17.

14. This core meaning is so old it predates the first English, Latin, and Ancient Greek uses, having its origin in two Indo-European words, *bheue* and *gen,* both also meaning "emergence" and "growth." The Greek *physis* and *phuein* (to bring forth) both derive from the similarly voiced *bheue,* which is still echoed in a range of modern English words: physical, physics, physician, phylum, neophyte, and so forth. *Natura* and *kynde* are both derived from the Indo-European *gen,* which obviously gave us quite a few words: gene, genital, generate, genesis, gender, genre, progeny, pregnancy, and the like. *Gen* directly emerged in Anglo Saxon as *cyn,* then in Middle English as *kynde,* which in turn became our word *kind,* as well as a host of others including *kin,* such as kin, kid, kindred, and kinship. In one of its forms with the addition of a suffix, as *gna-sko, gen* gave rise to the Latin *gnasci* and its past participle *natus,* which also means birth, from which we get nascent, natal, nativity, innate, nation, noel, and many others including, of course, "nature." A quick look at some of these outgrowths of *bheue* and *gen* confirms that their core meaning of birth and growth is, thousands of years later, still alive and well today.

15. Because it is the most recent of the three, *kynde* retained this original meaning even into the late Renaissance. For example, as Chaucer's "Second Nun's Tale" opens, we learn that "Cecilie, as hir lif seith, / Was comen of Romayns and of noble kynde," meaning of course that Cecelia was of noble birth. Similarly, the "Tale of Melibee" contends that "Oon of the gretteste adversitees of this world is / when a free man by kynde or by burthe is constreyned by poverte." Here Chaucer conveniently defines *kynde* for us as birth. Not only had this meaning survived into Chaucer's era, it persisted into Spenser's, and even into Milton's. For example, Spenser, affecting an archaic mode, makes *kynde* into a verb signaling birth, as in book V of *The Faerie Queene,* where Radigund is described as forgetting that she "was not borne / Of Beares and Tygers [but]...was of men kynded." Similarly, in *Eikonoklastes* Milton describes Charles I as imitating what "he seems to have learnt, as it were by heart, or els by kind," or birth, from his grandmother Mary Queen

they took on a staggering range of meanings over time.[16] Even though *physis* was well on its way to losing this original meaning by the time of Plato and Aristotle, both thinkers realized that it and related words (and Socrates offers quite a few possibilities) still echoed an ancient perspective on what was originally signaled by "nature." What is nature? It is birth, growth, and passing away, the endless process of process, whereby everything everywhere is ever coming into and out of being.

Well, perhaps not everything. According to Socrates in the *Cratylus* and elsewhere, moral Ideas like Beauty and Justice are here to stay. Thus we have a very different answer to our question. What is nature? *True* nature, according to Socrates, lies beyond the ever-changing physical environment. In the *Cratylus* (389c), Plato underscores this striking re-definition of *physis,* which turns the old one on its head, by arguing that *physis* and *idea* are one and the same. In order to explain how Socrates had reversed the name-givers, as well as the original meaning of *physis,* in the *Cratylus* (and elsewhere) Plato surprisingly extends his realm of Ideas to include certain sense objects: works created by human beings. For example, according to Plato, a wooden shuttle used in weaving is made to represent the Idea of a perfect shuttle (*Cratylus,* 389c), even though he is doubtful there is an Idea representing the tree from which it is made. The distinction here involves the direction of the representation. Even though each particular shuttle is obviously unique, because human beings created them all from a common Idea, they represent that Idea; however, Plato suspects it likely impossible to represent an ideal "tree" from untold millions of unique examples adrift in relentless change. As we shall see directly by way of Hannah Arendt, the shuttle represents an Idea because that is precisely what it was fashioned to do by the work of human beings, hence the Idea precedes the representation, while individual trees, preceding any representation and endlessly in flux, resist attempts at representation.

of Scots. *The Complete Poetry and Prose of Geoffrey Chaucer,* ed. John H. Fisher (New York: Holt, Rinehart, and Winston, 1977), "Second Nun's Tale" ll.120–21; "Tale of Melibee" ll.1566–67. *The Faerie Queene,* ed. A. C. Hamilton (Harlow, UK: Pearson, 2001), Book 5.5.40. *The Riverside Milton,* ed. Roy Flannagan (New York: Houghton Mifflin, 1998), 1094.

16. Although Arthur Lovejoy and George Boas teased out thirty-nine different categories of meanings for our word *nature,* along with another twenty-six specific to ethics, politics, and religion, even they had admitted that the list was by no means complete. *Primitivism and Related Ideas in Antiquity* (Baltimore: Johns Hopkins Press, 1935), 447–56.

Thus, in a general way, Plato presages a distinction often first attributed to Cicero (*De Natura Deorum,* ii. 152) between "first nature," existing separately from human intervention (i.e., the tree used to make the shuttle), and "second nature," which includes crafted objects like the shuttle. In terms of the two answers to the question of what is meant by "nature," a fallen tree without human intervention, caught in the endless flux of *physis,* will soon pass away with nary a trace. However, given a "second nature" by a human being working it to represent the Idea of the shuttle, the tree reborn as shuttle is, at least for a time, saved from this fate and the ravages of *physis* as it enters into, and in the process thereby sustains, a human world.

To explore this further, it will be helpful to consider two twentieth-century thinkers: Martin Heidegger and Hannah Arendt. Heidegger was aware both that *physis* originally signaled birth and endless becoming to the Greeks,[17] and that Socrates and Plato had reversed this meaning.[18] To Heidegger, who is in part responsible for making this reversal famous, it marks a turning point in Western thinking by inaugurating a "metaphysics of presence," which privileges constant presence, such as Plato's Ideas, over the endless play of absence and presence that the Greeks named *physis.* Following Heidegger, a great many thinkers, perhaps most famously Jacques Derrida, doubting that words are firmly linked to fixed presences, have questioned (like Cratylus) how successful we are in our representational enterprises. However, by considering the environmental implications of the quest for constant presence, Heidegger goes further than most of those who followed him.

Heidegger argues that modern technology is the completion of metaphysics. To support such a claim, he famously considers a hydroelectric power plant being built on the Rhine, which was actually set into the river as a great dam with the intention of making the otherwise sporadically flowing river constantly present. In another example, he draws attention to "the coal that has been hauled out in some mining district.... It is stockpiled: that is, it is on call, ready to deliver the sun's warmth that is stored in it."[19] Heidegger

---

17. See, for example, *An Introduction to Metaphysics,* trans. Ralph Manheim (New Haven: Yale University Press, 1959), 14.

18. "The Question Concerning Technology," in *The Question Concerning Technology and Other Essays,* trans. William Lovitt (New York: Harper and Row, 1977), 30.

19. Heidegger considers the dam and coal in "The Question Concerning Technology," 15.

argues that because of its relentless desire to stockpile and store, "modern technology is a challenging, which puts to nature the unreasonable demand that it supply energy that can be extracted and stored as such. But does this not hold true for the old windmill as well? No. Its sails do indeed turn in the wind; they are left entirely to the wind's blowing...the windmill does not unlock energy drawn from the air currents in order to store it."[20]

But why should Heidegger put such emphasis on storage? Why is it an "unreasonable demand that it [nature] supply energy that can be extracted and stored as such"? Would the "old windmill" whose "sails...turn in the wind" be so very different if it had some sort of contrivance to store the wind's energy? To Heidegger, the shift to storage is profoundly important, representing the completion of metaphysics itself, as the sporadically flowing Rhine, relentlessly in flux, is, by being converted into a reservoir, transformed into a constant presence not unlike one of Plato's ideas. Although Heidegger does not explicitly make the connection, it is difficult not to see his example as a response to the endlessly streaming stream referenced by Heraclitus and Cratylus, itself a near-perfect example of *physis,* which in the case of the Rhine has literally been reshaped into a reservoir in order to transform it into a physical manifestation of Socrates' dream of constant presence. Thwarting *physis,* the dam enacts metaphysics. Given that technological cultures rely almost exclusively on constantly present solar energy, which is stored in coal and other fossil fuels, Heidegger's observation presumably has profound environmental consequences. However, Hannah Arendt makes clear that, in assuming that this is a recent turn of events, Heidegger is simply being naïve.

The human condition, responds Arendt to Heidegger, depends wholly on our ability to set up enduring worlds on the earth. If we stop short of that goal, she argues, we are simply not being human. Following Heidegger, by "world" Arendt means something akin to our original Old English *weor-old:* literally an "age (*old*) of humanity (*weor*)." A "world" in this sense is a specific historic-cultural context set on the earth, not the earth itself. Heidegger spent a great deal of his life considering how such ages of humanity have always been striving against the earth. His preferred icon of the Western world is an ancient Greek temple, which defiantly stands, like one of

20. Ibid., 14.

Plato's Ideas, as a constant presence against the ebb and flow of *physis.*[21] As Arendt eagerly unfolds the idea, "the man-made world of things becomes a home for mortal men, whose stability will endure and outlast the ever-changing movement of their lives."[22] On an earth endlessly adrift in *physis,* constantly present worlds are erected through human works, which persist through "the ever-changing movement." True, individual human beings come and go, but human worlds endure through their abiding works.

More than just enthusiastically accepting Heidegger's notion of "world," Arendt goes further by boldly declaring that unless a people willfully establish enduring worlds on the ever-shifting earth through their works, they are simply not being human. Indeed, when we labor without creating lasting works, we are, to Arendt, merely subhuman *animal laborans* who not only fail to create works, but worlds as well, as "labor's products, the products of man's metabolism with nature, do not stay in the world long enough to become a part of it."[23] To Arendt, any people "bound to the reoccurring cycles of nature," whose works (tools, housing, unwritten literature, and so forth) generally do not endure for generations, have failed both to create a world and to live up to their potential of being human.[24] In contrast to *animal laborans,* who merely labors, Arendt offers what she sees as a true human being, "*homo faber,* fabricator of the world [whose ideals]...are permanence, stability, and durability."[25] In the following passage, in which she perceptively quotes from Locke's *Second Treatise of Civil Government,* Arendt explains how these two ways of relating to nature differ:

> Nature seen through the eyes of the *animal laborans* is the provider of all "good things," which belong equally to all her children, who "take [them] out of [her] hands" and "mix with" them in labor and consumption. The same nature seen through the eyes of *homo faber,* the builder of the world, "furnishes only the almost worthless materials as in themselves," whose whole value lies in the work performed upon them.[26]

---

21. "The Origin of the Work of Art," in *Poetry, Language, Thought,* trans. Albert Hofstadter (New York: Harper and Row, 1971), 41–43.

22. "Labor, Work, Action," in *The Portable Hannah Arendt,* ed. Peter Baehr (New York: Penguin, 2000), 178.

23. *The Human Condition* (Chicago: Bantam, 1958), 118.

24. Ibid., 98.

25. Ibid., 126.

26. Ibid., 134–35. Parenthetical additions to the *Second Treatise of Civil Government* (sections 28 and 43) are by Arendt.

Arendt sees *homo faber* as always acting violently toward nature and argues that "this element of violation and violence is present in all fabrication, and *homo faber,* the creator of human artifice, has always been a destroyer of nature."[27]

Although Arendt was herself engaged in a critique of technological modernity,[28] her former teacher Heidegger, perhaps not surprisingly, was skeptical. Heidegger continued to accept Plato's claim that what we mean by "nature" had been largely reversed by a single individual, Socrates, and furthermore believed that this change in thinking put into motion events that eventually led, through the desire to enact metaphysics (the pursuit of constant presence), to the emergence of technological modernity and our modern environmental crisis. However, as Arendt makes clear, this desire by no means began with Socrates, but rather is so basic and ancient that it marks our transition from being animal to human.[29] In so doing, Arendt clearly finds Heidegger and other individuals (including, perhaps, certain modern environmentalists), who imagine a time when human beings had a far better relationship with the earth, naïve and simplistic. Indeed, according to Arendt, when we reach back in history that far, we find laboring animals, not human beings.

Because Arendt puts such emphasis on the role of human works in creating worlds, she agreed with Plato's claim that these works, such as wooden shuttles, represent ideas. In fact, as works representing such ideas form the basis of human worlds—and, as Arendt would have it, our humanity itself—these ideas have enormous transformative power as our world comes to represent them. In the case of texts, even though they do not have the same sort of concrete existence as a Greek temple, they have the potential to rival such works in endurance. Some, like Plato's dialogues, have

---

27. Ibid., 139.

28. Arendt actually champions *homo faber* in the fight against dehumanizing technology, as she imagines technological modernity reducing human beings (*homo faber*) to the nonhuman status of *animal laborans* because we are no longer primarily directing ourselves toward the fabrication of enduring, world-making works, but rather to making objects that barely last beyond the moment of their fabrication. A handmade chalice handed down from one generation to the next has the ability to form a world around it; a modern paper cup has no such power.

29. In some sense, Heidegger himself hinted as much through his example of the Greek temple standing firm against its ever-changing surroundings, suggesting that a culture prizing such works would, not surprisingly, also give birth to a philosopher like Socrates, who would imagine *physis* as strikingly like such an enduring temple. This was an idea to which Heidegger does not sufficiently attend, perhaps because doing so would overturn his thesis that Socratic thinking changed his (and the Western) world; rather, by this view, that world produced Socratic thinking.

endured well beyond the worlds that created them and into ours, which to some degree is still representative of them.

What is nature? To Arendt and Heidegger, nature is the earth's never-ending processes (which is what *physis, natura,* and *cyn* signaled to early Greeks, Romans, and Anglo-Saxons). However, according to Arendt, to be human is to put an end, by violently forcing the earth to steadfastly represent the ideas of the world (as does Heidegger's temple), to what would otherwise be an endless play of absence and presence. Of course, as George Herbert reminds us in his little poem "Church Monuments," even temples will one day turn to dust, but, for a time, they shape worlds by representing ideas that defiantly, like the temple itself, resist nature.

But where does this leave the poet and artist looking to nature? How does an artist go about representing nature in this original sense, when the resultant work, entering into and sustaining a human world, boldly makes a stand against *physis* itself, nature's endless play? One possibility, which has been explored by modern environmental artists such as Andy Goldsworthy, is to use materials such as cut flowers to create landscape installations that barely last beyond their moment of creation, thereby drawing attention to nature as fleeting process. However, in so doing Goldsworthy hardly creates works, let alone representational works, as the installations do not endure long enough to enter into the world. Faced with this difficulty, Goldsworthy photographs the scene before it fades, thereby creating lasting works that capture (as we say, "for posterity") the moment. The obvious consequence, however, is that these photographic works in no way avoid the representational difficulties we have been considering. True, those individuals fortunate enough to view the original installation would have had their attention drawn to nature as process (for example, by means of cut flowers strewn into a stream, thereby revealing the stream's stream as they stream down its length), but the photograph is still just a representation—and in this case a rather poor one, as such works face enormous challenges in representing a scene so alive with process.

There is, however, another alternative available to the poet and artist: Cratylus's option. Had Cratylus wished to make the stream's stream apparent, he would have simply pointed to it. In fact, that is exactly what Goldsworthy's streaming flowers succeed at doing: they gesture to the streaming stream, thereby drawing attention to the Heraclitean streaming of *physis*. In part because of Plato's influence, we tend to think of art as works that represent the world. However, art does not need (1) works to do what it does, (2) to be representational, and (3) to direct itself to human worlds. Had Goldsworthy stopped at his Cratylic gesture to the stream's stream, and not gone on to create a work of photographic representation, his artistic gesture would have largely avoided all three. This is not to say that all or any of these need to be avoided by the artist making such a gesture. As we shall see in the following chapter with Virgil's first Eclogue, a representational work concerned with very worldly matters can also make Cratylic gestures. In fact, the world entering the scene may well prompt the gesture. To understand how, it will be helpful to respond to the title question of Paul Alpers's enormously influential *What Is Pastoral?* with one of our own, the central question of this book: What *else* is pastoral?

2

What Else Is Pastoral?

"It has become something of a truism," noted Nancy Lindheim well over a decade ago, "that Vergil's first Eclogue is the most influential work in the tradition that governs Renaissance pastoral. Paul Alpers, for example, notes that Sidney's *Apology for Poetry* defends the genre solely on the basis of *Eclogue 1,* and Annabel Patterson virtually defines pastoral since Virgil in terms of the use of this one poem."[1] Like many, many critics who followed Alpers and Patterson, Lindheim fully accepts this "truism." Given the critical climate of Renaissance studies in the 1980s and 1990s, this acceptance should come as no great surprise. After all, if what Sidney argued in his 1592 *Apology,* namely, that pastoral literature often cleverly conceals "under pretty tales of wolves and shepherds the misery of people under hard lords and ravening soldiers,"[2] is true, then Renaissance

---

1. Nancy Lindheim, "Spenser's Vergilian Pastoral: The Case for September," *Spenser Studies* 11 (1994), 1.

2. Philip Sidney and Geoffrey Shepherd, eds., *An Apology for Poetry; or, the Defence of Poesy, Nelson's Medieval and Renaissance Library* (London: T. Nelson, 1965), 29–30. This particular

pastoral—as a highly figurative literary mode that obviously owes a massive debt to Virgil's first Eclogue—has the capacity to conceal the sort of political commentary that has so interested literary critics in recent years. As many books and articles have attested in the past few decades, pulling aside the pleasant pastoral veil to reveal underlying political controversies has given Renaissance studies many dramatic moments. Not surprisingly, the view championed by Alpers and Patterson still holds great sway.

While not denying the political nature of classical and Renaissance pastoral, such works, as we shall see, are often also deeply concerned with literal landscapes. Even Virgil's politically suggestive first Eclogue is very much environmentally preoccupied. To understand how, it will be useful to reconsider Alpers's *What is Pastoral?* which largely derives its enormously influential thesis from his 1982 *Critical Inquiry* article of the same title.[3]

Alpers reads Virgil's first Eclogue, on which he argues "formal pastoral" is based, as establishing pastoral's founding paradigm because it reflects a sober awareness of political and cultural realities through its two characters, Meliboeus and Tityrus. In his reading of this eclogue (and of much subsequent pastoral), Alpers suggests that, although acting out their lives against the scenic backdrop of beech trees, groves, and grassy hills, Virgil's shepherds could represent nearly any two human beings, living anywhere, who find themselves caught up in a web of political and economic power. While acknowledging that the "scene-agent ratio" often gives a certain amount of "importance ... to [the] natural setting (as the setting of *A Midsummer Night's Dream* is more important that that of *As You Like It*) ... whatever the specific features and emphasis, it is the representative anecdote of the shepherds' lives that makes certain landscapes pastoral," and not the landscape itself (27–28, parenthetical comment by Alpers). Admittedly a powerful notion, in that it brings forward the cultural and political backdrop behind familiar texts (which is why scholars in the 1980s and 1990s quickly embraced it), this view relegates depictions of the environment in pastoral art to a mere background status.

---

passage from Sidney's *Apology* has, not surprisingly, been cited literally dozens of times in the past two decades in connection with pastoral literature.

3. In order to consider Alpers's more mature thinking on the subject of pastoral, I will be using the somewhat revised version of his 1982 article as it appears in his 1996 book *What is Pastoral?* (Chicago: University of Chicago Press). Unless otherwise noted, all references to Alpers are to this text and are cited parenthetically.

On the subject of backgrounds, Heidegger's thinking is again helpful. In *Being and Time,* Heidegger argues that when it comes to the intelligibility of the backdrop of our lives, we generally lack thematic awareness of this "availableness" (*Zuhandenheit*). However, if there should be a conspicuous malfunction (*auffällig*), an obstinate temporary failure (*Aufsässigkeit*), or most serious of all, an obtrusive total breakdown (*Aufdringlichkeit*) of this availableness, we would suddenly gain awareness of the backdrop as occurrent (*Vorhandenheit*), as that which emerges at hand as a presence, although ironically only belatedly at the moment it falls away from us. Although harshly criticized for this instrumental view of the environment in *Being and Time,* Heidegger meant simply to direct us to the backdrop of our lives that normally escapes notice. Applying this approach to the world of human cultures are analyses of background cultural phenomena such as patriarchy: cultural realities that are always there, yet have historically often managed to escape our attention—unless we bring about at least their partial or temporary breakdown, thereby pulling them out of the background to make them more apparent. Heidegger, however, was also considering the physical environment's availableness.

This is not to say that the environment only becomes something we notice at the moment it is threatened. The point is simply that at such times the backdrop of our existence, which we all too often take for granted, becomes especially apparent and capable of being known more thematically. Consider the metaphor of a play (mentioned in my Introduction): as the action of the players takes center stage, we rightfully say that a play's scenery fades into the background. In fact, we simply call it the "background." This is not, of course, to say that it is no longer there, but simply that we often ignore that it is. But at those moments when the scenery changes before our eyes—and, with respect to scenery, these are the moments that should interest us most—suddenly our awareness shifts from the human action on stage to the scenery behind it, not only to the previous backdrop now being moved away, but also to the new one coming into place. Because the scenery risks fading once more into the background as the actors again take the stage, these scene changes are crucial. While the actors themselves are responsible for the scenery changes in this metaphor, we must not put too great an emphasis on this human action, lest we lose sight of the receding and emerging backdrops as they make their short-lived emergence into appearance.

Returning to Virgil's first Eclogue, it is Tityrus who is of particular interest to Alpers, as his pastoral song departs significantly from that of his companion Meliboeus. Although both friends are subject to political and economic forces largely beyond their control, in contrast to Meliboeus, whose life is shattered as he is exiled from his farm, Tityrus's life remains largely stable, although he, as Alpers observes, is acutely aware that this depends on the actions of his patron in Rome. Tityrus's awareness of the larger political forces acting on his life becomes crucial to Alpers, establishing for him the defining paradigm of all subsequent pastoral: "The natural scene, with its wandering herd, is the setting for Tityrus's freedom, but it is not central to his representation of it. The focus is rather on the human condition [which]...both indicates his dependence on his patron and...brings out...the problematic relations of freedom and dependency" (25). Yet Meliboeus, whose estranged situation should presumably elicit an even greater interest in the inner workings of power, seems nearly oblivious to it. Although Alpers astutely (if somewhat conventionally) notes that "Meliboeus's idyllic [is]...colored by his sense of separation" (25), there is something more going on here.

Out of an obtrusive, total collapse of the availableness (*Zuhandenheit*) of the natural backdrop, caused by his exile from it, Meliboeus directs himself from the first lines he speaks to the startling appearance of that background—of which Tityrus seems nearly oblivious, as no such collapse has occurred for him. (If we are to believe classical commentators such as Aelius Donatus, this may in part have been what motivated Virgil in the writing of the work, as he, like Meliboeus, lost his own farm.)[4] Virgil is not looking back to some sort of golden age, but rather to an historically situated, contemporary moment when the environment becomes the subject of thematic awareness at the very moment of its withdrawal. Indeed, a central feature of this new version of pastoral is revealed through Meliboeus's persistent attempts to enable Tityrus both to see what he sees (to catch sight of the countryside as it falls away from him) and to feel the horror of knowing that there is little he can do to stop it.

---

4. The issue of Virgil losing his farm has been well covered by critics, such as Annabel Patterson in her *Pastoral and Ideology: Vergil to Valéry* (Berkeley: University of California Press, 1987), 31–32.

What else is pastoral? In addition to the concealed political allegory that interests Alpers and many other critics, Virgil's first Eclogue, in a pivotal moment in the history of pastoral, raises and answers a surprisingly modern question: What is environmental consciousness?[5] It is when we, like Meliboeus, become thematically aware of our environment, which sadly may, as it does for Meliboeus, also signal the moment of its withdrawal.

The emergence of such an environmental consciousness appears as early as the opening lines of Virgil's text, in which Meliboeus draws attention to the natural scene with its "spreading beech...woodland Muse...sweet fields [and]...woods," now falling away from him:

> Tityre, tu patulae recubans sub tegmine fagi
> silvestrem tenui musam meditaris avena;
> nos patriae finis et dulcia linquimus arva.
> nos patriam fugimus; tu, Tityre, lentus in umbra
> formosam resonare doces Amaryllida silvas.

> You, Tityrus, under the shelter of a spreading beech,
> Tune the woodland Muse on your slender reed,
> We are leaving our county's borders and our sweet fields,
> We leave our country; you, Tityrus, relaxing in the shade,
> Teach the woods to echo again "fair Amaryllis."[6]

In a move that he will repeat throughout the poem, Virgil has Tityrus respond by drawing attention to the political situation (lines 6–10) while remaining oblivious to Meliboeus's persistent attempts to foreground the background, of which he has lately become extraordinarily aware. When Meliboeus continues by observing in some detail how "undique totis / usque adeo turbatur agris" (11–12, "in the fields everywhere there is so much turmoil"), Tityrus again ignores the fields as he returns to a discussion of his

---

5. I have been avoiding the word *consciousness,* as the term has such a long and circuitous history, in favor of (following Heidegger) "thematic awareness." However, as the phrase "environmental consciousness" is now colloquially with us, I am using it here as roughly equivalent to "thematic awareness of the environmental."

6. While the original Latin is from *Vergil I, Eclogues, Georgics, Aeneid I–VI,* Loeb Classical Library, trans. H. Rushton Fairclough (London: W. Heinemann, 1916), lines 1–5, the translation is mine. All future references to the *Eclogues* in Latin are to this text cited by line number with my translations.

patron in Rome (19–25). True, Tityrus makes mention of "inter viburna cupressi" (25, "cypresses among wayfaring trees"), but having little to do with the actual surrounding countryside, this is simply an analogy explaining how Rome powerfully towers like a cypress over lesser cities. Not surprisingly, after listening to Tityrus pontificate about politics (27–35), Meliboeus observes that his friend has neglected his fields (36–39). In one of the most moving lines of the poem, Meliboeus declares that "ipsae te, Tityre, pinus, / ipsi te fontes, ipsa haec arbusta vocabant" (38–39, "the very pines, Tityrus, / the very springs, the very orchards called out for you!"). Unfortunately, Tityrus was not there to hear or answer their call. Not only has Tityrus neglected the maintenance of his fields, he is, much to Meliboeus's annoyance, oblivious to the environment right before his eyes—like an audience member so obsessed with the human action on stage that the scenery is completely ignored, even though something altogether extraordinary is happening there.

In one last attempt to facilitate the natural backdrop appearing for Tityrus as it has for him (in the language of the poem, to allow Tityrus "to hear it calling out to him"), Meliboeus launches into two protracted descriptions of the surrounding countryside. In the first of these long concluding speeches, Meliboeus attempts to draw Tityrus's attention to "flumina nota et fontis sacros…apibus florem depasta salicti" (51–54, "familiar streams and sacred springs…bees feeding on willow blossoms"), and a variety of birds. Although each of Meliboeus's descriptions, such as these specifically to "willow blossoms" and "palumbres" (57, "turtledoves"), underscore that these are literal, local plants and animals, Tityrus responds by again praising his patron.

> Ante leves ergo pascentur in aethere cervi
> et freta destituent nudos in litore pisces,
> ante pererratis amborum finibus exsul
> aut Ararim Parthus bibet aut Germania Tigrim,
> quam nostro illius labatur pectore vultus.
>
> Sooner, the nimble stag will graze in the air,
> And the seas will leave their fish on the ground;
> Sooner, each wandering through each other's land,
> Will the Persian drink the Arar, the German the Tigris,
> Than his countenance slips from my heart.
>
> (59–63)

Although Alpers draws a different conclusion from these lines, his initial observation regarding them in his early study of the *Eclogues* is squarely on the mark:

> What is striking about these *adynata* (the rhetorical term for such a catalog of impossibilities) is that, though they appear impossible to Tityrus, they are all too real for Meliboeus. His flock is hungry, he and it are being forced out of their element, he has left newborn lambs stranded on bare rock, and, most important, he too is condemned to wander in exile.[7]

In a striking collision of literal and figurative language, Tityrus responds to Meliboeus's literal descriptions of the countryside with figurative language that is intensively insensitive because on a literal level what is described is, as Alpers rightly notes, "all too real for Meliboeus." Nonetheless, in largely focusing on Tityrus's figurative language to the exclusion of Meliboeus's literal descriptions, readers such as Alpers repeat Tityrus's insensitivity in that they downplay the very real situation (the loss and belated appearance of the natural backdrop) to which Meliboeus—and, of course, Virgil—is repeatedly trying to draw attention.

In this sense, Virgil has placed in his text by way of Tityrus a warning of what can happen if the figurative is privileged over the literal. As we shall see in greater detail in chapter 4, reading the language of pastoral from Virgil's first Eclogue onward as either literal or figurative to the exclusion of the other will haunt the reception of the pastoral mode from at least the early Renaissance through today. To focus, like Alpers, on pastoral as political allegory does not even reveal half of the situation, nor will it do to just consider the emergence of environmental consciousness; rather, we need to explore how the cultural (sometimes political) situation veiled in figurative language has profound consequences for those individuals literally facing the loss of an environment. Any discussion of pastoral literature that does not explore how the figurative impacts the literal is simply incomplete.

The irony, seeming paradox, and epistemological insight of Virgil's first Eclogue is that while the natural backdrop appears to Meliboeus (who has lost it), as well as to the reader, it fails to make its appearance to Tityrus,

---

7. Paul Alpers, *The Singer of the Eclogues: A Study of Vergilian Pastoral* (Berkeley: University of California Press, 1979), 70.

who still has possession of it. If the eclogue is successfully conveying Meliboeus's sense of loss to us, then Virgil's text brings us face-to-face with the sobering realization that the natural backdrop is now increasingly absent as it falls away from us. As we saw in the last chapter, and shall see further in the next, this has profound implications, in that lavish mimetic images in pastoral poetry may not only be unnecessary, but actually counterproductive. If they are written in a mode governed by Virgil's first Eclogue, pastoral works should perhaps be less concerned with presenting an image of the now-absent natural backdrop than with making the reader aware of the distressing fact that the very real, literal natural environs outside of the text are withdrawing. Consequently, it should come as little surprise that Renaissance pastoral poetry does not generally contain the sort of lavish descriptions of the environment we have come to expect from writings of later periods.

In Virgil's eclogue, each character wishes for the other to understand what is happening. Meliboeus wishes to signal the appearance and loss of the natural backdrop, while Tityrus offers the political causes for its loss. Meliboeus finds Tityrus neglectful of his duty to his fields, while Tityrus repeatedly makes clear that Meliboeus has neglected his political obligations. These efforts play out on two levels, literal and figurative, with Meliboeus drawing attention to literal "willow blossoms" and "turtledoves" (54, 57), while Tityrus speaks figuratively of cities such as Rome towering like "cypresses among wayfaring trees" (25). And, of course, one of Virgil's great achievements is that Meliboeus's "shelter of a spreading beech" (1) can be read figuratively and Tityrus's suggestion that "the nimble stag will graze in the air" (59) can be read as all too real. While I have been focusing on Meliboeus and his literal images in part as a correction to critics such as Alpers and in part to underscore the often-ignored environmental component of Virgilian pastoral, any consideration of the first Eclogue and other similar pastoral works must take into account both the literal and the figurative: the natural environs and the political and cultural factors acting on them.

Alpers and those critics who followed him are certainly justified in championing Tityrus by contending that Virgil's eclogue involves cultural and political tension (it is, after all, the relation of the Roman world to the land that is central to Virgil), but to dismiss the environment as mere scenery is to overlook the counterpoint made by Virgil's Meliboeus, namely that this backdrop lost its scenery status as it was brought forward—and in the process, through its being foregrounded, provides evidence for an environmental consciousness on Virgil's part. This is not to discount the importance of pastoral as cultural and political allegory; it is simply to suggest that, from as early as Virgil's first Eclogue, it has been of central importance that the natural scene depicted in some pastoral art be understood as more than just mere scenery.

As to why the pastoral mode historically rises in importance when it does, even a cursory look to Roman literature from Virgil's era, such as that written by Cato and Varro (both of whom were widely read in the Renaissance; Cato was actually used as a school text to teach Latin),[8] reveals that the countryside surrounding Rome was undergoing unprecedented changes in the period. In this context, the reinvention of pastoral literature from its Greek roots in the form of the *Eclogues* is hardly surprising. Virgil's innovation, however, is to dramatize the feeling of loss for the vanishing countryside by embodying this emotion in the figure of Meliboeus. This exile motif allowed Virgil to underscore the emotional impact of the scene change, which he dramatized through Meliboeus's lament, as he changes scenes rather than having the scene change about him. This proved to be an exceptionally poignant literary device that will appear repeatedly throughout Western art, dramatically revealing the moment when a place is lost.

A striking early modern example of the exile motif used in a pastoral text to draw attention to the now receding natural backdrop is Aemilia Lanyer's "The Description of Cooke-ham." While critics have noted that this complex poem is fascinating for a host of reasons relating to cosmology and religion,[9] it also has an important environmental component. Written in honor of Margaret Clifford, the Countess of Cumberland, this poem (which along with Jonson's "To Penshurst" inaugurated the so-called "country-house" genre) describes the estate of Cookeham, which

---

8. See Marcus Porcius Cato's *On Agriculture,* and Marcus Terentius Varro's *On Agriculture,* both in the same edition by Loeb Classical Library, trans. by William Davis Hooper (Cambridge MA: Harvard University Press, 1967). Among other Renaissance texts, they are both found in the *Libri de re rustica, M. Catonis, Marci Terentii Varronis, L. Iunii Moderati Columellae, Palladii Rutilii, quorum pagina seque[n]ti reperies* (Paris, 1533).

9. For a detailed treatment of Lanyer and "The Description of Cooke-ham," see Barbara Kiefer Lewalski's *Writing Women in Jacobean England* (Cambridge, MA: Harvard University Press, 1993), 212–41.

the countess's brother leased from the Crown for a time and which, the lease having expired, both women must leave behind. Lanyer, who spent some time at Cookeham in the early 1600s, describes in her poem the place as she and Clifford had once experienced it, but which "never shall my sad eyes again behold."[10] What is surprising is that, while there is an early mention of "the house [that] received all ornaments to grace it" (19), and another in the conclusion, the house itself is largely absent from this so-called country-*house* poem. Rather, nearly all of the attention is given to the countryside. Addressed to "you (great Lady) mistress of that place" (11), the speaker, like Meliboeus in Virgil's first Eclogue, wishes for Clifford (as Meliboeus did for Tityrus) to see clearly the countryside that has appeared before her on receiving the news of her exile from it. While in the language of the first Eclogue, Meliboeus desires that Tityrus should hear the land calling out to him (38–39), in "The Description of Cooke-ham," Lanyer has the estate anthropomorphically acting to draw attention to its features by having them make their appearance before her:

> Hills, vales, and woods, as if on bended knee
> They had appeared, your honor to salute,
> Or to prefer some strange unlooked for suit:
> All interlaced with brooks and crystal springs,
> A prospect fit to please the eyes of kings:
> And thirteen shires appeared all in your sight,
> Europe could not afford much more delight.
> (68–74)

Of course, the speaker could not have seen "thirteen shires" from the estate.[11] What is seen is the land, as if for the first time. Indeed, the entire poem is Lanyer's lavish attempt to allow her mistress to see "Hills, vales, and woods [and everything else that to her]...had appeared."

Following Virgil, and in the process reclaiming the most environmentally significant innovation of the first Eclogue—and arguably of pastoral itself—Lanyer uses the exile motif to dramatize the sense of loss and

---

10. Lanyer's "The Description of Cooke-ham" is cited from *The Poems of Aemilia Lanyer: Salve Deus Rex Judaeorum,* ed. Susanne Woods (Oxford: Oxford University Press, 1993), line 9. All references to Lanyer are to this text and are cited parenthetically by line number.

11. See Lewalski's *Writing Women in Jacobean England,* 238.

catch the very moment when the natural backdrop moves forward for the speaker as it withdraws. In the striking language of the poem, it is the moment when the features of the withdrawing countryside, "their dying bodies half alive, half dead," collectively depart, "placing their former pleasures in your heart" as their last act (146, 154). Using the participial form of "place" to catch the moment when the place itself is placed into the exile as a presence now absent wonderfully underscores that a place has literally been lost, but lives on in memory.

What makes Lanyer's poem somewhat singular among Renaissance pastoral is that, while it has a metaphorical layer, it is not concerned with what was traditionally thought of as "politics" in pastoral literature. The situation bringing about the exile, which is never mentioned directly in Lanyer's poem, is that the speaker and her companion are, like Meliboeus, helpless in the face of those who wield power. What distinguishes Lanyer's from Virgil's poem is that it is not a powerful politician in Rome who is deciding the fate of the exiles, but rather, economic and domestic concerns. As Lanyer makes dramatically clear in her poem, the disinheritance of women in early modern England was at times strikingly similar to what disenfranchised, exiled men had been experiencing for at least sixteen hundred years.

Although my interest in this chapter is principally in how early modern texts were influenced by Virgil, to explore the pastoral mode further it will be helpful to very briefly move to a more recent text. Consider the very pastoral opening to Elizabeth Gaskell's novel *Mary Barton:*

> There are some fields near Manchester, well known to the inhabitants as "Green Heys Fields"... there is a charm about them which strikes even the inhabitant of a mountainous district, who sees and feels the effect of contrast in these commonplace but thoroughly rural fields, with the busy, bustling manufacturing town he left but half-an-hour ago. Here and there an old black and white farmhouse, with its rambling outbuildings, speaks of other times and other occupations than those which now absorb the population of the neighbourhood.[12]

While it is unlikely that Gaskell will ever be thought of as a nature writer, as Jonathan Bate and others have argued,[13] in so bringing attention to the

---

12. Elizabeth Gaskell, *Mary Barton* (London: John Lehmann, 1947), 13.

13. See Jonathan Bate's *Romantic Ecology: Wordsworth and the Environmental Tradition* (London: Routledge, 1991).

changing, indeed vanishing, countryside outside of England's expanding industrial cities, writers of her time reveal the emergence of an environmental consciousness. Although Gaskell is clearly concerned with political and cultural shifts, she nonetheless is in part chronicling the profound, unprecedented changes to the environment occurring outside of industrial cities in nineteenth-century England. Not surprisingly, then, the receding backdrop is not described as belonging to some long-past mythical age, but rather to a time so recent that we can still catch sight of it on the edge of the expanding industrial scene at Manchester. By placing the reader in the liminal space between emerging and receding backdrops, Gaskell is able to draw attention to both. Consequently, a work of this sort is not concerned with an individual (like Meliboeus) changing scenes, but rather with how the scene itself is changing. It has been argued, however, that changes to the environment in nineteenth-century England were unlike anything that had occurred before, making literature of the period fundamentally different from traditional pastoral. Nonetheless, if we look back 250 years before the 1847 publication of *Mary Barton,* it becomes clear that a similar story was already being told.

Like Gaskell, John Stow was interested in what was occurring outside of an English city: London, in 1597. In his tour of the city, called *A Survey of London,* he makes clear that, in order to understand the transformations happening in and around contemporary London, he needs to chronicle this scene change by considering both what the city had once been and what it was becoming. In order to present a picture of what London was in "auncient time," Stow translates from a twelfth-century account of the city's suburbs given by William Fitzstephen:

> On all sides, without the houses of the Suburbs, are the citizens gardens & orchard, planted with trees, both large, sightly, & adjoining together. On the north side there are pastures & plain medows, with brooks running through them, turning water mills, with a pleasant noise. Not far off is a great forrest, a well wooded chase, having good cover for Harts, Buckes, Does, Boores, & wild Bulles. The corne fields are not of a hungry sandie mould, but as the fruitfull fields of Asia; yielding plentifull encrease, & filling the barnes with corne.[14]

---

14. John Stow, *A Survey of London,* intro. and notes by Charles Lethbridge Kingsford (Oxford: Clarendon Press, 1908), II, 70. Fitzstephen is translated by Stowe. All references to Stow are to this text, cited parenthetically.

By 1597, this natural backdrop affectionately (and pastorally) described by Fitzstephen was nearly gone. While the causes of growth may have been different, early modern London experienced expansion similar to that of Victorian industrial towns such as Manchester. Indeed, some estimates have London's population growing tenfold from 1500 to 1700. Certainly during a portion of Stow's lifetime, from 1560 to 1600, the number of Londoners at least doubled. Perhaps not surprisingly then, Stow is repeatedly outraged by the suburban growth into the rural countryside described by Fitzstephen. In general, "the suburbs about London hath bin...mightily increased with buildings" (II, 70). For example, near Aldegate, "both sides of the streete bee pestered with Cottages, and Allies, euen vp to White chapel church: and almost a half mile beyond it, into the common field: all which ought to lye open & free for all men" (II, 72).

However, as Patrick Collinson astutely observes, something important needs to be noted about Stow's observations:

> Stow compresses the centuries. Having quoted Fitzstephen at length on orders and customs, "the estate of things in his time," Stow writes "whereunto may be added the present, by conference whereof, the alteration will easily appear." The implication is of a world which had remained more or less static until a vaguely defined moment which seems to correspond to the years of Stow's own childhood, the 1530s. The great changes which he alleges, and regrets, had all or mostly happened in his own lifetime, not in the four centuries which distanced him from [Fitzstephen].[15]

Collinson compellingly argues that although Stow purports to be looking back four centuries, he is, in fact, contrasting 1597 London to a period of time just decades earlier, his childhood.

This is consistent with the notion of pastoral we have been putting forth. Once changes to the scene have taken place, it is not surprising that the new backdrop takes on mere scenery status for the next generation born into it, suggesting that what is "natural" for each generation has traditionally often been the historically situated backdrop into which we are born. Stow, who like Gaskell witnessed in his lifetime a profound change in his

---

15. Patrick Collinson, "John Stow and Nostalgic Antiquarianism," in *Imagining Early-modern London: Perceptions and Portrayals of the City from Stow to Stype, 1598–1720*, ed. J. F. Merritt (Cambridge: Cambridge University Press, 2001), 28–29.

surroundings, is ideally positioned to chronicle such a scene shift. This is not to say that an imagined golden age cannot act as some sort of reference, as Fitzstephen's descriptions do for Stow, but what in large measure motivates such a project are the profound changes occurring to the environment in a single lifetime. (This also explains why writers as early as Shakespeare in *The Winter's Tale* and Friedrich Schiller in his 1795 essay "On Naïve and Sentimental Poetry" brought together the notion of a pastoral golden age and childhood.) Once attention is drawn to the shifted scene—once consciousness of the environment emerges and what counts as "natural" is fixed—a golden-age reference is often sought to help in charting the changes; nonetheless, what motivates this maneuver are the contemporary changes themselves. Not surprisingly, the two often become entangled, with an imagined golden age of London four hundred years past becoming equivalent in Stow's text to the relatively recent, remembered past of his own childhood.

But what exactly is the city's role in such pastoral works? Consider Heidegger's Greek temple (mentioned in the preceding chapter), which, in spite of being a work of art, "portrays nothing" as it

> holds its ground against the storm raging above it and so makes the storm manifest in its violence. The luster and gleam of the stone, though itself apparently glowing only by the grace of the sun, yet first brings to light the light of day, the breadth of the sky, the darkness of night.... The steadfastness of the work contrasts with the surge of the surf, and its repose brings out the raging of the sea.[16]

Buildings are not generally representational. True, certain churches represent crosses when viewed from above; however, Heidegger's "temple-work" is able to make a raging storm manifest not because it provides a representation of the storm, as might happen with a painting of the scene, but rather because the character of the temple reveals the contrasting character of its surroundings. Unlike Japan's Jingu Shrine, which is a series of wood structures accepted as being in a state of constant decay (and which, consequently, has been rebuilt every twenty years since the seventh century), Heidegger's stone temple is a work that seeks permanence: constant

---

16. "The Origin of the Work of Art," 41–42.

presence across time. To the extent that it succeeds (or at least appears as if it does), it reveals the impermanence of the backdrop shifting around it. "The steadfastness of the work contrasts with the surge of the surf" as well as with the ebb and flow of other aspects of the surrounding environment, such as the raging storm. The temple reveals this surrounding flux through its own contrasting permanence, not through attempts at representation, as it neither represents the rage of the storm, the surge of the surf, nor anything else.

If we expand the notion of "works," as does Hannah Arendt, to include not just works of art, but also architectural works like cities, then it becomes apparent that city works also have the power to reveal their surrounding environments in a way that is not principally representational, but rather gestural. Insofar as early modern London contrasted so strikingly with its surroundings, the endangered environment encircling the city would have been revealed (as it was for Stow) in an entirely new manner by this city work. While we might resist thinking of Stow's London or Gaskell's Manchester as artworks, such works can, as we have seen in the case of Heidegger's temple work, reveal much through gesture. In this sense, the explosion of pastoral artwork in sixteenth- and seventeenth-century London occurred in part because that city at that moment in its history was—precisely because it facilitated the emergence of an environmental consciousness in its citizens and artists—one of the greatest pastoral works ever created.

This raises an obvious question: Just what is the relationship of works such as cities to works that have traditionally been thought of as pastoral, such as bucolic poetry? Fortunately for us, as it speaks directly to the nature of pastoral, one of the most remarkable reflections on this question came just a few years after Stow's *Survey:* Ben Jonson's poem "To Penshurst."

3

What Else Was Pastoral in the Renaissance?

Once we realize what was occurring to London's surroundings in Stow's time, it quickly becomes apparent that it influenced a variety of works. Consider the opening of "To Penshurst":

> Thou art not, Penshurst, build to envious show
> Of touch or marble, nor canst boast a row
> Of polished pillars, or a roof of gold;
> Thou hast no lantern whereof tales are told,
> Or stair, or courts; but stand'st an ancient pile,
> And these grudged at, art reverenced the while.
> Thou joy'st in better marks, of soul, of air,
> Of wood, of water; therein thou art fair.[1]

---

1. Jonson's "To Penshurst" is cited from *Ben Jonson,* ed. C. H. Herford and Percy Simpson (Oxford: Clarendon Press, 1925-) vol. 8, lines 1–8. All references to Jonson are to this text and are cited parenthetically by line number.

Jonson here establishes a number of features that will come to define the genre of the country-house poem. Most noticeably, he compares Penshurst to the grand country houses of the time. With their lanterns (glass turrets) and rows of pillars, they are models of excess, built merely for "envious show" and entertaining the court. Unlike Penshurst, they are newly built, not standing on an "ancient pile."

It is, however, crucial to consider where these houses were being built. Written shortly before Jonson's poem, Stow's 1597 *Survey* introduced many of the elements Jonson will employ—but in Stow's case this is explicitly a critique of suburban expansion outside of London's walls: "But now we see the thing in worse case than euer, by meanes of inclosures for Gardens, wherein are builded many faire summer houses, and as in other places of the Suburbes, some of them like Midsommer Pageantes, with Towers, Turrets, and Chimney tops, not so much for vse or profite, as for shewe" (II, 78). While Stow's attack on London's sprawl touches on a number of issues that will repeatedly reappear in country-house poems, one of the most important, somewhat surprisingly, involves literal foundations.

From "To Penshurst" to "Upon Appleton House," a recurring feature of many country-house poems is the notion that the houses being extolled are either ancient or built on an ancient pile (foundation). To understand the significance of this inclusion, it is important to realize that Stow and Jonson were hardly the first to notice and object to the suburban scene-change taking place around London. In fact, distressed at what was happening outside of the city's walls, from 1580 onward Elizabeth, James I, Charles I, Cromwell, and Charles II (not to mention various Parliaments and mayors) attempted unsuccessfully to not only curb, but actually outlaw, all building in London's suburbs. A feature common to all these various schemes was an order that no new houses could be built, the one exception being that they could be constructed where there had recently been houses, on existing foundations. For example, a proclamation of Elizabeth's from July 1580 notes that

> the Queene's Majestie perceiving the state of the Citie London (being anciently termed her Chambre) and the suburbs and confines to increase dayly...her Majestie by good and deliberate advice of her Council...doth charge and straightly command all manner of Persons...to desist and forbeare from any new building of any house or tenement within three miles

from of any gates of the said citie of London, to serve for Habitation or Lodging for any person where no House hath been knowen to have been in the memories of such as are now living.[2]

To a contemporary reader aware of the rampant, notorious development in London's suburbs, the opening lines of "To Penshurst" could not be a more obvious contrast. Seen in this original context, the fact that a country house is applauded for being built on an "ancient pile" is not just a figurative device designed to legitimately ground the dwelling in some distant past that is only imagined (as critics such as David Riggs have argued),[3] but rather is an effort to give it credibility in the face of what officially was seen as the illegal development of the previously rural suburbs. Indeed as time went on, in spite of literally dozens of attempts to check London's ever-expanding growth, including the imposition of stiff fines and mandatory demolition of newly erected buildings, there was little that could be done to curtail it—in spite of the fact that the "no-building" zone kept increasing. In 1615 James I expanded Elizabeth's three-mile ordinance to include "New Buildings with[in] seven miles of the town"; by 1657 Cromwell introduced an "act for preventing Multiplicity of Buildings in and about the suburbs of London and within ten miles thereof."[4] Penshurst, which, given its position outside of the suburbs, would have been excluded from even the most far-reaching of the later antidevelopment ordinances, could not be a greater contrast, both in location and character, to the ring of opulent prodigy houses circling the city.

While there is a mention of "country stone" walls (45) from within which "fires / Shine bright on every hearth" (77–78), the house of Jonson's patrons, the Sidneys, is otherwise so strikingly absent from "To Penshurst" that one reader, Alastair Fowler, aptly suggests that the entire genre is misnamed and might better be called country-"estate poems."[5] At a time when changes in London's suburbs were increasingly drawing attention to (and prompting civil action on behalf of) previously rural locales, "To

2. Quoted from Sir Laurence Gomme's *The Making of London* (London: 1912), 214–17.

3. David Riggs, *Ben Jonson: A Life* (Cambridge, MA: Harvard University Press, 1989), 183–87.

4. From Norman G. Brett-James's *The Growth of Stuart England,* (London: George Allen & Unwin, 1935), 90.

5. Alastair Fowler, *The Country House Poem: A Cabinet of Seventeenth-Century Estate Poems and Related Items* (Edinburgh: Edinburgh University Press, 1994) 1.

Penshurst" and similar poems were simultaneously drawing attention to country estates as not only extant, but thriving, rural environments. While Stow repeatedly lamented the loss of "fayre hedgerows of Elme trees [and]... pleasant fields, very commodious for Citizens to walke, shoot, and otherwise recreate" (I, 127), Jonson conversely begins his commendation of Penshurst's surroundings by noting that "Thou joy'st in better marks, of soil, of air, / of wood, of water; therein thou art fair" (7–8). At a time when this countryside was announcing its appearance in the suburbs at the very moment of its withdrawal, Jonson spends a great deal of time in "To Penshurst" drawing attention to a scene, a rural country estate, just beyond the edge of this suburban transformation (literally just a few miles south of it) where the environment was, at least as he imagined it, still intact, from the wilderness of old-growth forests containing "the broad beech and chestnut" (13), through the very pastoral "lower land [where]... Thy sheep... do feed" (22–23), to "Thy [clearly georgic] orchard fruit" (39). Jonson is certainly convoluting his view of Sidney's estate with a golden age, but what emerges is far more (and far more contemporary) than the pleasant place "where Pan and Bacchus their high feasts have made" (11).

But what exactly is responsible for the appearance of this environment? It is, of course, in part sprawling London that facilitated the emergence of the countryside to Jonson. Consequently, since the new backdrop moving onto the scene (London as it moved into its surroundings) would have been as apparent as the one withdrawing, Jonson could certainly have chronicled the emergence of this expanding city and the life taking place there. And in other works he did just that. But in "To Penshurst," Jonson, like Heidegger, shifts his attention away from the striking work of architecture before him to the even more startling sights now silhouetted along its boundaries. To hold this pastoral focus, Jonson never looks to the city in "To Penshurst." Or more precisely, though he opens the poem with an indirect reference to the city's sprawl, he never directly mentions the suburban prodigy houses. Instead, he obliquely draws attention to them as what "Thou art not, Penshurst." Nonetheless, this would have, as Jonson no doubt intended, quickly invoked suburban sprawl in the mind of his contemporary reader.

In the same way that cities like London reveal their environment, the house at Penshurst (as Jonson imagines it) reveals its surrounding estate, though positively and more in the manner of Heidegger's temple.

Although I have unabashedly appropriated Heidegger's example for my own purposes, it must be remembered that he calls on the Greek temple as a means of catching a work of art at work. To return to the spirit of Heidegger's example of an artwork, we might think of one of Frank Lloyd Wright's designs, such as the house at Fallingwater, Pennsylvania, which from its foundation of locally quarried stones (which draw attention to surrounding outcroppings of the same) upward is designed to gesture to its surroundings. Indeed, the house's very name underscores that it gestures and draws attention to the waters it spans rather than to itself. If the house is making such gestures successfully, first-time visitors would leave having not only seen an unfamiliar house, but also a familiar landscape as if for the first time.

Similarly, on approaching the house Jonson imagines at Penshurst (which, admittedly, may bear little relation to reality), from a distance visitors might be unsure if they were seeing a house made of "country stone" (45) or simply natural formations of the same. On moving closer and recognizing it as a house, the placement of local stone in its walls would bring attention to the stone itself, not only in the walls, but also in surrounding outcroppings of the same. Because of this gesture, the house would illuminate and be responsible for the appearance of aspects of the surrounding environment, although, of course, not by means of representation. Consequently, the house would be responsible for both the environment's appearance (emergence into awareness) to us and its appearance (its specific look) to us. It is well accepted that artworks representing landscapes, including certain paintings, can influence how such landscapes appear to us; however, a work such as the house at Penshurst, in addition to facilitating greater awareness of the countryside, also has the ability to affect how that countryside appears. If a writer wished to draw attention to this phenomenon, perhaps the best approach, which indeed was Jonson's, would be to begin the poem by introducing the house as the work responsible for this phenomenon, then to quickly move to an extended treatment of the countryside revealed by this dwelling. In order to hold the pastoral focus on the surrounding estate, descriptions of the house, if present at all, should be kept to an absolute minimum.

In striking contrast to London's suburban growth, which, as Stow made clear, was endangering its surroundings, in "To Penshurst," Jonson not only suggests that the title house is responsible for the appearance of the surrounding estate, he argues that the dwelling actually protects that countryside. As both Stow and Jonson argue through their attacks on contemporary prodigy houses, part of the problem was that the resources of their surrounding estates could not sustain such lavish dwellings. One can imagine standing before one of these houses and, though suitably impressed, being aghast at the surroundings: Many of the estate's trees would have been cut for lumber, while needed cash for the imported marble and gold would have been collected by overfishing streams, selling off livestock and the remaining timber, and working tenant farmers and their fields into ruin. Avoiding all this, the relatively humble house Jonson imagines at Penshurst would be surrounded by an explosion of life: plant, animal, and human.

This explosion of life is the environment to which Jonson introduces us, beginning with plants and animals: the old-growth "broad beech and the chestnut" tree (12) and plentiful "sheep... bullocks, kine and calves" (23). While it could be (and frequently has been) argued that "The painted partridge... for thy mess willing to be killed" (29–30) anthropocentrically suggests that the plants and animals of the estate are there merely so that they might be used by human beings, fabulous images of "Bright eels" who "leap on land / Before the fisher, or into his hand" (37–38) suggest (admittedly in an over-the-top way) that Penshurst is a place of remarkable fertility and fecundity precisely because of the sensitivity of the human beings who live in the place. Not only would the plants and animals suffer if the lord of Penshurst did not dwell there with care, but the tenant farmers would suffer as well. But fortunately, because the walls of Penshurst are judiciously made of simple "country stone, / They're reared with no man's ruin, no man's groan; / There's none that dwell about them that wish them down" (45–47). In Jonson's poem, the Sidney house does not overtax—literally or otherwise—the people, animals, or plants of the place; rather, such a dwelling is portrayed as adding wealth and fertility to the countryside.

In his *The Country and the City*, Raymond Williams famously saw in "To Penshurst" the harsh reality of class struggle that made such an estate possible;[6] however, Jonson might also be seen as offering careful environmental prescriptions to Sidney through these golden-age descriptions.

---

6. See Raymond Williams's *The Country and the City* (London: Chatto and Windus, 1973) 27–34.

Given that the images are so excessive, they can be seen as offering a pre-scribed goal of fertility and fecundity that can never be realized but at which Sidney should nonetheless aim. By this reading, not only is Williams's po-sition justified, it is actually the point of "To Penshurst," as Jonson offers his patron Sidney a model and goal not only of greater environmental re-sponsibility but of more equitable class relations at a time when they were sorely needed. Taken in this sense, although Jonson describes the walls of the house as "reared with no man's ruin, no man's groan" (45–46), he is perhaps suggesting that this should be the model followed by Sidney. Alternately, these passages can be read simply as hyperbolic descriptions, in which case Jonson is praising Sidney for having already done much to improve class relations. The difficulty with the position taken by Williams et al. is that, dating as it does to a time when critics doing historical analy-sis of literary texts often ignored the intentions of the individual artist (it first appeared in 1973), this approach makes a blanket statement regard-ing early modern class relations. It therefore ignores the possibility that Jonson, aware of the class problem, is either proposing specific changes himself or praising changes that Sidney had already implemented, such as not taxing tenant farmers into ruin to finance the extravagance of the land-owner. Given Jonson's own complex and ambiguous class position, neither suggestion should come as a great surprise.

It is worth pausing to consider the environmental implications of what Jonson's poem celebrates. In modern terms we might call it "sustainable yield." Although not named as such, this concept was well understood in Renaissance England. For example, because as much as 80 percent of En-gland's forests had already been destroyed by the eleventh century, measures were put into place in the centuries leading up to the Renaissance in order to conserve remaining stands of wood. Because manufacturers of charcoal (which provided the fuel for iron foundries) from coppice wood could not transport their fragile product more than a few miles, they selectively cut (rather than clear-cut) their forests in order to ensure that the foundries were circled by a long-term supply of potential fuel.[7] When such careful stewardship of resources was not practiced, as in the years leading up to

---

7. See Michael W. Flinn's "The Growth of the English Iron Industry: 1660–1760," *Economic History Review* 11.1 (1958): 144–53, and his "Timber and the Advance of Technology: A Reconsid-eration," *Annals of Science* 15.2 (1959): 109–20.

the civil war in the Forest of Dean,[8] those in control of the woodlots were frequently censured. In the case of the Forest of Dean scandal, a 1649 Act by Parliament temporarily excluded the cutting and sale of certain forests until a policy ensuring sustainable yield could be put into place, which resulted in passing the Act for the Deforestation, Sale, and Improvements of the Forests in November 1653. Jonson's inclusion of old-growth forests containing "the broad beech and chestnut" in "To Penshurst" (13), as well as streams that are clearly anything but overfished, establishes a country-house model of careful stewardship ensuring sustainable yield—a feature that will reappear repeatedly in later examples of the genre.

In the concluding line of "To Penshurst" ("their lords have built, but thy lord dwells"), Jonson explores such stewardship by suggesting that the human activity of dwelling is vastly different than a structure. Others build buildings, lasting artifacts, but the lord of Penshurst is imagined as prudently engaged in the ongoing act of dwelling on the land. To catch a glimpse of the lord of Penshurst's dwelling—both his act of living on the estate as well as the structure in which he lives—we need to look to the place where he dwells to see the impact of the dwelling (both as activity and structure). The continuing activity of such active dwelling surpasses even such extraordinary buildings as Wright's house at Fallingwater. Wright's house may facilitate the appearance of its surrounding countryside, but the responsible way in which Jonson imagines Sidney dwelling at Penshurst ensures that this particular environment, which includes plants, animals, and human inhabitants, is not asked to yield more than it can sustain.

Jonson cleverly makes this point by concluding his argument and poem with the suggestion that some "May say, their lords have built [solidly placing the activity of building, which, now completed, has left a habitable artifact behind, in the past], but thy lord dwells," leaving us at poem's end with the open, ongoing activity of Sidney dwelling in his country dwelling. If we hold Jonson's pastoral focus, we are left not with an image of

---

8. As John Taylor noted in 1641, the "iron milles in the forrest of Dean does eate up all the wood there (as hath already done reasonably well and ill) within these few yeares, if [coal cannot be delivered there]...it is feared that many rich men will bee glad to blow their fingers ends in the winter through want of fiering, and numbers of poore will perish with extreme cold; the complaints and cryes are grievous already; which if I had not heard and seene I would not have beleeved." From John Taylor's *Travels through Stuart Britain: The Adventures of John Taylor, the Water Poet* (Stroud, UK: Sutton, 1999), 198.

Sidney's dwelling (understood in either sense, as activity or artifact), but rather, silhouetted along the boundaries of the dwelling (in both senses) and facilitated by it, with the striking appearance of the environment, the true subject of his poem, which emerges, not belatedly at the moment of its withdrawal, but rather as enduring, because of the responsible dwelling taking place there. While similarly revealing the environment, Sidney's dwelling is thus in striking contrast to London.

Generalizing Jonson's distinction between a structure and the act of dwelling by way of the related but broader distinction Hannah Arendt makes between "work" and "labor," we can say, following Jonson, that not only lasting works (artifacts, such as cities or houses) can reveal the countryside through gesture, but that the very activity of human "labor" (which, as Arendt makes clear, in both etymology and colloquial use, is a word signaling a process that produces no lasting works or artifacts)[9] can serve the same illuminating role. In so doing, Jonson's epiphany challenges Arendt's project, in that she contends that only lasting works, principally artworks, have this ability. If we follow Jonson's shift from offensive works (buildings) at the beginning of "To Penshurst" to the activity of dwelling praised at poem's end, it becomes clear that the labor of dwelling can do the revelatory work that we normally associate with works of art, yet need not necessarily produce an enduring work.[10] True, the labor of the Sidney family produced a lasting work in the form of its house, but it is the ongoing labor that Jonson privileges over the artifact at the end of his poem. The implication, that labor can do the work of art without producing a work of any kind, let alone what we would rank as a work of art, is startling.

---

9. For Arendt's distinction between "work" and "labor," see *The Human Condition,* (Chicago: Bantam, 1958) 7, 96–126, and elsewhere. In a sense, Arendt's entire project derives from this "distinction between [the words] *labor* and *work,* which our theorists have so obstinately neglected and our languages have so stubbornly preserved" (94, emphasis added). Indeed, "every European language, ancient and modern, contains [a similar pair of]…etymologically unrelated words for what we have come to think of as the same activity, and retains them in the face of their persistent synonymous usage" (80). Although intimated by Locke, Hegel, and Marx (80 ff.), it is Arendt who first thematically attends to this distinction hidden in our languages.

10. In Jonson's poem, much of this labor can be attributed to Robert Sidneys's wife Barbara Gamage, as it is "the just reward of her high housewifery" (85). In fact, we now know that Gamage and the steward employed by the Sidneys performed much of the managerial labor at Penshurst. For Barbara Gamage's management of the Penshurst estate, see Barbara Kiefer Lewalski's *Writing Women in Jacobean England* (Cambridge, MA: Harvard University Press, 1993), 235–37, 399 n.60.

It is clear that we will not "have a far truer idea of pastoral if we take its" true story "to be the herdsmen and their lives, rather than landscape" (Alpers 22); on the contrary, certain pastoral poems, such as "To Penshurst," explore how we become conscious of a landscape at the moment of its endangerment. But is this done representationally? Is the landscape actually represented in Jonson's poem? Of course it is. But might Jonson's poem, like the house at Penshurst, facilitate the appearance of the environment without lavishly representing it? Even works that work in part by means of representation might be doing some, perhaps most, of their work by gesture.

In this sense, a pastoral poem such as "To Penshurst" works like a human nature guide walking beside us, making Cratylic gestures at every turn: "Look, 'the broad beech and the chestnut'" (12), "Look, 'the purple pheasant with the speckled sides'" (28), "Look, 'the painted partridge lies in every field'" (29), and so forth. Before having our attention drawn to the pheasant as it was brought forward into appearance for us gesturally, not only might it have entirely escaped our attention and failed to make its appearance, but its appearance as "purple…with the speckled sides" might also have escaped notice. Jonson's poem would have acted similarly to such a guide to the owner of Penshurst, Robert Sidney, as well as friends who knew his estate. One can imagine Jonson's patron walking about the grounds of the estate, poem in hand, noticing features of the environment illuminated by the gesturing work of art. This raises an important observation about topographic poems made by Angus Fletcher:

> The topographic poem typically points to a *specific* place.... The problem is that if you emphasize the topographic as traditionally understood, you neglect the broader notion of environment, and you lose track of the medium by which all visions of external reality must be presented to the reader. You lose track of description.[11]

However, with Jonson's poem, which predates those that Fletcher references, we "lose track of description" precisely because we need not subscribe to the notion that "all visions of external reality must be presented to the reader" by way of representation. In fact, the notion that any vision

---

11. *A New Theory for American Poetry,* 32 (Fletcher's emphasis).

of an "external reality" wildly in flux can successfully be "[re]presented to the reader" has, from at least as early as the philosopher Cratylus, been questioned. In contrast, by making Cratylic gestures to the environment, poems such as Jonson's do not "neglect the broader notion of environment," but rather work diligently to make us conscious of a very specific local environment, perhaps at the moment of its endangerment, which may in the bargain lead to a general, "broader notion of environment" (i.e., environmental consciousness).[12] Consequently, poems, especially those in the Renaissance, that are moored to specific locales may not chiefly be, as they are often characterized, "loco-descriptive," but also (and perhaps mainly, as in the case of "To Penshurst") loco-gestural.

Pastoral works such as "To Penshurst" can be responsible for the appearance of an environment (and, with it, the emergence of environmental consciousness) while doing very little to represent it. Descriptions, such as the partridge being "painted," are of course present in the work, but what is far more important is what is revealed silhouetted outside of the text. Not only is there much outside of such a text, the text crucially gestures to what lies outside. Thus, such a Cratylic work works best if it does not draw excessive attention to itself or its own representational images: if a nature guide walking beside us gave in to the temptation of representation by lavishly describing the countryside around us, it would not only be superfluous, as the scene itself would now be present at hand, it would risk being counterproductive by detracting from the surrounding environment. Certainly some representations may be helpful in gesturing to the scene, such as it being a "*painted* partridge" (29), but as Jonson makes clear with this single-word (and only vaguely descriptive) modifier, a little representation can go a long way. As we shall see in the following chapter, although having often escaped modern critical attention, this was a maxim well understood by Renaissance nature writers.[13]

---

12. Consequently, to subsequent generations of readers not familiar with these surroundings, poems such as "To Penshurst" can similarly direct us to our own environments.

13. This is not to say that this maxim would not be challenged. Contrast Pope's lavish description of a pheasant in "Winsor Forest" with Jonson's simple "purple pheasant with the speckled sides":

> See! from the brake the whirring pheasant springs,
> And mounts exulting on triumphant wings:
> Short is his joy; he feels the fiery wound,
> Flutters in blood, and panting beats the ground.

And it was also understood long before the Renaissance. In his first Eclogue, in which Meliboeus persistently attempts to draw Tityrus's attention to the appearance of the surrounding environs, Virgil also offers few mimetic images of the countryside. In fact, throughout this eclogue Virgil keeps his descriptions of the natural environs to an absolute minimum. Consider Meliboeus's closing remarks, spoken to his livestock:

> non ego vos posthac viridi proiectus in antro
> dumosa pendere procul de rupe videbo;
> carmina nulla canam; non me pascente, capellae,
> florentem cytisum et salices carpetis amaras.

> No longer will I, stretched out in a cavern of green,
> Watch you in the distance hanging on a bushy rock.
> I'll sing no songs. Not with me as shepherd, my goats,
> Will you feed on flowering clover and bitter willows.
>
> (75–78)

In his final, and arguably most moving, description of the surrounding environment, as Meliboeus remembers the scene now lost to him, he offers few descriptive images, yet makes clear that these are real, local features of the countryside. For example, although he had a number of words to describe clover at his disposal (such as *medica* and *melilotos*), he chooses to invoke a particular type of bushy clover that goats feed on when it flowers ("florentem cytisum"). Meliboeus performs his role of nature guide by using as few words as possible to direct Tityrus (as Virgil does his readers) to the natural backdrop, which he makes clear is real rather than just figurative. Using an extraordinary economy of language to draw attention to the specific natural environs is not only a shared feature of Virgil's first Eclogue and Jonson's "To Penshurst," but of much of the nature writing that came between them.

Rather than attempting descriptions of the countryside, what is perhaps more important is that a work (or labor) such as Virgil's first Eclogue

---

> Ah! what avail his glossy, varying dyes,
> His purple crest, and scarlet-circled eyes,
> The vivid green his shining plumes unfold,
> His painted wings, and breast that flames with gold?

"Winsor Forest" by Alexander Pope, in *Selected Poetry and Prose,* ed. by Robin Sowerby (London: Routledge, 1988), lines 10–17. As we shall see in the close of chapter 3, such lavish descriptions of the natural world would flourish from the eighteenth century onward.

or Jonson's "To Penshurst" creates a mood. This is especially important for those individuals who will not experience the actual countryside of the work. Consider the mood created by Wright's aforementioned house at Fallingwater. Everything about the structure, from its carefully chosen natural materials to the extraordinary attention to detail involved in working those materials into a house, conveys the sense that the surrounding environs are deeply respected. This is similar to the mood Jonson creates for Penshurst. Alternately, consider a modern tract house built in the desert: from its massive air-conditioning unit to its necessarily irrigated plants, it conveys a deep sense of fear. It is making a stand against the desert, attempting to stave off what is obviously perceived as an environment hardly capable of sustaining human life. Although an extreme example, this is similar to the mood Jonson creates for London's suburban prodigy houses, which he sees as warring against the countryside.

The extent to which Renaissance pastoral works avoid mimesis is a complicated question. Certainly this issue cannot be explored adequately by means of a single "country-house" poem. However, we might provisionally see why asking this question is important by turning to Theodor Adorno, who provocatively suggested in his *Aesthetic Theory* that "art, the rescue of nature, revolts against nature's transitoriness."[14] In the simplest sense, by this Adorno meant that nature as process, as forever unfolding and transitory (an ongoing play of absence and presence), can seemingly be given permanence in art. However, this presents a problem in that "the tension between objectivating technique and the mimetic essence of artworks is fought out in the effort to save the fleeting, the ephemeral, the transitory in a form that is immune to reification and yet akin to it in being permanent."[15] Because artworks by their very nature should resist reification far more than most objects (by inviting ongoing subjective encounter, lest they become hardened and dead), the fact that "the mimetic essence of artworks" seeks permanence is clearly problematic. As Tom Huhn concisely explains Adorno's dilemma:

> The task for the artwork—or, perhaps we might now just as readily say, the task for *mimesis*—is to objectivate the momentary in such a way that

---

14. Theodor Adorno, *Aesthetic Theory,* eds. Gretel Adorno and Rolf Adorno (London: Athlone, 1997), 184.

15. Ibid., 219.

it stands in contrast to reification. Yet the very technique of art, what we might call its inseparability from form, is in tension with its mimetic essence. The trick for art—and since art is the refuge for *mimesis,* the task for *mimesis*—is to somehow objectivate without reification, to express without expressing something, and to think without being too well thought.[16]

This is a true dilemma because, as Adorno notes, "the greatest justice that was done to the mimetic impulse becomes the greatest injustice, because permanence, objectification, ultimately negates the mimetic impulse." This was not historically brought about "by art's putative decline but," worrisomely, "by the very idea of art itself."[17]

This raises an important question, so seemingly self-evident that it often goes unasked: Does art represent nature? Setting aside the sticky question of how successful works of art can ever be at representing nature wildly in flux, certain art, and this includes some pastoral poetry, has the ability to sidestep this problem as it facilitates and attempts to govern the appearance of nature through gesture, rather than, revolting against nature's transitoriness, attempting its preservation through representation. In fact, approaches such as Jonson's underscore transitoriness, as they draw attention to nature in the process of profound change. True, one could attempt to lavishly portray an environment as it once was in a vain effort to mimetically hold off its inevitable change and loss, but such a reified image would, sadly, offer little opportunity for subjective encounter.[18] Works such as "To Penshurst" are important because, gesturing to environments undergoing change so profound that they are becoming lost to us as we knew them, they have the potential to bring about in the reader the sort of environmental consciousness that prompted their creation.

The cultural implications of all this are profound. If a pastoral work is capable of leading us away from itself to the emerging, yet receding backdrop, what happens when this movement is literally enacted by large

16. Tom Huhn, Introduction to *The Cambridge Companion to Adorno,* ed. Tom Huhn (Cambridge: Cambridge University Press, 2004), 13.

17. Ibid.

18. As Adorno explained when he opened this discussion of mimesis: "That today any walk in the woods, unless elaborate plans have been made to seek out the most remote forests, is accompanied by the sound of jet engines above that not only destroys the actuality of nature as, for instance, an object of poetic celebration. It affects the mimetic impulse. Nature poetry is anachronistic not only as a subject: Its truth content has vanished." Ibid.

groups of people? In the case of early modern London, this happened regularly, especially on holidays. Stow notes that in times past, "in the month
of May, namely on May day in the morning, euery man, except impedi-
ment, would walk into the sweet meadowes and greene woods, there to
rejoice their spirits with beauty and sauour of sweete flowers, and with the
harmony of birds" (I, 98). The reason for this exodus from the city was that
Londoners regularly needed to "recreate and refresh their dulled spirits
in the sweete and wholesome ayre" after spending time in the dismal city
(I, 127). Not only did the clean air of early modern London's surrounding environs appear because of the city's horrific air-pollution problem
(which will be taken up in detail in chapter 5), but its citizens went out in
droves to experience for themselves what had appeared. In so doing, these
individuals provide evidence for the mass emergence of an environmental
consciousness in the Renaissance, as early modern London's citizens not
only increasingly became conscious of their environment, but also became
aware of it as withdrawing and endangered.

What distressed Stow was that Londoners could no longer experience
these meadows and fields, which "within a few yeares [had been] made
a continuall building throughout" (I, 127).[19] So important was access to
this quickly withdrawing countryside outside of the city that Stow reports
that a riot broke out when it was suggested "that no Londoner ought to
goe out of the City, except in the high Waies" (II, 77). Not only did this
riot lead to a citizen-initiated campaign to maintain the local fields, "the
Moorfields," but a 1580 Device prepared by the Lords of Council declared
that "the City of London hath ever had, and now ... should have, their free
and open walks in the fields about the City, and namely in Moorfields, and
some other fields, where groundes have been enclosed for gardens, and
new dwellings there builded." This initiative was so successful that in 1603
James commended the citizens for "things that doe concern the ornament
of that our Cittie as namely in the walks of Moorefields, a matter both of

19. Laura Williams compellingly argues that as London expanded and there were no longer
fields within an easy walk, there was a "shift of focus away from peripheral open fields, meadow
and pasture for walking and recreational use, and towards more ordered and formal sites," which
led to the establishment of England's first true intraurban parks in the seventeenth century. "To
recreate and refresh their dulled spirits in the sweete and wholesome ayre: green space and the
growth of the city," in *Imagining Early-modern London: Perceptions and Portrayals of the City from
Stow to Stype 1598–1720,* ed. J. F Merritt (Cambridge: Cambridge University Press, 2001), 186.

grace and greate use for the recreation of our people."[20] Perhaps not sur-prisingly, it is the Moorfields that Stow laments were being built up with suburban prodigy houses boasting "Towers, Turrets, and Chimney tops, not so much for vse or profite, as for shewe" (II, 78).

Because the pastoral impulse was responsible for a mass movement of individuals away from the city to its appealing surroundings, that impulse ironically endangered those very environs. Indeed, the reason that it was first suggested that Londoners should not make day trips out into the sub-urbs was because they were leaving behind "donge, fylthe [and]...rub-byshe" that threatened the place (Stow, II, 77). However, according to both Stow and Jonson, those individuals who stayed and built opulent prodigy houses did far more lasting damage. The Moorfields provide an example of the countryside emerging into appearance because of the city, but—surprisingly—efforts to preserve the countryside were undertaken by citizens of the very city endangering it. As we have seen, these preser-vation efforts included Stow's somewhat awkward attack on the devel-opment of the Moorfields, as well as Jonson's highly sophisticated poem. Moreover, rioting day-trippers themselves, who were part of the problem, also took on themselves the task of preserving the Moorfields.

Ironically, the very building of the prodigy houses themselves was an effort at preservation insofar as these buildings were often situated within enclosed gardens that mimicked the retreating backdrop, as these garden houses were often built by individuals who in some sense appreci-ated the newly emerging countryside. However, these enclosed gardens (which many other writers, such as Marvell in "The Mower against Gar-dens," railed against in the seventeenth century)[21] are not so much an ef-fort to preserve the countryside as they are carefully constructed living

---

20. See *The Growth of Stuart England,* 453, 73.

21. As the speaker in Marvell's "The Mower against Gardens" makes clear, his feeling toward suburban gardens was one of profound disgust:

> He first enclosed within the gardens square
>   A dead and standing pool of Air:
> And a more luscious Earth for them did knead,
>   Which stupefied them while it fed.

Andrew Marvell, "The Mower against Gardens," *The Poems of Andrew Marvell,* ed. Nigel Smith (London: Pearson Longman, 2003), lines 5–8. In his *Marvell's Pastoral Art,* Donald Friedman aptly notes of this passage that

representations of it. Such gardens make clear the risks involved in attempting representations of the countryside, in that a variety of cultural
and economic factors can so distort the mimetic work that it becomes far
removed from what it purports to represent. To give but one example,
as early as 1584, the Belgian theologian Justus Lipsius argued in his *De
Constantia* (translated by John Stradling in 1594 as *Tvvo Bookes of Constancie*) that wealthy individuals "vaingloriously hunt after strange hearbs
& flowers, which having gotten, they preserue and cherish more carefully
than any mother doth her child."[22] This criticism, which is echoed nearly a
century later by Marvell, makes clear that the same propensity toward af-
fectation of wealth that motivated the building of the prodigy houses also
affected their gardens. In this case, however, it was not exotic materials
such as gold and marble that went into the work, but equally rare and
costly plants. While such gardens represented the countryside, their real
purpose was the lavish representation of wealth.

Works (or labors) that do the work of art at least partly free of mimesis, as does "To Penshurst," somewhat sidestep this problem because
they cannot misrepresent what has not been represented. Of course, historic and cultural contexts forcefully enter the text by means of even brief
images like the description of Jonson's "broad beech" (13, which can be
seen as referencing Virgil's oft-cited sheltering shade tree, receding old-
growth forests, a natural resource of enormous commercial potential in the
seventeenth century, and so forth); however, insofar as these are kept to a
minimum, the problem is mitigated. This is not to deny, of course, that the
issue of cultural context reemerges in individuals who read (or otherwise
experience) the pastoral work in the form of their ongoing encounter with
the newly appearing environs. Obviously, not only is that unavoidable, it

---

the diction of these four lines is almost an exercise in the expression of disgust. As if "dead"
and "standing" were not enough to convey the sense of stifling decay, Marvell intensifies
the underlying image of a stagnant pond by applying it to the air itself, making the garden
enclosure even more unnatural and repellant.... The measure of man's treachery is found
in the idea of "a more luscious Earth"; the process of nourishment is perverted, not by di-
verting or interrupting it, but by intensifying it to the point where fertility lapses into sa-
tiated, sterile stupefaction.

Marvell's Pastoral Art (London: Routledge, 1970), 125.
    22. Justus Lipsius, John Stradling, Rudolf Kirk, and Clayton Morris Hall, *Tvvo Bookes of
Constancie* (New Brunswick, NJ: Rutgers University Press, 1939), 134.

can be the point of the work. Moreover, if the work (or labor) success-fully expresses a mood, as does "To Penshurst," it can set up the conditions governing the experience. This is not to say that the work or labor can entirely dictate the encounter, assuming artistic intention is involved at all. The surprisingly similar response that Jonson, the day-trippers, and the suburban builders had to London resulted in the city's surroundings ap-pearing to them in one way, but it would have seemed vastly different to other individuals at the time (many of whom, as we shall see in the second half of this book, saw the newly appearing backdrop as in need of sweep-ing agricultural changes). The challenge for the artist is to set the mood for the encounter. In this respect, what distinguishes what we tradition-ally think of as artworks (such as "To Penshurst") from other works (like London), is that efforts have carefully been made to influence the encoun-ter in the former case. As we have observed, this need not necessarily in-volve descriptions of what is seen, but rather suggestions as to how it might be experienced. By prescribing a dwelling that he imagines as capable of holding off the withdrawal of the natural backdrop, Jonson obviously goes further.

The complex relationship to the environment explored in this chapter—our becoming conscious of its presence often only at the moment of its in-creasing absence at our hands; our literally rushing out to catch sight of its belated appearance, yet ironically in the process often hastening its with-drawal; and finally, in order to save it from us, our overdue and often inef-fectual attempts to preserve it from falling away—although a distinctive condition of material and technological modernity, was obviously already well known in the Renaissance. We should not, however, mistake this phe-nomenon for the appearance, which signals the disappearance, of "nature" or "wilderness." As we have seen, because what is "natural" for each of us is often the backdrop into which we are born (making its loss, and the backdrop that replaces it, seem accordingly and distinctly unnatural), it matters little if the "nature" lost is wilderness, rural, suburban, urban, or some combination of these. However, as time went on and this process re-peated itself across England, it was perhaps inevitable that the far reaches of the island (and the globe) were scoured to find the environs freest of human habitation, which were imagined as "true wilderness." These lo-cales would become the fetish objects of generations of pastoral writers in the centuries following the Renaissance.

4

Pastoral and Ideology, and the Environment

Paul Alpers played a major role in shifting critical interest in pastoral away from landscape to what are essentially, as mentioned in the preceding chapters, political concerns. I have attempted to show not only that Alpers's reading of Virgil's first Eclogue is too restrictive, but that poems such as "To Penshurst" and "The Description of Cooke-ham" reclaimed the original force of this Eclogue, which in fact has a great deal to do with landscapes. Readers who have patiently followed the arguments of the preceding chapters might, even if persuaded that these two early modern poems have an environmental component, still reject the notion that Renaissance pastoral on the whole is largely anything other than a figurative mode. This is hardly surprising, as it is generally accepted that, while pastoral will one day deal extensively with landscapes, that day lies a century and a half after Jonson with the Romantics.

Nonetheless, while not denying the political and allegorical character of much of Renaissance pastoral, my objective in the present chapter is, through a discussion of a variety of early modern texts, to make clear that

a broad range of Renaissance pastoral works do indeed frequently concern themselves with literal landscapes, and that these works often do their
work as art, as suggested in the previous chapters, without significantly
employing mimesis. This is not to reverse Alpers and say that "we will
have a far truer idea of pastoral" if we assume that it is more concerned
with landscapes than politics; rather, my aim is simply, by moving landscapes out of the margins of current critical debate, to demonstrate the
validity of an ecocritical reading of Renaissance pastoral.

However, separating landscapes from politics in Renaissance pastoral
is no easy task. At the end of the sixteenth and beginning of the seventeenth centuries, pastoral writing was frequently used to develop a political
distinction between "court and country." An obvious example is Spenser's
Collin Clout Comes Home Again. Such writings often have very little to
do with literal landscapes; rather, an ideal, highly stylized country life is
used as a foil in order to construct an image of the court, often as a place of
duplicity and treachery. This type of pastoral is not only political commentary, but in the first quarter of the seventeenth century, it actually helped
consolidate the opposition forces in Parliament, as men like the third Earl
of Southampton professed that far from court they were actually living
the pastoral ideal: "I have been wholly a country man and seldom seen
either the court or London.... In this life I have found so much quiet and
content, that I thinke I should hardly ever brook any other."[1] Many such
examples could be given.[2] In fact, as Perez Zagorin made clear in what
was once an enormously influential work, appropriately entitled *The Court
and the Country,* prior to the reign of Charles I, opposition forces, which
were already beginning to form a political "proto-party," did not generally
call themselves "patriots" or "parliamentarians," but rather took on the
moniker "country" in order to stand against the court.[3] Although, as many

1. C. C. Stopes, *The Life of Henry, Third Earl of Southampton: Shakespeare's Patron* (Cambridge: Cambridge University Press, 1922) 449.

2. Among parliamentarians who styled themselves (and were styled by others) as living the
pastoral ideal in opposition to the court, the first Lord Spencer was described as living in the
country where "his Fields and Flockes broughts him more calme and happie contentment, than
the various and mutable dispensations of a Court." (Arthur Wilson, *The History of Great Britain* ...[London, 1653], 162–63.) Perez Zagorin gives many such examples in his *The Court and the
Country: The Beginning of the English Revolution* (London: Routledge & K. Paul, 1969).

3. Zagorin, *Court and the Country,* 33, 75, and elsewhere.

historians have noted,[4] Zagorin's argument is problematic for a variety of reasons (not the least of which being that many of these "country gentle-men" also lived in London), from the point of view of literary studies, it is an interesting case of pastoral literature supplying the ideal through which an emerging political party styled itself.

In another obvious example of pastoral literature serving a political use, in the middle of the seventeenth century, retreating royalists and others began to invest the word *retreat* with an altogether new meaning, as it now stood for both a place and a literal withdrawal to the country, away from public life and politics.[5] Not surprisingly, the traditional pastoral mode was used to describe the rural retreat. Annabel Patterson largely devotes the third chapter of her *Pastoral and Ideology* to making clear that the phenom-enon was exceptionally widespread.[6]

With the pastoral mode of writing being used by parliamentarians to consolidate a sense of self as a group in opposition to the court in the begin-ning of the seventeenth century, as well as by retreating royalists and others in opposition to parliamentarians a few decades later, it becomes clear that pastoral literature can serve a wide range of political uses. It is largely this fact that prompts Patterson to suggest that

> it is not what pastoral *is* that should matter to us. On that, agreement is impossible, and its discussion inevitably leads to the narrowing strictures of normative criticism, statements of what constitutes the "genuine" or the "true."...What can be described and, at least in terms of coverage, with

---

4. For major revisions of Zagorin's *The Court and the Country,* see Conrad Russell's *Parlia-ments and English Politics, 1621–1629* (Oxford: Oxford University Press, 1979); Richard Cust's and Ann Hughes's *Conflict in Early Stuart England: Studies in Religion and Politics, 1603–1642* (Lon-don: Longman, 1989), 13–14; and Dwight D. Brautigam's essay "The Court and the Country Re-visited," in *Court, Country, and Culture: Essays on Early-modern British History in Honor of Perez Zagorin,* eds. Bonnelyn Young Kunze and Dwight D. Brautigam (Rochester, NY: University of Rochester Press, 1992), 55–64.

5. See *OED,* definition 4b for the 1646 emergence of "retreat" as "the act of withdrawing from society, public life, business, or office."

6. See Patterson's *Pastoral and Ideology: Vergil to Valéry* (Berkeley: University of California Press, 1987), 133–78. Unless otherwise noted, all references to Patterson are to this edition and are cited parenthetically. As Patterson notes, "During the civil war...many royalists, of course, now found themselves in the position of [Virgil's] Meliboeus, and if they themselves were not actually in exile in France, their estates were frequently 'sequestrated' (confiscated) by the Long Parliament" (151). Not surprisingly then, the pastoral mode was well suited to describing the rural retreat.

some neutrality, is what pastoral since Virgil can do and what always has done; or rather, to put the agency back were it belongs—how writers, artists, and intellectuals of all persuasions have *used* pastoral for a range of functions and intentions.[7]

As each new political situation arises, pastoral is marshaled into use to serve new political ends. In this view, it thus makes little difference if a reversal of fortune takes place among groups engaged in generating pastoral literature, as it did in the seventeenth century; rather, what is most important is to see the political situation hidden beneath pleasant pastoral landscapes.

But there is a problem here: such an approach to Renaissance pastoral focuses chiefly on the changing political scene. But might this literature be also serving some other use—which did not waver in spite of the changing fortunes of politics—in the seventeenth century? A clue to the answer lies with the aforementioned third Earl of Southampton who professed that "I have been wholly a country man and seldom seen either the court *or London.*"[8]

While the population of many Renaissance cities such as Rome remained relatively unchanged between 1500 and 1700, in the same period, as noted earlier, London's population grew tenfold by some estimates. There had never been anything even remotely like this in European history. As we saw earlier and shall see throughout this study, the extraordinary growth of this city not only had profound cultural and ecological implications, but also played a remarkable role in shaping Renaissance pastoral. In spite of repeated efforts by governments from Elizabeth through Cromwell and Charles II, London's expansion simply could not be controlled. While the pastoral mode was used in relation to political controversies throughout this period, something far bigger was also going on: a cultural, environmental phenomenon that none of the various political factions had a hope of controlling. True, idealized landscapes often stood in opposition to courtly power in Renaissance pastoral, but the idealized—and increasingly realistic—landscapes of pastoral art in the seventeenth century often also literally stood in opposition to London's unprecedented urban expansion. As I argued in connection with Jonson's "To Penshurst," London was in part responsible not only for the extraordinary growth of pastoral art in

---

7. Ibid., 7 (emphasis in Patterson).
8. *Life of Henry, Third Earl of Southampton,* 449. Emphasis mine.

Renaissance England but also for the appearance (both as "emergence" and as "look") of the English landscape in those works.

While exceptions can certainly be given, Renaissance pastoral in England is largely a London phenomenon. Indeed, since nearly every writer in England significantly contributing to pastoral's development in the early modern period lived in or near London at some point, exceptions are few. Even writers on the outer fringes of the empire, such as Edmund Spenser, spent time in London. Consequently, London, whether named or simply referenced as the "city" or the "town," looms large in Renaissance England's pastoral art. This phenomenon becomes especially apparent if we look to the ways in which another paradigmatic pastoral text, Horace's second Epode, was translated into English in the seventeenth century.

Patterson suggests that in the Renaissance Virgil's first Eclogue was not only "what Michel Foucault...called a discursive practice," but that it is "a rare instance of a discursive practice that permeates the culture while being fully intelligible to those who practice it at the time" (140–41). In part because this eclogue was used in schools to teach Latin grammar, it was so well known, Patterson argues, that it became a discursive practice because

> brief quotations could stand for larger arguments or even an entire ideology, and the text could be splintered into what, borrowing a phrase from Fredric Jameson, we might call *ideologemes*.... [Consequently,] writers, statesmen, and even kings grasped the capacity of the original to contribute to their own debates. (141)

While arguably true, this is by no means a "rare instance" of such a discursive practice. Certainly the same can be said of Horace's second Epode. Not only was this epode also used to teach Latin grammar in schools, it was translated by an even greater number of writers in the seventeenth century, including Ben Jonson, Henry Rider, Sir John Beaumont, Thomas Randolph, John Smith, Sir Richard Fanshawe, Abraham Cowley, Katherine Phillips, John Harrington, Alexander Brome, Thomas Creech, John Dryden, and others. As the century progressed, the opening phrase *Beatus ille* ("Happy is he") became what Patterson, borrowing from Jameson, calls an ideologeme, as this brief quotation also "could stand for larger arguments or even an entire ideology." In her *Pastoral and Ideology*, Patterson refers to Horace once, and only briefly; nonetheless, the poet's second Epode had an enormous influence on Renaissance pastoral.

While the "happy-man" ideology always involved life in the country, such a life increasingly began to be contrasted to the city in the seventeenth century. Consider the opening two lines of Horace's second Epode, here translated by Ben Jonson:

> Beatus ille qui procul negotiis,
> ut prisca gens mortalium,

> Happie is he, that from all Businesse cleere,
> As the old race of Mankind were,[9]

To a Latin-reading audience, the first line ends in an obvious play on words, as *negotiis* (*negotium*) is being contrasted with the leisure of *otium,* which, of course, is a mainstay of pastoral literature, describing leisurely country occupations. Jonson, who is here offering a rather literal line-by-line translation, wonderfully catches this wordplay by translating *negotiis* as "Businesse," which still echoed its Middle-English meaning of "busy-ness."[10] In his 1629 translation, Sir John Beaumont contrasts the "busy life" with country *otium* even more explicitly:

> He happy is, who farre from busie sounds,
> (as ancient mortals dwelt)[11]

These are near-perfect renderings of the Latin, signaling to the English-reading audience (as the original does to Latin readers) that busy occupations are going to be contrasted with the leisure of country employment. But in 1638 Thomas Randall offers another term, *city:*

> Happy the man which farre from city care
> (such as ancient Mortals were)[12]

---

9. The original Latin is from *Horace: The Odes and Epodes, with an English Translation,* Loeb Classical Library, trans. Charles E. Bennett (London: W. Heinemann, 1929), while Jonson is quoted from *Ben Jonson,* ed. C. H. Herford and Percy Simpson (Oxford: Clarendon Press), 289. Jonson titled his translation of Horace's second epode "In Praise of Country Life."

10. See *OED* for "business," definition I.1.

11. Sir John Beaumont, *Bosworth-field* (London, 1629), 47.

12. Thomas Randall, *Poems* (Oxford, 1638), 33.

Similarly, in 1649 J[ohn] S[mith] renders the lines:

> Happy is he who far from Cities toile
> Like the worlds golden-Infancy[13]

There is no classical precedent for translating *negotiis* as "city." In Horace's time *negotium* could mean business, employment, occupation, trade, labor, or even pain and difficulty, but it never meant "city."[14]

In the opening of the epode (which by the end we find is being related, ironically, by a usurer) Horace offers one occupation (*negotium*) after another, such as soldier, seafarer, and lawyer, in contrast to the *otium* of rural employment.[15] In short, the epode begins by taking as its subject contrasting occupations—or, to be more specific, it contrasts various occupations with *otium*. Although we might assume the occupations that offer the greatest contrast to country *otium* would take place in the city, Horace selects as his opening examples (soldier, seafarer, and lawyer) occupations that not only need not, but, in the case of seafarer, simply cannot take place in a city. Similarly, soldier is generally not an urban occupation. Clearly then, Horace is praising leisurely rural occupations above all others, regardless

---

13. J [ohn] S [mith], *The Lyric Poet, Odes and Satyres Translated out of Horace into English Verse* (London, 1649), 114.

14. See the *OLD* for *negotium*.

15. Here are the lines (3–8) in which Horace introduces the occupations he initially contrasts with *otium* (again followed by Jonson's translation):

> paterna rura bobus exercet suis
>   solutus omni faenore,
> neque excitatur classico miles truci,
>   neque horret iratum mare,
> Forumque vitat et superba civium
>   potentiorum limina.

> With his owne Oxen tills his Sires left lands,
>   And is not in the Userers bands;
> Nor Soldier-like started with rough alarms,
>   Nor dreads the Seas inraged harmes;
> But flees the Barre and Courts, with the proud bords,
>   And waiting chambers of great Lords.

Horace is again quoted from the Loeb edition and Jonson from the Herford and Simpson edition of the *Poems*.

of where they are practiced. This reading of Horace's second Epode was widespread even early in the Renaissance. Petrarch, for example, spends entire chapters in his *De Vita Solitaria* (*The Life of Solitude*) condemning the "busy" life.[16] To overlook this obvious reading is both to ignore the opening *neg-otium / otium* play on words, as well as Horace's carefully selected examples of occupations; yet, seventeenth-century translators such as Randall and Smith not only did just that, but also began to put extraordinary emphasis on Horace's descriptions of country life. Consider lines 23–28 of the epode, here again with Jonson's translation:

> libet iacere modo sub antiqua ilice,
>   modo in tenaci gramine.
> labuntur altis interim ripis aquae,
>   queruntur in silvis aves,
> fontesque lymphis obstrepunt manantibus,
>   somnos quod invitet leves.

> Then now beneath some ancient Oake, he may,
>   Now in the rooted Grasse, him lay,
> Whilst from the higher Bankes doe slide the floods,
>   The soft birds quarrel in the Woods,
> The Fountaines murmure as the stream does creepe,
>   And all invite to easie sleep.[17]

With the exception of substituting the local oak for the Mediterranean *ilex,* Jonson again offers a rather literal, line-by-line translation, which gives him little latitude for interpretation.

However, a few decades later, these lines are given new life. Consider Abraham Cowley's 1668 rendering:

> With how much joy do's he beneath some shade
> By aged trees rev'rend embraces made,

---

16. Horace's condemnation of the "busy" life is the subject a number of chapters in Petrarch's *De Vita Solitaria* (*The Life of Solitude*), such as: "Of the wretchedness of the busy man and the happiness of the retired man when evening falls" and "Almost every busy man is unhappy, though there are some few who are worthily employed." *The Life of Solitude,* trans. Jacob Zeitlin (Urbana: University of Illinois Press, 1924), 118, 125.

17. Horace is again quoted from the Loeb edition and Jonson from George Burke Johnston's edition of the *Poems.*

His careless head on the fresh Green recline,
His head uncharg'd with Fear or with Design.
By him a River constantly complaines,
The Birds above rejoyce with various strains
And in the solemn Scene their *Orgies* keep
Like Dreams mixt with the Gravity of sleep,
Sleep which does alwaies there for entrance wait
And nought within against it shuts the gate.[18]

The original six lines have grown to ten. The single *antiqua ilice,* Jonson's "ancient Oake," has now not only multiplied into "aged trees," but these ancient trees are themselves imagined in a "rev'rend" lover's embrace.[19] Although clearly drawing on the pastoral tradition, the sight of this man's "careless head on the fresh Green" grass (*gramine*) pillow beckons the reader, through an expansive description of the scene, to "Loafe with me on the grass," as Whitman will interpret these lines nearly two hundred years later in his "Song of Myself."[20] It is, of course, possible to see Cowley's translation entirely in political terms, as he retreated to the country and the metaphorical shade of sheltering trees to avoid the political quagmire in the years following the Civil War. (Both royalists and parliamentarians found Cowley suspect at various points in his career; by 1668, when his translation of Horace's epode appeared, he had not received from Charles II the favor he had expected.) Yet such a reading does little to explain why Cowley's translation spends so much time on the happy man's natural setting, such as the expansion of the simple line *queruntur in silvis aves* into "The Birds above rejoyce with various strains / And in the solemn Scene their *Orgies* keep," which obviously makes no effort at holding a political focus.

In fact, by 1668, Cowley and many other writers were interpreting the classical pastoral of Horace and others in very literal terms dealing with England's rural landscape. For this to have happened, however, a major

---

18. Abraham Cowley, *Plays and Sundry Verses,* ed. A. R. Waller (Cambridge: Cambridge University Press, 1906), 412.

19. Cowley's 1668 embracing trees may have been influenced by Milton's "Vine" in *Paradise Lost* who "wed her Elm; she spous'd about him twines / Her marriagable arms." *The Riverside Milton,* ed. Roy Flannagan (New York: Houghton Mifflin, 1998), 5.216–17. Unless otherwise noted, all future references to Milton are to this text and are cited parenthetically in the text.

20. Walt Whitman, "Song of Myself," from *Leaves of Grass* (Brooklyn, NY: [s.n.], 1855), l. 84.

shift in the way the natural world was perceived had to occur. We can see this more clearly by moving back three hundred years to Petrarch.

Patterson suggests that Petrarch, who arguably contributes more to pastoral's popularity and development in the early Renaissance than any other writer, saw the pastoral mode as not only entirely allegorical, but as "primarily *subversive*" (44, her emphasis). In large measure her argument is based on Petrarch's own disclosure from his unpublished *Epistolae sine nominee:*

> Though truth has always been hated, it is now a capital crime. It is a fact that the hatred of truth and the kingdom of flattery and falsehood has increased in proportion to the growing sins of mankind. I remember often having said this, and sometimes even writing it, but it ought to be said and written more often. The lament will not cease before the grief. This idea led me some time ago to the *Bucolicum Carmen,* a kind of cryptic poem which, though understood only by a few, might possibly please many; for some people have a taste for letters so corrupt that the well-known savor, no matter how sweet, offends them, while everything mysterious pleases them, no matter how harsh.[21]

Patterson finds this passage of "central importance" to Petrarch's interest in pastoral, in spite of the fact that in a letter to his brother the poet himself gives altogether different reasons for this fascination. Although aware of this letter, Patterson dismisses it parenthetically (without mentioning its content):

> Making due allowance for the revisionary effects of reminiscence (a letter to his brother at the beginning of the project suggests a more therapeutic motive for turning to pastoral in 1346, and the eclogues were composed over a six-year period, during which Petrarch became increasingly pessimistic), this statement [from the above-cited passage of the *Epistolae sine nominee*] is nevertheless of central importance. (44)

Certainly Petrarch saw that the pastoral mode could be used to create "a kind of cryptic poem" that could "subversively" deal with political issues.

---

21. Norman P. Zacour, trans., *Petrarch's Book without a Name: A Translation of the Liber Sine Nomine* (Toronto: Pontifical Institute of Mediaeval Studies, 1973), 27. This letter is also cited by Patterson on her pages 43–44.

However, as he explains in the abovementioned letter to his brother, this "use" of pastoral was not what originally motivated his writing of the *Bucolicum Carmen*. Rather, while staying near the rural source of the Sorgue River in France, he writes to his brother that

> the nature of that spot in the retreat in the woods, where I would often go at dawn, urged on by oppressive cares, and whence I was only driven back by the return of the night, gave me the idea to compose some woodland song there. So I began to write something I had already in mind earlier, a Bucolic Song, divided in twelve Eclogues, and it is incredible in how short a time I finished that; such was the stimulus provided by my environment for my spirit.[22]

Petrarch further explains to his brother his choice of names for the characters in his pastoral poem:

> I am Silvius and you are Monicus. The reason behind the names chosen is as follows: of the first, because the poem's setting is in the woods and, moreover, because of my hate, inveterate from my early youth onwards, of the Town, and love of the woods—this is why many of my friends call me in all their talk more often "Silvius" than "Franciscus."[23]

Although clearly "a kind of cryptic [political] poem," Petrarch's *Bucolicum* was from the very start also conceived of as a pastoral work about the appearance (as both "emergence" and "look") of the rural landscape as it stood in opposition to the "town."

Not only in this letter, but repeatedly throughout the body of his work, Petrarch puts great emphasis on the natural environs and his personal relation to them, as well as on the contrast between them and the town. In his *De Vita Solitaria* (*The Life of Solitude*), in a chapter that takes its argument as its title, "Woods, fields, and streams are of great advantage to the solitary," he begins:

---

22. Cited in *The Echoing Woods: Bucolic and Pastoral from Theocritus to Wordsworth* (Amsterdam: J. C. Gieben, 1990), 248. This letter also appears in *Letters on Familiar Matters: Rerum familiarium libri IX–XVI,* trans. Aldo S. Bernardo (Baltimore: Johns Hopkins University Press, 1982), 71.

23. *Letters on Familiar Matters.*

Let provision first be made that, after the prosperous conclusion of his mental toil, one may be enabled to put off the burden of his weariness by having access to woods and fields and, what is especially grateful to the Muses, to the banks of murmuring streams, and at the same time to sow the seeds of new projects in the field of his genius.[24]

Furthermore, while considering his own visit to the Alps, Petrarch reflects on the fact that other writers, such as Cicero and Virgil, also "adhered to this practice" of retreating to more rural settings for poetic inspiration:

I have said to myself, "Thou hast tasted the grass of the Alps, thou comest from above."

But to make an end of this point at last, both Cicero and Vergil, without cavil the chiefs of Latin eloquence, adhered to this practice. The former on many occasions, but especially when he came to compose his treatise on the Civil Laws, sought out leafy oaks and delicious retreats for his labor, and I remember that he makes mention there of a shady bank and lofty poplars, and the caroling of birds, and the rippling of waters, and a little island much like this one of mine in the middle of a stream which it cuts in half. And Vergil when about to celebrate in a pastoral poem his Alexis, whoever he may be, did it walking continually, "Where, piles of shadows, thick the beeches rose," alone among the mountains in the woods.[25]

Although Petrarch could certainly have focused on the allegorical nature of Virgil's poem, he did not. Similarly, Petrarch notes that "throughout his life" St. Augustine "took pleasure in quiet and solitary places, such as the retirement of Mount Pisano, where he is believed to have passed extended intervals in the condition of a hermit."[26] Not surprisingly, this love of nature and withdrawal from the town repeatedly appears in Petrarch's poetry, as in the opening of Song 129 of his *Canzioniere:* "From thought to thought, from mountain to mountain love guides me.... Among high mountains and through harsh woods I find some rest; every inhabited place is a mortal enemy to me."[27]

---

24. Petrarch, *Life of Solitude,* 157.
25. Ibid., 158.
26. Ibid., 210.
27. Francesco Petrarca and Robert M. Durling, *Petrarch's Lyric Poems: The Rime Sparse and Other Lyrics* (Cambridge, MA: Harvard University Press, 1976).

Given his fascination with rural landscapes, it should also come as no surprise that Petrarch's admittedly allegorical *Bucolicum Carmen,* referenced extensively by Patterson and many other critics since, should also be filled with praise of the countryside. For example, the mountains which he noted so interested Virgil and Augustine, are depicted as the home of Jove

> Who with His nod can temper the fostering heavens,
> Moderating the air, distilling dew in abundance,
> Scattering the icy snow and out of the clouds, life-giving,
> Bringing the thirsty grasses the gentle showers they long for,
> Thundering down and shaking the atmosphere with sharp flashes,
> When he is moved to giving seeds to the earth, to the stars each its season,
> Bidding the tides of the ocean to flow and the hills to be stable.[28]

As we saw with "To Penshurst," there are few descriptions of the natural environs here, which are instead limited to single-word modifiers, such as "thirsty" grasses and the "gentle" showers. Patterson, in order to foreground the use of pastoral as political allegory, not only marginalizes such strikingly beautiful passages, but also ignores the poet's own reflections on their importance.

These reflections, which are scattered throughout his personal letters, not only reveal much about Petrarch's attitude toward the landscape, but also serve as something of an indicator of the way those environs were generally perceived at the time. With respect to mountains, in a letter to Dionysus da Borgo, Petrarch describes a trip took with his brother to Mount Ventoux (near Avignon):

> The day was long, the air was mild, and the determination of our minds, the firmness and readiness of our bodies and the other circumstances were favorable to the climbers.... First of all, moved by a certain unaccustomed quality of the air and by the unrestricted spectacle, I stood there as in a trance. I looked back. Clouds were beneath me. And suddenly what I had heard and read about Athos and Olympus became less incredible to me when I looked out from this mountain of lesser fame.[29]

---

28. *Petrarch's Bucolicum Carmen,* trans. Thomas Goddard Bergin (New Haven, CT: Yale University Press, 1974) 13.

29. Petrarch's letter to Dionysus da Borgo San Sepholchro is found in *Rerum Familiarium Libri, I—Viii,* trans. Aldo S. Bernardo (Albany, NY: State University of New York Press, 1975), 175–76.

To critics like Raymond Williams, who contend that the Renaissance perception of mountains was exclusively one of fear and loathing—for example, John Evelyn's description of them in the 1640s as "strange, horrid and
fearful crags and tracts"—Petrarch among many others makes clear that
this was not always the case.[30] Petrarch explains in this letter to da Borgo
the real reason why the mountain view comes to give him discomfort:

> While I was admiring such things, at times thinking about earthly things
> and at times, following the example of my body, raising my mind to loftier
> things, it occurred to me to look into the *Book of Confessions* of St. Augus-
> tine, a gift of your kindness, which I shall always keep on hand in memory
> of the author and the donor....I opened it and started to read at random,
> for what can emerge from it except pious and devout things? By chance it
> was the tenth book of that work to which I opened....May God be my wit-
> ness, and my very brother, that my eyes happen to light where it was writ-
> ten: "And they go to admire the summits of mountains and the vast pillows
> of the sea and the broadest rivers and the expanses of the ocean and the rev-
> olutions of the stars and they overlook themselves." I confess that I was as-
> tonished...I closed the book enraged with myself because I was even then
> admiring earthly things after having been long taught by pagan philoso-
> phers that I ought to consider nothing wonderful except the human mind
> compared to whose greatness nothing is great.
>
> Then indeed having seen enough of the mountain I turned my eyes
> within.[31]

Nearly fifty years ago, in her study of the *Beatus ille,* or "Happy-Man," literature of the Renaissance, Maren-Sofie Røstvig perceptively suggested that
in the seventeenth century there was a "tendency to consider God as immanent rather than transcendent....A new attitude towards nature was
developed in the seventeenth century, and to this new attitude must be attributed a large part of the responsibility for making a retired life popular
among men of a pious and contemplative disposition."[32]

The difference in the way Cowley viewed the natural world three hundred years after Petrarch does indeed have to do with a shift that sees "God

---

30. Evelyn is quoted by Raymond Williams in *The Country and the City,* 128.

31. *Rerum Familiarium Libri,* 177–78.

32. Maren-Sofie Røstvig, *The Happy Man: Studies in the Metamorphoses of a Classical Ideal*
(Oslo: Akademisk forlag, 1954), vol. 1, 31–32.

as immanent rather than transcendent." Petrarch is such a fascinating figure because, as he proves with his prescriptions for the good life in *De Vita
Solitaria,* his nature descriptions in the *Bucolicum Carmen,* and his remi-
niscence of his visit to Mount Ventroux, he was on the verge of seeing the
natural world in an entirely new way, but as he literally looked down to
the book in his hand, he was thrown back a thousand years to Augustine's
suspicions of that fallen world. "Enraged" with himself, he turned away
from the astonishing sight before him. Although Røstvig generalizes too
broadly when she says that "in the medieval period, Nature—meaning the
creation after the fall—had been considered as belonging to the Satanic,
rather than the divine order of things,"[33] the natural world was nonetheless
viewed with suspicion by many in the early medieval period.

One of the difficulties with Alpers's and Patterson's approaches to
pastoral is that, neglecting such shifts in the way the natural world was
perceived, they fail to take into account the role these changes had in the
development of pastoral. Because a celebration of the fallen world often
presented theological challenges to Medieval Christian artists, it should
come as no surprise that they found other "uses" for the pastoral mode.
However, at the close of the sixteenth century, the natural world, though
often still seen as "inferior," was increasingly being celebrated by theologians and poets alike. Consider the following passage from the aforementioned Belgian theologian Justus Lipsius's 1584 *De Constantia,* as translated
by John Stradling in 1594 as *Tvvo Bookes of Constancie:*

[We cannot] behold the earth & her sacred treasures, nor the excellent
beauty of this inferior world, without an inward tickling and delight of
the senses....Pause I pray thee a little while and behold the multitude of
flowers with their dailie increasings, one in the stalke, one in the bud, another in the blossome. Marke how one fadeth suddenly, and another spring-
eth. Finally, observe in one kind of flower the beauty, the form, the shape
or fashion either agreeing or disagreeing among themselves thousand of
wayes. What mind is so sterne that amid all these will not bend it selfe with
some mild cognitions, and be mollified thereby?...O the true fountain of
joy and sweete delight! O the seat of *Venus* and the Graces. I wish to rest me
and lead my whole lyfe in your bowers. God grant me leave (farre from all

---

33. Ibid., 32.

tumults of townes) to walk with a gladsome and wandering eie amid these
herbes and Flowers...so that my minde being beguiled with that kind of
wandering recklessness, I may cast off the remembrance of all cares and
troubles.[34]

As this passage makes clear, Lipsius hardly finds his local environs in conflict with Christianity.

Recalling our observation that pastoral works need not work entirely
through mimesis, this passage, like Jonson's "To Penshurst," also works
like a nature guide directing us to what is appearing outside of early modern cities (or in this case, outside of the "tumults of townes"). Lipsius is not
so much offering us representations of the natural environs as he is guiding
us to "behold...Pause...behold...Marke...Finally, observe" the appearance of these environs, which are obviously outside the text. Although it
might at first seem as if the natural scene is being represented mimetically,
where are the images? Of "the multitude of flowers," for example, what
do we know of their color, size, shape, or smell? Anything? Rather, we
are urged to "observe in one kind of flower the beauty, the form, the shape
or fashion either agreeing or disagreeing among themselves thousand of
wayes." But what kind of flower? What beauty? What form? What shape?
What are the thousands of ways in which they agree or disagree with each
other? None of this is given to us. Rather, the poet repeatedly gestures
outside the text for its appearance, both in the sense of its specific look and
its emergence to us. And, if there is any doubt that the appearance of the
natural environs is worth seeking, and should not be scorned as fallen, its
astonishing aesthetic potential should put this to rest: "O the true fountain
of joy and sweete delight!"

Although Lipsius is in some sense guiding everyone to the appearance
of the natural environs, it is to poets that he especially directs himself:

Yea out of the walkes and pleasant allies of garden, spring those sweet
abounding rivers which with their fruitful overflowings have watered the
whole world. For why? The mind lifteth up and advanceth itself more
to those high cogitations, when it is at libertie to behold his owne home,

---

34. Justus Lipsius, *Tvvo Bookes of Constancie,* trans. John Stradling (New Brunswick, NJ:
Rutgers University Press, 1939), 133.

heaven: then when it is enclosed within the prisons of houses or townes. Here you learned Poets compose yee some poems worthy of immortalite. Here let all the learned meditate and write.[35]

Lipsius finds the natural backdrop (which appears to him because of the "tumults of townes" and the "prisons of houses or townes") not in opposition to heaven, as had so many medieval theologians, but rather the appearance of the natural environs helps him to "behold his owne home, heaven." Certainly Petrarch had similarly suggested in his *De Vita Solitaria* that the artist should "put off the burden of his weariness by having access to woods and fields,"[36] but he succumbed to Augustine as he closed his copy of the *Confessions,* "enraged with myself because I was even then admiring earthly things."[37] The extent to which Lipsius breaks from this tradition of condemning the fallen world becomes clear when—in a way that strikingly presages Thoreau's opening chapter of *Walden*—he turns to condemn those preoccupied with things *other* than their surrounding natural environs: "So soon as I put my foote within that place, I bid all the while servile cares abandon me, and lifting up my head as upright as I may, I contemne the delights of the prophane people, & the great vanitie of human affairs."[38] Not only is an aesthetic appreciation of the natural world not now in opposition to God, it is framed as standing against what traditionally was seen as opposing God.

Although Stradling's 1594 translation of the *De Constantia* did not have an enormous influence on Renaissance pastoral art in England, Lipsius's closing prescription was prescient: "Here [in the garden] you learned Poets compose yee some poems worthy of immortalite. Here let all the learned meditate and write." While, even at the beginning of the sixteenth century, this was happening with writers like Nicholas Grimald, who noted of his garden that "it allures, it feeds, [and] it glads the spirits,"[39] throughout both the sixteenth and seventeenth centuries many writers broke free of the medieval tradition of seeing the natural world as fallen, choosing instead to

35. Ibid., 136.

36. *Life of Solitude,* 157.

37. *Rerum Familiarium Libri,* 178.

38. *Tvvo Bookes of Constancie,* 136.

39. Grimald is quoted from *Recusant Poets,* eds. Louise Imogen Guiney, Geoffrey Bliss, and Edward O'Brien (New York: Sheed & Ward, 1939), 92.

view it as ordained by God for humanity's delight. Consider William Forrest's "The Marigolde" from the 1550s:

> The God above, for man's delight,
> Hath heere ordaynde every thing,
> Sonne, Moone, and Sterres, shinyng so bright,
> With all kinde fruites that here doth spring,
> And Flowrs that are so flourishyng.[40]

Fifty years after Forrest, in a work that would have extraordinary influence on Izaak Walton, John Dennys considers God's "creation":

> The lofty woods the forest wide and long,
> Adornd with leaues and branches fresh and greene,
> In whose coole bow'rs the birds with chaunting song,
>
> * * *
>
> All these and many more of his creation,
> That made the heauens, the Angler oft doth see,
> And takes therein no little to delection,
> To think how strange and wonderfull they be,
> Framing therein an inward contemplation,
> To set his thoughts from other fancies free,
> And whiles hee lookes on these with joyfull eye,
> His minde is rapt above the starry skye.[41]

More than a hundred years after Forrest, this trend continues with Henry
Vaughan's poem "Religion," although now, as an angel appears at each "*juniper...myrtle...oak*" or bubbling brook, this appreciation of the environment seems inseparable from the Christian religion itself.

> My God, when I walke in those groves
> And leaves thy spirit still doth fan,
> I see in each shade that there grows
> An Angel talking with a man.

---

40. Ibid., 149.
41. Ibid., 33.

Under a *juniper,* some house,
Or the cool *myrtle's* canopy,
Others beneath an *oak's* green boughs,
Or at some *fountain's* bubbling on high.[42]

It is noteworthy that these selections from Forrest, Denny, and Vaughan, like those from Virgil's *Eclogues,* contain few mimetic images of the environment to which they gesture.

But the reassessment of the natural world in the English Renaissance involved more than reevaluating its relationship to the Christian God and spiritual world. Consider Thomas Lodge's 1585 poem "In Commendation of a Solitary Life":

Sweete solitarie life thou true repose,
Wherein the wise contemplate heaven aright,
In thee no dread of warre or worldly foes,
In thee no pompe seduceth this mortall sight,
In thee no wanton eares to win with words,
No lurking toyes which Citie life affords.

* * *

Whether with solace tripping on the trees
He sees the citizens of Forest sport,
Or midst the withered oake beholds the Bees
Intend their labor with a kinde consort:
Downe drop his tears, to thinke how they agree,
Where men alone with hate inflamed be.
Taste he the fruites that spring from *Tellus* womb:
Or drinke he of the christall springs that flowes:
He thanks his God.[43]

Lodge touches on a number of points that will repeatedly appear in Renaissance pastoral: the opposition of rural environs to the "Citie"; the belief that "the wise contemplate heaven" or God by experiencing their natural

---

42. Henry Vaughan and Alan Rudrum, *The Complete Poems [of] Henry Vaughan* (New York: Penguin, 1976), 155.
43. Lodge is cited from *Recusant Poets,* 242.

environs; the *Walden*like suggestion that "no pompe seduceth" someone who truly appreciates the natural world; the belief that this appreciation is brought on by more than just an ocular-aesthetic experience, as lines like "Taste he the fruites" invite a wider range of connection and sensory involvement; the echoing of certain classical phrases and motifs, such as the "withered oake" (Horace's *antiqua ilice*) and Virgil's "Bees" from the *Georgics;* a deep appreciation for plants and animals, sometimes leading to anthropomorphism, such as "Bees / [who] Intend their labor with a kinde consort"; a striking and general lack of lavish mimetic images of the natural environs, as Lodge, merely mentioning trees, birds, and bees, offers few descriptions of them; the notion that one can have a deeply personal aesthetic appreciation of such environs, to the point that "Downe drop his tears..."; and the suggestion that one should experience for oneself the appearance of the environs to which the artist is gesturing, rather than simply reading his work. Regarding this last point, although Lipsius had offered a series of prescriptions ("Pause...behold...Marke...Finally, observe"),[44] Lodge offers us an example of the prescribed behavior as the person described "*sees* the citizens of Forest sport...*beholds* the Bees...*thinke[s]* how they agree" (emphasis mine).

In addition to Lodge's 1585 "Commendation," in the first half of the seventeenth century several works appeared on the scene that incorporated many, if not all, of these elements. In 1630, for example, Alexander Ross not only commends the country life as providing the place where the mind may "talke freely with her Maker" with "no help of Priest or Romish Baker," but limits his mimetic images of the natural environs to a single line ("hills and dales, woods, groves, and christall springs"), which are described simply as

> The best delight of transitory things.
> I more esteeme your *Tempe* shades and flowers,
> Then Princes Courts, proud towns, & loftly towres.
>
> * * *
>
> Here is not to be found that Misery,
> Which reigns in Citties, I mean Usery.

---

44. *Tvvo Bookes of Constancie,* 133.

No envy here, no wrongs, no vanity,
No treason, slander, variety, nor flattery.
But innocence, truth, and a quiet life,
Are found in woods; in Citties care and strife.[45]

Although heavily drawing on Horace's second Epode and other classical tropes, as well as placing the country in its conventional opposition to
"Princes Courts," it is clear from this passage that Ross has a profound appreciation for his natural surroundings. Like Lodge, through very sparse images he invokes a world in opposition to the city, one in which he talks freely
with his God and has an intense aesthetic experience of the environs, which
he recommends to others. Ross was hardly alone in expressing these senti-
ments. Also influenced by Horace's second Epode, William Drummond's
1630 "The Praise of a Solitarie Life" reveals much the same attitude:

Thrice happy he, who by some shady grove,
Far from the clamorous world, doth live his own;
Though solitary, who is not alone,
But doth converse with that eternal love.
O how more sweet is birds' harmonious moan,
Or the hoarse sobbings of the widowed dove,
Than those smooth whisperings near a prince's throne,
Which make good doubtful, do the evil approve!
O how more sweet is zephyr's wholesome breath,
And sighs embalmed, which new-born flow'rs unfold,
Than that applause vain honour doth bequeath!
How sweet are streams to poison drunk in gold!
The world is full of horrors, troubles, slights;
Woods' harmless shades have only true delights.[46]

While we could read these passages metaphorically or politically, to do so
exclusively would be to ignore the intense appreciation of the environment
being conveyed here.

---

45. Alexander Ross, *Three Decades of Diuine Meditations...With a Commendation of the Priuate Countrey Life* (London, 1630), 30–31.

46. William and Peter Cunningham, *The Poems of William Drummond of Hawthornden: With
Life, by Peter Cunningham* (London: Cochrane and M'Crone, 1833), 137.

One of the difficulties in approaching English Renaissance pastoral as a largely figurative mode is that we risk ignoring the fact that English writers living in the rural countryside were often—it should come as no surprise—writing about the rural English countryside. What is surprising is that literary critics have, for decades now, largely ignored this obvious use of Renaissance pastoral. While such writings borrow from classical pastoral, they also represent a new phenomenon which itself had an enormous influence on seventeenth-century pastoral. As in the case of Lodge above, these writings were often characterized by a general lack of lavish mimetic images, a sense of the country being opposition to the city, belief in an immanent God, a deep appreciation for plants and animals, and intense feelings for the environment.

While nearly all of these features repeatedly appear throughout the seventeenth century, it is important to realize that the belief that nature writing should eschew lavish mimetic imagery would also be challenged throughout the century. It is often suggested that highly descriptive nature writing in England did not appear before the work of writers like James Thomson in the eighteenth century. Thomson is often cited as inaugurating a new movement because his work directs attention to the natural world in what is generally argued to be an entirely new way. This can be seen, for example, in his descriptions of birds as "feathery people...feathered game...plumy nations ... aerial tribes ... plumy people ... gay troops ... tuneful nations ... coy quiristers ... glossy kind ... fearful kind ... soft tribes ... feathered youth ... plumy burden ... soaring race ... gentle tenants of the shade ... feathered eddy ... merry minstrels ... swarming songsters," and so forth.[47] Because there had never been a catalogue like this in classical literature, many critics have argued that Renaissance nature-poetry, which in their view never moves beyond endless repetition of tired classical metaphors and conceits, had seemingly stopped devising new ways of directing attention to the natural world. Accordingly, appreciation of nature in the Renaissance is sometimes thought to have stalled as well.

Nonetheless, a shift in literary style need not necessarily reflect a deeper appreciation of the natural world. Viewed through the lens that Thomson helped consolidate, Renaissance nature writing may indeed seem sparse,

---

47. James Thomson and J. Logie Robertson, various poems from *The Complete Poetical Works of James Thomson* (London: Henry Frowde, 1908).

hardly presenting images of the natural world at all. However, as I hope to have shown, this can more constructively be read as a strategy for directing attention away from the text to the natural world itself, as well as an anxiety, still echoing from Plato, over the challenges that come with representing nature endless in flux. Nonetheless, the new, highly representational form exemplified by Thomson clearly emerges in the English Renaissance. With respect to Thomson's seemingly revolutionary approach to describing birds, for example, consider the following catalog: "brutish band...rude quests of Aire, and Woods and Water...wandring Heards Of Forrest people...irefull Droues that in the Desarts roare...earthly Bands...Flocks and Droues couer'd with woll and haire...Forrest-haunting Heards...inhabitants of the Sea, and Earth, and Ayre...savage heards." This is not the work of a Romantic poet, but rather Josuah Sylvester's 1605 translation of Guillaume de Salluste Du Bartas.[48]

Sylvester's translation of Du Bartas pointed to the future of English nature writing. Profoundly influential on Milton and others, Du Bartas's highly descriptive literary approach to the natural world would appear in scenes like the description of Eden in *Paradise Lost:*

> Thus was this place,
> A happy rural seat of various view:
> Groves whose rich trees wept odorous Gumms and Balme,
> Others whose fruit, burnished with Golden Rinde,
> Hung amiable—*Hesperian* fables true,
> If true, here only, and of delicious taste.
> Betwixt them Lawns, or level Downs, and Flocks
> Grazing the tender herb, were interpos'd,
> Or palmie hillock, or the flowerie lap
> Of som irriguous Valley spread her store,
> Flours of all hue, and without Thorn the Rose.
> Another side, umbrageous Grots and Caves
> Of cool recess, o'er which the mantling vine
> Lays forth her purple Grape, and gently creeps
> Luxuriant; meanwhile murmuring waters fall
> Down the slope hills dispersed, or in a Lake,

---

48. Guillaume de Salluste Du Bartas, Josuah Sylvester et al., *Du Bartas His Deuine Weekes and Workes*... (London: By Humfrey Lownes, 1613).

> That to the fringed Bank with Myrtle crowned
> Her chrystal mirror holds, unite thir streams.
> The Birds their quire apply; aires, vernal aires,
> Breathing the smell of field and grove, attune
> The trembling leaves.
>
> (5.246–65)

While such solid studies as Barbara Lewalski's *Paradise Lost and the Rhetoric of Literary Forms* have made clear that Milton's depiction of Paradise owed much to the pastoral tradition,[49] as demonstrated in this expansive description of Paradise, Milton's work also points to a future, more mimetic form of nature writing. With respect to the descriptions of birds in Du Bartas, even early in his career, in *L'Allegro,* Milton paints an expansive scene containing the "Lark" and the "Cock:"

> To hear the Lark begin his flight,
> And singing startle the dull night,
> From his watch-towre in the skies,
> Till the dappled dawn doth rise;
> Then to com in spight of sorrow,
> And at my window bid good morrow,
> Through the Sweet-Briar, or the Vine,
> Or the twisted Eglantine.
> While the Cock with lively din,
> Scatters the rear of darknes thin,
> And to the stack, or the Barn dore,
> Stoutly struts his Dames before.[50]

This is not just the description of a classical scene. The "twisted Eglantine," which the *Oxford English Dictionary* credits Milton for identifying with the local plant honeysuckle,[51] is not a classical reference, nor is the "milkmaid" of line sixty-five. This is in fact a lush, expansive description of a contemporary barnyard. Not only a visual scene, it is alive with the

---

49. Barbara K. Lewalski, *Paradise Lost and the Rhetoric of Literary Forms* (Princeton: Princeton University Press, 1985).

50. *L'Allegro* is cited from the *Riverside Milton,* lines 39–52. Additional references to this poem are cited parenthetically to this edition.

51. See *OED* "eglantine," definition 2.

sound of the Lark's singing, which "startle[s] the night," and the Cock's crow, which "Scatters the rear of darknes thin," as well as bringing to life the taste of the "savory dinner set / Of Hearbs, and other Country Messes" (84–85), and the smell of "Sweet-Briar" and honeysuckle. Throughout the poem, Milton appeals to the senses in order to describe a local scene with mimetic lushness. While we can, of course, broadly see forerunners to this approach in Chaucer and others, this would become a technique that dominated writings dealing with the countryside in the centuries following Milton. However, it is also important to realize that, in the seventeenth century, there were a variety of environmental crises that were already threatening the picturesque countrysides of such descriptions. Because, as I have been arguing, these crises are in part responsible for the emergence into appearance of the English countryside, they will be the subject of the rest of this book.

Part II

ENVIRONMENTAL PROBLEMS

5

REPRESENTING AIR POLLUTION
IN EARLY MODERN LONDON

When confronted with the description of a literal dark cloud of air pollution hanging over Coketown in Dickens's *Hard Times,* many readers are immediately persuaded not only that our current environmental crisis has its roots in the nineteenth century, but that it was clearly making its appearance in the literature of the day. However, turn the clock back two centuries, to Spenser, Jonson, and Milton, and many of the same readers are remarkably resistant to the notion that the roots of the crisis could possibly reach back so far—at least with respect to such "modern" environmental problems as air pollution. Nonetheless, as the seventeenth century opened, London had a serious problem with air pollution (resulting from the burning of coal with high sulfur content), which Charles I and others soon realized was not only eating away at the fabric of buildings but also killing animals and fish, causing the local extinction of entire species of plants, and according to some midcentury accounts, second only to the Plague as the leading cause of human deaths in London.

Certainly human beings had been burning fossil fuels for thousands of years, but never before even remotely on the scale of seventeenth-century London. Unlike other English cities (such as Manchester) that would come to have similar air-pollution problems a century or two later, what is fascinating about Renaissance London is that it was not, generally speaking, an industrial city. This not only because the protoindustrial practices of the time were not truly "industrial" in the sense that historians today use the term,[1] but also because, in contrast to cities like Manchester, London's economy never depended chiefly on protoindustrial practices. Rather, London's wealth principally came from its role as an international trading hub and from agricultural ventures, since many of its prosperous citizens often had considerable real-estate holdings.

Because there was no extensive industry in the city, we now know that seventeenth-century London's air-pollution problem was caused principally by its citizens themselves, who by the end of the sixteenth century had almost exclusively adopted coal with high sulfur content as their primary energy source for both residential heating and cooking. More than just an environmental issue, air pollution so produced created a corresponding representational challenge for early modern writers. After all, how exactly does one portray a problem that no one wishes to acknowledge because everyone is in fact its cause? As we shall see, the solution would come in 1661 with the publication of John Evelyn's *Fumifugium,* the first work to take as its subject modern air pollution. *Fumifugium* transferred the blame for the environmental crisis from consumer to industry. Although an obvious misrepresentation of the facts, this maneuver established a questionable model for much modern environmental activism.

To understand how Londoners woke up to their pollution problem, and the role that the literature of the day played in this awakening, it will be helpful to review the city's history with air pollution, which is surprisingly extensive, though it has largely escaped the attention of literary critics.

---

1. John K. Walton has compellingly argued that late-eighteenth-century Lancashire has "a strong claim to having become the first full-fledged industrial society" on the planet. While the actual locale of this event is still hotly debated by historians, the fact that the "first full-fledged industrial society" emerged in eighteenth-century England is now generally accepted. See "Proto-Industrialization and the First Industrial Revolution: The Case of Lancashire," in *Regions and Industries,* ed. Pat Hudson (Cambridge: Cambridge University Press, 1989), 41.

In many respects, air pollution in London was poised to become a significant issue in the fourteenth rather than the seventeenth century. The issue centered on coal. Because of increased deforestation and the availability of cheap coal, known as "sea coal" (so called because it was shipped to London from the coast), many groups, such as brewers, began switching from wood use to coal as early as the eleventh and twelfth centuries. It was already widely known, however, that sea coal not only created a great deal more smoke than wood, but also that this smoke was particularly toxic to human beings. Consequently, in 1286, the first of many commissions was set up to study the air pollution problem in London. By 1307, a proclamation made it illegal to burn sea coal in certain parts of the city "for the use of which sea-coal an intolerable smell diffuses itself throughout the neighborhood places and the air is greatly infected, to the annoyance of the magistrates, citizens, and others dwelling there and to the injury of their bodily health."[2] Individuals found violating the law would be subject to "heavy forfeiture." In spite of such efforts, given the dwindling supply of wood in the area surrounding London, it is quite possible that sea coal use would have risen throughout the fourteenth century—had not another environmental crisis intervened.

Fourteenth-century England lost half of its population to plagues, as well as to famines as its grain-based economy collapsed. Consequently, the island not only enjoyed an abundance of wood for fuel, but for the first time in centuries actually experienced a period of reforestation, as previously cultivated fields were abandoned and whole areas imparked. With forests comparatively plentiful, even the period from 1500–1550 saw the cost of wood falling. However, by the close of the sixteenth century England's population had nearly rebounded and was consuming its forest at a startling rate.[3] As a result, the cost of wood experienced unprecedented

---

2. *Calendar of Close Rolls,* Edward (1302–7), 5.537.

3. With regard to deforestation near the end of the seventeenth century, a 1574 survey of eight Kent parishes found that a mere 607 of their combined 55,000 acres had not yet been deforested. (See Michael Zell's *Industry in the Countryside: Wealden Society in the Sixteenth Century* [Cambridge: Cambridge University Press, 1994], 127–28.) Similarly, in 1580 William Harrison wrote that the deforestation was so great that a person could ride ten or twenty miles and see no trees "except where the inhabitants have planted a few elms, oaks, hazels, or ashes about their dwellings." (William Harrison, *The Description of England: The Classic Contemporary Account of Tudor Social Life,* ed. Georges Edelen [Washington, DC: Folger Shakespeare Library and Dover, 1994], 275.) Although Harrison correctly prophesized in 1580 that "if woods go so fast to decay in the next

inflation: by some estimates it rose as much as 700 percent between 1550 and 1630.[4] "So rapid an increase in the cost of any commodity in common use," notes historian John Nef, may "have been without precedent in the history of western civilization."[5]

Sea coal, however, experienced no such inflation. Not surprisingly, then, in spite of sea coal's known health risks, its use increased dramatically in the sixteenth and seventeenth centuries because of a range of economic factors (a fact Adam Smith would observe in *The Wealth of Nations*).[6] As Sir William Cecil noted in 1596, "London and all other towns near the sea...are mostly driven to burn coal...for most of the woods are consumed."[7] In fact, the total consumption of sea coal in the Thames Valley was just beginning to rise: from 1575–80 it was a mere 12,000 tons, by 1651–60 it grew to 275,000, and by 1685–99 it reached a staggering 455,000 tons—an increase of nearly 3,800

---

hundred year of grace as they had done and are likely to do in this...it is to be feared that" there would no longer be any for fuel (Ibid., 280–81), and proposals to replant forests were often put forth, little was actually done. See Arthur Standish, *The Commons' Complaint* (London, 1611).

4. For the increase in the price of wood from 1550 to 1630, see John E. Neff, *The Rise of the British Coal Industry* (New York: George Routledge & Son, 1932), 158.

5. Ibid. As John Hatcher further explains, "Expressions of acute anxiety about the diminishing availability of firewood and timber, as woodland suffered from the twin depredations of consumers and cultivators, were to be heard from the far west and the far north as well as from the heartlands of England and the traditionally thinly wooded and thickly peopled southern and eastern regions. Coal offered timely compensation for the insufficiency of conventional fuels and, in some instances, salvation from a prolonged crisis." John Hatcher, *The History of the British Coal Industry* (Oxford: Clarendon Press, 1993), 7.

6. *Wealth of Nations,* "Coals are a less agreeable fuel than wood: they are said to be less wholesome. The expense of coals, therefore, at the place where they are consumed, must generally be somewhat less than that of wood." *Wealth of Nations* (London: Everyman's Library, 1991), Book 1, chapter 2. This was already borne out by the middle of the sixteenth century: as John Leland observed, "Although between Cawood and Rotherham there is a good supply of wood, yet the inhabitants [of Rotherham] burn predominantly coal, which is found in great abundance there, and is sold very cheap." *John Leland's Itinerary: Travels in Tudor England,* ed. John Chandler (Phoenix Mill, UK: Alan Sutton, 1993), 523–24.

7. Cecil is quoted from John Perlin's *A Forest Journey: The Role of Wood in the Development of Civilization* (New York: Harper and Row, 1989), 186. Similarly, in 1615 Edmund Howes observed that the problem extended well beyond London:

Through the great consuming of wood as aforesaid, and the neglect of planting woods, there is so great a scarcity of wood throughout the whole kingdom and not only the City of London, but in all haven-towns and in very many parts within the land, the inhabitants in general are constrained to make their fires of sea-coal.

John Stow and Edmund Howes, *The Annales, or, Generall Chronicle of England* (London, 1615), 33.

percent in just over one hundred years.[8] Still, as early as the mid sixteenth century, John Leland had already noticed nearly a dozen large-scale coal mining operations during his tour of England.[9] By the end of the seventeenth century Celia Fiennes not only provided a far more extensive list but was astonished when on a "hill 2 mile from Newcastle I could see all about the Country which was full of Coale pitts."[10] John Taylor outlined (somewhat imaginatively) the remarkable scope of one of these mines in 1618. It was

> a wonder: for my selfe neither in any travels that I have been in, nor any history that I have read, or any discourse that I have heard, did never see, reade, or heare of any work of man that might parallell or be equivalent with this unfellowed and unmatchable worke.... [Within a circular stone wall that was designed to keep out tidal water,] workmen ... did digge more then fourtie foot downright, into a rocke, at last they found what they expected, which was sea-cole, they following the vein of the mine, did digge forward still: So that in the space of [roughly] ... nine and twenty yeares they have digged more then an English mile under the sea, so that when men are at worke belowe, an hundred of the greatest shippes in Britiane may saile over their heads.... Many poore people are there set on worke, which would otherwise through the want of imployment perish.[11]

Although Taylor was obviously intrigued by the undersea mine, he nonetheless was quick to bring attention to the environmental fallout of such large-scale operations:

> As for the River Severne, it is almost as much abus'd as it is us'd, for an instance, there are coale-mines neere it ... some of those cole-mines doe yield

---

8. *Rise of the British Coal Industry,* 80.

9. Leland noted coal-mining operations at Gateshead (153), Weardale (158), West Derbyshire (270), Bolton (270), Coquet Island (338), Murton (345), Cowhill (346), Mendip (430), Wednesbury (444), Staffordshire (470), and near Pontefract (530).

10. Celia Fiennes, *Through England on a Side Saddle in the Time of William and Mary* (London: Field & Tuer, 1888), 175. During her tour through England, Fiennes noted coal mines in Mindiffe (4), Yorkshire (75), Darbyshire (77), Woolsley (89–90), Boudezworth (138), Flintshire (151), Newcastle (175), Shopshire (192), Bristol (199), Staffordshire (285), and elsewhere.

11. John Taylor and John Chandler, *Travels through Stuart Britain: The Adventures of John Taylor, the Water Poet* (Stroud, UK: Sutton, 1999), 34–35. Given the obvious problems of draining such ocean-front operations, it was, as historian D. C. Coleman reminds us, "the problem of mine draining which stimulated, right at the end of Stuart times [1698], the momentous innovation of the atmospheric engine, precursor of the steam engine." *Industry in Tudor and Stuart England: Studies in Economic and Social History* (London: Macmillan, 1975), 49.

neere 1000 tunnes of rubbish yearely, which by reason of the nearenesse of
the river is all washed into it, and it makes so many shallowes, that in time
Severne will be quite choaked up.[12]

Because of such flagrant abuse of the environment, coal miners were ordered by the Commissioners of Sewers to remediate such river damage as
early as 1575.[13]

While laws prohibiting sea coal's use remained on the books, perhaps
because it was the only energy source readily available, sea coal burners
were rarely fined. However, in 1578, when Elizabeth refused to go into
London because she was "greved and annoyed with the taste and smoke of
sea cooles," a brewer and dyer who had set up shop in Westminster were
imprisoned.[14] Exploiting Elizabeth's dislike of sea coal smoke, the president of the Council of Marches pleaded with his queen for permission to
harvest wood from the royal Forest of Deerfield, so as not to be "compelled
to burn that noxious mineral pit-coal [sea coal]."[15] Similarly, a number of
coal-burning brick kilns were shut down in 1631 because they were offensive to Charles I.[16]

As the seventeenth century opened, Londoners were almost wholly relying on an energy source that for centuries had been known to be dangerous. And it was increasingly clear that the danger extended not to
only human beings, but to plants and animals as well. In 1627 a petition
argued that acid rain from coal burned for alum works outside the city

---

12. Taylor, *Travels through Stuart Britain,* 198.

13. In 1575, after James Clifford "made a coaldelf or coal pit in his lordship of Broseley at a
place called Tuckeyes, and cast all the rubbish, stone and earth into the deepest part of the Severn,"
he was ordered by the Commissioners of Sewers to remove it at his own cost. From the *Transac-
tions of the Shropshire Archeological Society* 11: 425–26; reprinted by Barrie Stuart Trinder in *The
Industrial Revolution in Shropshire* (London: Phillimore, 1981), 6.

14. Elizabeth is quoted from *Calendar of State Papers, Domestic Series,* Elizabeth I (1578), 612.

15. The president of the Council of Marches is quoted from William Rees's *Industry before the
Industrial Revolution: Incorporating a Study of the Chartered Companies of the Society of Mines Royal
and of Mineral and Battery Works* (Cardiff: University of Wales P, 1968), 413.

16. See Norman George Brett-James's *The Growth of Stuart London* (London: G. Allen &
Unwin, 1935), 111. It important to note, however, that it was widely known that other types of coal
did not present the same health risks as sea coal. Anthracite, which is generally less toxic because
of its much lower sulfur content, was readily available in Wales, Scotland, and across parts of Europe. As George Owen noted in 1602, "This kind of coal is not noisome for the smoke, nor nothing so loathsome for the smell as the running coal [sea coal] is." *The Description of Pembrokeshire,*
ed. Dillwyn Miles (Llandysul, Wales: Gomer Press, 1994), 90.

was "tainting the pastures and the very fish in the Thames."[17] However, it would not be until 1665 that the horrific scope of the danger to human beings became clear. John Graunt (who is regarded by many as the founder of modern statistics), while collecting data for the London Bills of Mortality, noticed an increased death rate in London: "Little more than one of 50 dies in the Country, whereas in London it seems manifest that about one in 32 dies, over and above what dies in the *Plague*."[18] Since many of the deaths in London came from respiratory illness, Graunt concluded that London was "more *unhealthful* ... partly for that it is more populous, but chiefly because ... *Sea-Coles* [are now] ... universally used." Simply put, some people "cannot at all endure the smoak of London, not only for its unpleasantness, but for the suffocations it causes."[19]

Although Graunt offered statistical proof that linked sea coal smoke with respiratory illness (which helped lead to his appointment to the Royal Society at the recommendation of Charles II), in 1655 Margaret Cavendish was already theorizing that coal was composed of uniquely dangerous "*atoms sharpe*."[20] An acquaintance of Cavendish's, Sir Kenelm Digby, possibly influenced by her speculations, later theorized that sharp coal atoms were responsible for both "pyisicall and pulmonicall distempers."[21] It was also well known that inhaling smoke in general was harmful. One of many examples comes from Thomas Platter, who in 1599 argued that tobacco smoke was so noxious that "I am told that the inside of one man's veins after death was found to be covered in soot just like a chimney."[22]

---

17. *Calendar of State Papers, Domestic Series,* Charles I (1627–28), 270. With respect to air pollution impacting the Thames, in 1661 John Evelyn realized quite correctly that "the very Rain, and refreshing Dews ... precipitate this impure vapour" of sea coal smoke (*Fumifugium* [London, 1661], 6). As Evelyn makes clear, it was common knowledge to anyone bathing in the Thames that rain carries sea coal smoke "down in greater proportion, not only upon the Earth, but upon the *Water* also, where it leaves a thin Web ... dancing upon the Surface of it, as those who go to bathe in the Thames ... do easily discern and bring home upon their Bodies" (Ibid., 14). We now know that roughly half of the sulfur dioxide and nitrogen oxide released in the atmosphere returns to earth as acid rain—a fact which likely would not have surprised Evelyn.

18. John Graunt, *Natural and Political Observations ... with reference to the Government, Religion, Trade, Growth, Air, Diseases, and the several Changes of the said City,* 5th rev. ed. of 1676, reprinted in William Petty, *The Economic Writings of Sir William Petty,* ed. Charles Henry Hull (Cambridge, 1899), 2:393.

19. Ibid., 2:394.

20. Margaret Cavendish, *Poems and Fancies* (London, 1655), 73.

21. Sir Kenelm Digby, *Of the Sympatheticƙ Powder* (London, 1669), 23.

22. Thomas Platter and Clare Williams, *Thomas Platter's Travels in England, 1599* (London: J. Cape, 1937), 171.

Building on Digby's early speculations, in 1661 John Evelyn wrote *Fumifugium or The Inconvenience of the Aer and Smoak of London Dissipated. Together with some Remedies Humbly Proposed.* In this pioneering work, Evelyn appeals directly to the new king for immediate action because, thanks to a perpetual cloud of sea coal smoke, "the city of London [now] resembles the face rather of *Mount Aetna,* the *Court of Vulcan . . .* or the Suburbs of *Hell,* then an Assembly of Rational Creatures."[23] The mention of Hell in reference to air pollution from sea coal, however, would have been nothing new to Charles II and many early modern readers.

What makes the smell of sea coal smoke immediately apparent and particularly noxious is that, as the product of a coal with high sulfur content, it reeks of sulfur. Drawn from Latin, in English the word *sulfur* emerges on the scene in the late fourteenth century. However, in Old English, the word *brynstan,* which meant not only "sulfur," but literally the "burning stone" (*bryn-stan*), sulfur or coal, was already in use. During one of London's early bouts with air pollution caused by sulfurous coal, in the year 1300, *brynstan* enters Middle English as the word *brimstone.*[24]

In countries and regions where coal with high sulfur content was not in general use, such as Italy, there is often little or no premodern mention of sulfur or brimstone in connection with Hell.[25] Dante's *Inferno,* for example, contains no such references. This is hardly surprising given that early modern England likely mined and burned three to four times more coal than all of Europe combined.[26] However, because sea coal had been in use throughout England for centuries, when medieval and early modern English writers wanted to depict Hell as particularly noxious and unpleasant, they often invoked images of sulfur smoke. As early as Tundale's 1149 *Vision,* which contains perhaps the most detailed description of Hell prior to

---

23. John Evelyn, *Fumifugium or The Inconvenience of the Aer and Smoak of London Dissipated. Together with some Remedies Humbly Proposed* (London, 1661), 6. Unless otherwise noted, all references to Evelyn are to this edition and are parenthetically cited in the text.

24. See the OED, "brimstone," definition 1a.

25. This is not to say, however, that Italians did not envision Hell in terms of mines and metalworking. As John Rudolph Theodore Schubert notes, in 1470 Antonio Filarete compared an Italian foundry to the house of Pluto. *History of the British Iron and Steel Industry from C. 450 B.C. to A.D. 1775* (London: Routledge & K. Paul, 1957), 230.

26. As E. M. Carus-Wilson noted, "on the eve of the Civil War, three or four times as much coal was probably produced in Great Britain as in the whole of continental Europe." *Essays in Economic History* (London: E. Arnold, 1954), 98.

Dante, it is sulfurous smoke itself that is one of the greatest punishments: "The soul was unable to see anything in the darkness, but he could hear the sound of sulfur flaming and of great howling in the depths of endurance. The smoke rose back up fetid from sulfur and bodies and exceeded any punishments that he had seen before."[27] Such depictions were common in medieval English literature.[28]

In Hebrew, the reference to "fire and brimstone" in Genesis 19:24 is to the word *gophriyth,* which meant neither a stone nor coal nor sulfur, but rather "Jehovah's breath." Similarly, the "brimstone" of Revelation 19:20 in New Testament Greek is *theion,* which meant merely "divine incense." But by the beginning of the seventeenth century, when a rapidly expanding London was experiencing a new, unprecedented wave of sea coal air pollution, both *gophriyth* and *theion* became "brimstone," as the translators of the Authorized Version of the Bible envisioned a Hell engulfed in a sulfurous cloud—like the one descending on London. Similarly, Shakespeare coined the word *sulfurous* in *Hamlet* to describe the flames of Hell: "When I to sulfurous and tormenting Flames must render up my selfe" (I.v.3). And in 1604 Thomas Bilson sees no reason to question why his God would wish to further the torment in Hell by adding brimstone to the mix: "If God will have *Brimstone* mixed with *Hell Fire* to make it burne not onely darker and sharper, but also more loathsommer, and so to grieve the sight, smell, and taste of the wicked...what have you or any Man living to say against it?"[29] Milton's repeated use of "brimstone," "sulfur," and "sulfurous" to describe the outward state of Hell would have been commonplace by the time he wrote *Paradise Lost.*[30] Because the smell of sulfur was known in premodern England chiefly from the burning of

---

27. Tundale's *Vision* is quoted from Eileen Gardener's *Visions of Heaven and Hell before Dante* (New York: Italica Press, 1989), 157. Moreover, not only does Tundale directly link this smoke to "burning coals" that tormented murderers, but his crowning image, that of the "Prince of Shadows" himself, describes Satan seated in a coal-fired forge: "The horrible stooping spectacle was seated on a forged iron wicker-work placed over coals inflamed by the inflated bellows of an innumerable number of demons." Ibid., 156, 178.

28. See Gardener's *Visions* for similar medieval accounts of "pits boiling with pitch and brimstone" by Charles, king of Swabia, 128, as well as "baths of pitch and sulfur" by the Monk of Evesham, 205.

29. Thomas Bilson, *The Survey of Christ's Sufferings for Mans Redemption* (London, 1604), 46–47.

30. For Milton's use of "brimstone," "sulfur," and "sulfurous" to describe Hell in *Paradise Lost,* see 1.69, 1.171, 1.350, 2.69, and elsewhere.

sulfurous coal, literary references to Hell in terms of these words would
have initially conjured up such a horrific image of air pollution from sea
coal that it now seemed hellish.

By the beginning of the seventeenth century, the mining of coal itself
was associated with Hell. In part this can be attributed to the fact that, as
Dud Dudley noted in his 1665 *Metallum Martis,* the seventeenth century
saw a dramatic shift away from the strip mining of coal deposits on or near
the surface, which were quickly becoming depleted, to increasingly dangerous pit mining, which often required reaching to depths of sixty feet or
more.[31] To commemorate his aforementioned 1618 visit to the undersea pit
mine, John Taylor composed a poem:

> I was in (would I could describe it well)
> A darke, light, pleasant, profitable hell.
>
> * * *
>
> To guide us in that vault of endlesse night,
> There young and old with glim'ring candles burning,
> Digge, delve, and labour, turning and returning,
> Some in a hole with baskets and with baggs,
> Resembling furies, or infernall haggs:
> There one like Tantall feeding, and there one,
> Like Sisiphus he rowles the restlesss stone.
> Yet all I saw was pleasure mixt with profit,
> Which prov'd it to be no tormenting Tophet;
> For in this honest, worthy, harmelesse hell,
> There ne'r did any Damned Divell dwell:
> And th' owner of it gaines by 't more true glory,
> Then Rome doth by fantastick Purgatory.[32]

Not everyone, however, found such mines to be an "honest, worthy,
harmelesse hell." Given that in 1661 Evelyn had already drawn attention
to the sooty, sulfurous plumes emerging from industrial smokestacks, it is
perhaps not surprising that just a few years later Milton, whose vision of

---

31. Dud Dudley, *Metallum Martis, or, Iron Made with Pit-Coale, Sea-Coale...* (London,
1665), 26–27.

32. Taylor, *Travels through Stuart Britain,* 36.

Hell is paved in "firm brimstone," has a sulfur-filled hill spewing out thick smoke in *Paradise Lost:*

> There stood a Hill not far whose griesly top
> Belch'd fire and rowling smoke; the rest entire
> Shon with a glossie scurff, undoubted sign
> That in his womb was hid metallic Ore,
> The work of Sulfur.[33]

Like Ovid, Pliny, Seneca, and Spenser before him,[34] Milton objected to mining, as he demonstrates on three separate occasions in *Paradise Lost:* the industrious devils who "Op'nd into the [above mentioned] Hill a spacious wound" in order to build Pandemonium; future generations of human beings, who "with impious hands / Rifl'd the bowels of thir mother Earth / For Treasures better hid"; and the devils who "turnd / Wide the Celestial soile" of Heaven for the raw materials needed to create their weapons of mass destruction.[35] But Milton, writing at a time when air pollution had become a significant issue, not only linked the mining of minerals with that of sulphurous "scurff," but associated the entire mining operation, and the smelting that came after it, with "Belch'd fire and rowling smoke." Milton's sulfur-smoke belching hill, incidentally, was not the only way to imagine smokestacks. Spenser embodies the Hell mouth in *The Faerie Queene* as a dragon spewing smothering sulfur smoke: "A cloud of smoothering smoke and sulfure seare / Out of his stinking gorge forth steemed still / That all the ayre about with smoke and stench did fill."[36]

More than just playing on the popular notion that the burning of sea coal had made London hellish, in *Fumifugium,* John Evelyn systematically undertook to describe London's air pollution problem and to offer up solutions. "For when in all other places the *Aer* is most Serene and Pure, it

---

33. *Paradise Lost* 1.350, 1.670–74. According to the *Oxford English Dictionary,* definition 3, "scurff" was "a sulphurous deposit."

34. For Ovid's, Pliny's, and Seneca's objections to mining in *Metamorphoses, Natural History,* and *Natural Questions* (respectively), see Merchant's *The Death of Nature,* 29–34. In a passage that likely influenced Milton (Book 2, canto 7, verse 17 of *The Faerie Queen*), Spenser describes how Mammon had the "Sacriledge to dig" into "the quiet wombe / Of his great Grandmother [earth] with steele to wound." *The Faerie Queene,* ed. A. C. Hamilton (Harlow, UK: Longman, 2001), II.vii,17.

35. *Paradise Lost,* 1.689, 1.686–88, 6.509–10.

36. *The Faerie Queene,* I.xi.13.

is here [in London] Eclipsed with such a Cloud of Sulfure, as the Sun it self...is hardly able to penetrate" (6). Although sea coal was in widespread use both industrially and residentially, Evelyn places the blame for air pollution squarely on industry: "Sea-coals alone in the city of *London,* exposes it to one of the lowest Inconveniences and reproches [which comes]...but from some few and particular Tunnels and Issues, belonging only to *Brewers, Diers, Lime-burner, Salt,* and *Sope-boylers*" (6).[37] Because a legal precedent dating from the fourteenth century had attempted to mitigate the smoke problem by requiring large-scale sea coal burners to construct increasingly tall chimneys, in order to discharge the smoke away from irritated neighbors, these smokestacks, which Evelyn calls smoke "tunnels," had become towering icons of industrial air pollution by the middle of the seventeenth century.

Perhaps because the billowing smoke these tunnels produced was so obviously visible rising above the city, Evelyn argues that they—and not residential sea coal burning—are largely responsible for London's air pollution problem. His proof is that when industrial operations are interrupted, such as on Sundays, the pollution dramatically decreases:

> Let any man observe it, upon a Sunday, or such times as these Spiracles cease, that the Fires are generally extinguished, and he shall sensibly conclude, by the clearnesse of the Skie, and universal serenity of the *Aer* about it, that all the [residential] Chimnies in *London* do not darken and poyson it so much, as *one* or two of those Tunnels of *Smoake*. (16)

Perhaps not surprisingly, then, Evelyn believes that a provisional solution to the problem is to place industry at a comparatively safe distance

---

37. As historian John U. Nef notes, the list of industries relying on coal was far more extensive than Evelyn noted:

> During the early decades of the seventeenth century coal came into widespread use, not only in the domestic hearths of the English and Scottish, and in their laundry-work and cooking, but in the extraction of salt and the manufacture of glass, bricks and tiles for building, anchors for ships, tobacco pipes...the dyers, the hat-makers, the sugar-refiners, the brewers [and so forth].

"Coal Mining and Utilization," in *A History of Technology,* ed. Charles Joseph Singer (Oxford: Clarendon Press, 1956), 76–77.

from London: "I propose therefore, that by an *Act* of this present *Parliament*...that all those *Works* be removed five or six miles distant from *London* to below the River of *Thames*" (16).

What is striking about his approach to London's air-pollution problem
is that, like many modern environmentalists, Evelyn realized that casting blame away from his readers to industry was a highly effective rhetorical device. However, we now know—and it is likely that Evelyn also
knew—that far more than half of the sea coal burned in London prior to
1700 was for residential, not industrial use. In fact, London's sixteenth-
and seventeenth-century residential skyline owed much to this fact. When
William Harrison penned his 1587 *Description of England,* he noted that
something had been "marvelously altered in England within [the]...sound
remembrances" of older inhabitants: it was

> the multitude of chimneys lately erected, whereas in their young days there
> were not above two or three, if so many, in most uplandish towns of the
> realm (the religious houses and many places of their lords always being ex-
> cepted, and peradventure some great personage), but each one made his fire
> against a reredos [back of a hearth] in the hall.[38]

Because smoke from wood fires was not nearly as noxious as coal smoke
(and actually considered pleasant by some), the traditional English home
prior to the sixteenth century often did not have a fireplace with a chimney, but rather a place for fire on the floor under an opening in the roof.[39]
Because the smoke from coal was too noxious for such an arrangement,
residential chimneys, as Harrison noted, soon became ubiquitous. Not
coincidentally, the chimney sweep soon entered the public imagination.
While we might associate the depiction of such individuals with Blake or

---

38. Harrison, *Description of England,* 200–201.
39. "With so smoky a fuel" as sea coal, notes historian John U. Nef, "the English had to abandon their early crude habit of building the family fire in the center of the room and allowing fumes
to circle about before they escaped through the opening of the roof," *Rise of the British Coal Industry,* 199. Not surprisingly then, as John Hatcher has argued, residential building (and rebuilding)
from the "ascension of Elizabeth to the outbreak of the Civil War...ran parallel to the massive increase in domestic coal consumption. It is not coincidental that this rebuilding incorporated fun-
damental changes to numbers, location, and design of fires and chimneys," *History of the British
Coal Industry,* 410–11.

Dickens, in 1635 William Strode penned what may be the first "Chimney-Sweeper's Song":

> The street doth cry, the news doth fly
> The boys they think it thunders.
> Then up I rush with my pole and brush,
> I scour the chimney's jacket;
> I make it shine as bright as mine,
> When I have rubbed and racked it.

> * * *

> The scent, the smoke, ne'er hurts me,
> The dust is never minded;
> Mine eyes are glass, men swear as I pass,
> Or else I had been blinded.
> For in the midst of chimneys,
> I chant my lays in Vulcan's praise,
> As merry as the swallow.
> Still up I rush...

> * * *

> Mulsak I dare encounter
> For all his horn and feather;
> I'll lay him a crown I'll roar him down,
> I think he'll never come hither.
> The boys that climb like crickets
> And steal my trade, I'll strip them;
> By privilege I, grown chimney high,
> Soon out of town will whip them.
> Then I will rush...[40]

Read with a concern for environmental justice, Strode's "Chimney-Sweeper's Song" makes clear that the individuals of the working class performing this job suffered—as the poor generally still do today—from the dangers that come with working with toxic chemicals far more than

---

40. William Strode's "Chimney-Sweeper's Song" is reprinted in Lawrence Manley's *London in the Age of Shakespeare: An Anthology* (London: Croom Helm, 1986), 330–31. The Mulsak of the poem was a famous chimney sweep.

wealthier individuals. In this case, specifically in the form of long-term ex-
posure to creosote residue in chimneys, which we now know can cause serious convulsions, kidney and liver damage, and a range of other health
concerns, most notably cancer. With biting irony, Strode draws attention to
the risks of the trade: "The scent, the smoke, ne'er hurts / The dust is never
minded." Moreover, written 150 years before Blake's poems that take up
the same subject, Strode makes clear that, unchecked by a guild system,
children ("The boys that climb like crickets / And steal my trade") were
already being enlisted for the work.

The reason Evelyn felt so strongly about the air-pollution problem was
twofold. First, like Digby and others who influenced him, Evelyn was
concerned about the effect of sea coal smoke on human beings: "Those
who repair to *London,* no sooner enter it, but they find a universal altera-
tion to their Bodies" (9). Indeed, Evelyn professes that he undertook to
write *Fumifugium* in part because the new king's sister, "the Dutchess of
Orleans...did in my hearing, complain of the Effects of this Smoake both
in her Breast and Lungs" ("The Epistle"). Sea coal smoke was particularly insidious to Evelyn because "it kills not once, but always, since still
to languish, is worse then Death itself. For there is under Heaven such
Coughing and *Snuffing* to be heard, as in the *London* Churches and As-
semblies of People" (10). However, Evelyn had a second reason for under-
taking the project. Although he never finished his proposed great work,
Elysium Britannicum, Evelyn devoted much of his energy to horticultural
reform. His interest in gardening led Evelyn to ponder the extensive effect of smoke from sea coal on plant and animal life: it "kills our *Bees* and
Flowers abroad, suffering nothing in our gardens to bud, display themselves, or ripen; so as our *Anemonies* and many other choycest Flowers,
will by no Industry be made to grow in London" (7). But if the smoke was
removed, as

> was by many observ'd...in the year when *New-castle* was besieg'd and
> blocked up in our late Wars, so as through the great Dearth and Scarcity of
> Coales, those fumous Works many of them were either left off, or spent but
> few Coales in comparison to what they now use: Divers Gardens and Or-
> chards planted even in the heart of *London*...were observed to bear such
> plentiful and infinite quantities of Fruits, as they never produced the like
> before or since, to their great astonishment. (7)

It had long been known that sea coal smoke was harmful to plants, but Evelyn was persuaded from his experience as a gardener that it had indeed led to the local extinction of a variety of species. By the beginning of the eighteenth century, this was commonplace knowledge among London's gardeners.[41] And, of course, Evelyn places the blame firmly with "those fumous Works" of industry.

Given Evelyn's interest in gardening, his further solution to London's air-pollution problem is perhaps not too surprising: to surround London with a contiguous

> Plantation...elegantly planted, diligently kept and supply'd, with such *Shrubs* as yield the most fragrant and odoriferous *Flowers,* and are apt to tinge the *Aer* upon every gentle emission at a great distance. Such as are (for instance among many others) the *Sweet-briar,* all the *Perclymena's* and *Woodbinds;* the Common *white* and *yellow Jessamine,* both the *Syringa's* or *Pipe trees,* the *Guelder-Rose,* the *Musk,* and all other *Roses.* (24)

Counteracting the coal smoke, the fresh air produced by these plants would "penetrate, alter, nourish, yea, and to multiply Plants and Fruits" growing in and about London, while at the same time such a "Lurid and noble *Aer,* clarifies the Blood" of human beings and animals.[42] As Robert Burton noted in a similar vein in 1621, "A clear air cheers up the spirits, exhilarates the mind; a thick, black, misty, tempestuous, contracts, [and] overthrows." It is unlikely that Burton's mention of "thick, black, misty" air could be anything other than a reference to smoke.[43] Karen Edwards has noted in her *Milton and the Natural World,* in the aptly entitled chapter "The Balm of Life," that "the assumptions behind Evelyn's plan for a vast, 'odoriferous' hedge around London are similar to those behind Milton's representation of the garden of Eden. Just as foul air produces disease, so clean air

---

41. In 1722, Thomas Fairchild noted that there are certain places in London where "perhaps the constant rising vapors from the River helps plants against the poisonous quality in the City smoke," *The City Gardener: Containing the Most Experienced Method of Cultivating and Ordering Such Ever-Greens, Fruit-Tress, Flowering Shrubs, Flowers, Exotick Plants, &C., as Will Be Ornamental, and Thrive Best in the London Gardens* (London, 1722), 470.

42. Ibid., 7, 3.

43. Robert Burton, *The Anatomy of Melancholy: What It Is with All the Kinds, Causes, Symptoms, Prognostics, and Several Cures of It in Three Partitions: With Their Several Sections, Members, and Subsections, Philosophically, Medicinally* (London: Chatto and Windus Piccadilly, 1883), 334.

promotes good health."[44] Indeed, the assumption that the balm from plants might cure the damages of sulfurous air pollution is one that Milton's Beelzebub makes in Hell when he first learns of earth:

> Or else in some mild zone
> Dwell not unvisited of heaven's fair light
> Secure, and at the beginning orient beam
> Purge off this gloom; the soft delicious air,
> To heal the scar of these corrosive fires
> Shall breathe her balm.[45]

True to Beelzebub's speculation, when Satan first encounters the "circling row / Of goodliest Trees loaden with fairest Fruit, / [and] Blossoms" that surround Eden, "pure now purer aire / Meets his approach."[46] Moreover, in the same way that Evelyn had brought attention in *Fumifugium* to the fact that the scent of certain flowers, such as rosemary, can be perceived from some miles off—they "are credibly reported to give their scent above thirty Leagues off at Sea," thereby making them ideal for Evelyn's vast "odoriferous" plantation circling London—Milton argues that Eden's "balmie spoiles" are similarly discernable:

> As when to them who saile
> Beyond the *Cape of Hope,* and now are past
> *Mozambic,* off at Sea North-East windes blow
> *Sabean* Odours from the spicies shoare
> Of *Arabie* the blest, with such delay
> Well pleas'd they slack thir course, and many a League
> Chear'd with the grateful smell of old Ocean smiles.
> So entertaind those odorous sweets the Fiend.[47]

Given that Milton's examples are so similar to Evelyn's, it is provocative to think that he may indeed have read *Fumifugium;* however, it may simply

---

44. Karen Edwards, *Milton and the Natural World* (Cambridge: Cambridge University Press, 1999), 196.

45. *Paradise Lost,* 2.397–402.

46. Ibid., 4.146–154.

47. John Evelyn, *Fumifugium,* 24 (misnumbered 14); *Paradise Lost,* 4.159–66.

be the case that London's air pollution problem had become such common knowledge that these were familiar ways of addressing the issue.

It is only from this context of early modern London's air pollution problem that some of the strangest lines in *Paradise Lost* become understandable. When Milton's Satan first enters Eden he is described

> As one who long in populous City pent,
> Where Houses thick and Sewers annoy the Aire,
> Forth issuing on a Summers Morn, to breathe
> Among the pleasant Villages and Farmes
> Adjoynd, from each thing met conceaves delight,
> The smell of Grain, or tedded Grass, or Kine,
> Or Dairie.[48]

A "populous City"? In prelapsarian Eden? In one of the few occasions in *Paradise Lost* in which the narrator appeals directly to the contemporary experiences of the reader, here we not only have a "populous City" like London compared to Hell because of its air quality, but, in contrast, the fresh air of the countryside is used as an analogy to better understand the effect of Eden on Satan.

In fact, Milton was hardly the only popular writer to deal with the air-pollution problem. In his poem *Cooper's Hill,* which was enormously successful in the middle of the seventeenth century, Sir John Denham deals with the problem in a variety of ways. Denham was, incidentally, a close personal friend of Evelyn and was acquainted with other seminal thinkers on the subject of London's air pollution. From Evelyn's diary, we know that on at least one occasion Denham, Evelyn, and Digby all met together. Moreover, Denham also knew and was quite fond of Margaret Cavendish.[49] But he was closest to Evelyn.

Cooper's Hill has had a strange history with readers. Having put the poem through five major revisions from 1642 to 1655, Denham so transparently casts a hunted stag as "a declining Statesman, left forlorne / to

---

48. Ibid., 4.445–51.

49. For Denham's meeting with both Evelyn and Digby, see Brendan O'Hehir's *Harmony from Discord: A Life of Sir John Denham* (Berkeley: University of California Press, 1968), 100. Similarly see O'Hehir for Denham's relationship to Margaret Cavendish (242).

his friends pity" (1642, 275–76),[50] that many readers in 1642 would have
known that this was no longer a metaphor, but rather a literal description
of the recently beheaded statesman Thomas Wentworth—and in the 1655
draft, of Charles I, who suffered the same fate. Similarly, when the speaker
of *Cooper's Hill* explains that "I see the City [London] in a thicker cloud /
Of businesse, then of smoake" (1642, 28–29), contemporary readers would
have at once recognized this as a literal description of an environmental
crisis already centuries in the making. After imagining himself raised well
into the "aire, secure from danger and feare" (1642, 26), the speaker describes London:

> So rais'd above the tumult and the crowd
> I see the City in a thicker cloud
> Of business, then of smoake; where men like Ants
> Toyle to prevent imaginarie wants;
> Yet all in vaine, increasing with their store,
> Their vast desires, but make their wants the more.
> As food to unsound bodies, though it please
> The Appetite, feeds only the disease;
> Where with like haste, though several waies they runne:
> Some to undoe, and some to be undone:
> While Luxury, and wealth, like Warr and Peace,
> Are each the others ruine.

* * *

> In tumults seek their peace, their heaven in hell,
> Oh happinesse of sweet retir'd content![51]

---

50. Sir John Denham, *Cooper's Hill* is quoted from Brendan O'Hehir's *Expans'd Hieroglyphicks: A Critical Edition of Sir John Denham's* Cooper's Hill (Berkeley: University of California Press,
1969). All references to *Cooper's Hill* are to this edition and are cited parenthetically in the text by
line number with reference to the year of the draft being quoted.

51. *Cooper's Hill,* 1642, 27–47. Readers familiar with Thoreau's *Walden* will immediately recognize here the central argument of the opening "Economy" chapter—and indeed of the work
itself. "The mass of men lead lives of quiet desperation," argued Thoreau, because, as Dedham
had already realized, "their vast desires, but make their wants the more," Henry David Thoreau,
Walden, ed. J. Lyndon Shanley (Princeton: Princeton University Press, 1971), 7. Of course, basking
in the "sweet retir'd content" of country life, while contrasting it with the complexities of a con-
temporaneous "modern world," has been a cornerstone of pastoral at least since the Greek Theocritus first penned his *Idylls.* But what ironically distinguishes the reception of *Cooper's Hill* from
that of *Walden* is that while Dedham's poem (which critiques an increasingly modern, capitalist

Readers at the time would have immediately recognized London's air-pollution problem in Denham's description of the city. However, by the eighteenth century, Samuel Johnson, while acknowledging that *Cooper's Hill* conferred on Denham "the rank and dignity of an original author...of a species of...local poetry," both marginalized the political references as merely "embellishments" and read the descriptions of landscape solely as a type of nature writing.[52] Similarly, the dozens of eighteenth-century imitators of Denham's poem downplayed any political import, choosing to portray the landscape as bucolic in order to hold a tight pastoral focus. For example, William Crowe's 1788 *Lewesdon Hill*, which Wordsworth, Coleridge, and many others admired, concerns itself chiefly with praising the beauty of the title hill:

> How changed is thy appearance, beauteous hill!
> Thou hast put off thy wintry garb, brown heath
> And russet fern, thy seemly-colour'd cloak
> To bide the hoary frosts and dripping rains
> Of chill December, and art gaily robed
> In livery of the spring: upon thy brow
> A cap of flowery hawthorn, and thy neck
> Mantled with new-sprung furze and spangles thick
> Of golden bloom: nor lack thee tufted woods
> Adown thy sides: tall oaks of lusty green,
> The darker fir, light ash, and the nesh tops
> Of the young hazel join, to form thy skirts.[53]

So popular were such imitations of Denham's poem that, in the year in which *Lewesdon Hill* was published, *The Gentleman's Magazine* complained that readers were tiring of "seeing the Muses labouring up...many

---

world) has been taken by some critics to be traditional pastoral until recently, other critics, focusing largely on Thoreau's assessment of modernity, have overlooked the fact that *Walden* is thoroughly in the pastoral tradition. What distinguishes both *Cooper's Hill* and *Walden* from the pastoral that came before them is that the critiques they offer of their "modern world" also apply to our own capitalist, consumer society. This has, of course, long been noted of *Walden*, but perhaps because in the popular imagination the growth of large-scale capital remains very much a nineteenth-century phenomenon, the critique of consumerism offered in *Cooper's Hill* has largely escaped the interest of critics.

52. Samuel Johnson, *Lives of the Poets* (New York: Scribner, 1896), 4.312.
53. William Crowe, *Lewesdon Hill* (Oxford, 1788), ll. 20–31.

hills since Cooper's and Grongar, and some gentle Bard reclining on almost every mole-hill."[54]

Perhaps because readers were tiring of the hill poem, by the middle of the nineteenth century Denham's legacy was not faring so well: *Cooper's Hill* was rarely referenced and imitated even less. But interest in the poem renewed in the twentieth century, most recently in its depiction of contemporary political dramas. While such readings have done much to restore the poem to its original political context, they have unfortunately done little to situate it environmentally. For example, Bruce Boeckel has recently argued that "if Alexander Pope or Samuel Johnson...had traveled back in time to the scene of the poem's composition, they would have noticed a strong contrast between the pacific topography of the poem itself and the bellicose mental landscape of the poem's original audience."[55] While Boeckel's point regarding the "bellicose mental landscape of the poem's original audience" is not far from the mark, it is clear that much of the topography depicted in *Cooper's Hill* was hardly "pacific."

---

54. Quoted from Raymond Dexter Havens's *The Influence of Milton on English Poetry* (New York: Russell and Russell, 1961), 248. By the eighteenth century, the river meandering through the distant valley in the hill poem was generally depicted as a picturesque brook or clear stream, as it is in *Lewesdon Hill* the "clear stream...dost trip / Adown the valley, wandering sportively" (*Lewesdon Hill*, ll. 129–32). What strikingly contrasts *Lewesdon Hill* with Dedham's poem is that Crowe takes pains to make clear that the stream "flows along / Untainted with the commerce of the world" (*Lewesdon Hill*, ll. 136–37.)

Much has been made of the arrival of the railroad as a symbol of modernity in nineteenth-century fiction. It appears as such, for example, in *Middlemarch,* Émile Zola's *La Bête Humaine,* and of course *Walden,* although perhaps Dickens most vividly and famously describes it as a vehicle of commerce in *Dombey and Son:* "Crowds of people and mountains of goods, departing and arriving scores of times in every four-and-twenty hour, produced a fermentation in the place that was always in action" (Charles Dickens, *Dombey and Son* [New York: Penguin, 1970], 218.) But what the railway was to the nineteenth century, the river was to the seventeenth. As historian Frank Dix notes, "Following the exploratory voyages of Drake and Raleigh," shipping on the "Thames trebled and quadrupled [it]...must truly have looked like a 'forest of masts,' and the activity of loading and unloading must have been intense" (Frank Dix, *Royal River Highway: A History of the Passenger Boats and Services on the River Thames* [London: David and Charles Press, 1985], 23.) Aside from the international trade, as London's population doubled from 1560 to 1600 alone, the river was already choked with the movement of local goods. Not surprisingly, sea coal was the most common local commodity shipped on the Thames. Far from being a babbling brook, the Thames in the seventeenth century was likely the single greatest artery of commerce that the world had ever known, moving more goods than any railway ever would.

55. Bruce Boeckel, "Landscaping the Field of Discourse: Political Slant and Poetic Slope in Sir John Denham's *Cooper's Hill,*" *Papers on Language and Literature* 34.1 (1998): 57.

When compared to such eighteenth-century imitators as Crowe's *Lewesdon Hill,* what is immediately apparent is that Denham's poem contains no literal description of Cooper's Hill itself. Instead, the speaker lays out for the reader the landscape of the Thames Valley visible from the hill. Beginning with a view of St. Paul's cathedral, we move to London, then to Windsor Castle, St. Anne's Hill, a section of the Thames, Windsor Forest, a stag hunt on a washland meadow adjacent to the forest, and then finally conclude with the Thames overflowing its banks. True, Denham does compare the hill to the Greek Mount Parnassus, but this is obviously metaphorical, as the poet uses the comparison to support his opening authorial statement. The descriptions of landscape must wait until line thirteen, when "Exalted to this height, I first looke downe / upon Pauls" (1642, 13–14). As many critics have noted, the restoration of St. Paul's cathedral in London was a politically charged issue from at least as early as the 1620s, as Charles I was a leading proponent for a church restoration that many thought far too opulent. Consequently, it is hardly surprising that royalist Denham should praise the church that was "Preserv'd from ruine by the best of Kings" (1642, 24).

What critics have ignored, however, is why the restoration of St. Paul's was necessary in the first place. As Sir William Dugdale noted in his 1658 *The History of St. Paul's Cathedral in London,* Charles I believed (correctly, as we now know) that the "decayed fabrick" of St. Paul's was caused "by the corroding quality of the Coale Smoake, especially in moist weather, whereunto it had been so long subject."[56] As a consequence, as Dugdale notes, Charles's "princely heart was moved with such compassion to this decayed fabrick that for prevention of its neer approaching ruine...[Despite] considering with himself how vast the charge would be," he nonetheless spearheaded the drive to finance its reconstruction in the 1620s.[57] We now know that the burning of coal with high sulfur content releases sulfur dioxide into the atmosphere, which is highly caustic to building surfaces. As Evelyn concisely states in 1659, it is this "cloud of *Sea Coal.* ... This pestilent *Smoak,* which corrodes the very iron" of buildings.[58]

---

56. Sir William Dugdale, *The History of St. Paul's Cathedral in London* ...(London, 1658), 134.
57. Ibid.
58. John Evelyn, *A Character of London*... (London, 1659), 29–30.

Unfortunately, given the prevailing winds, St. Paul's was directly in the path of a sulfurous cloud of air pollution: as Evelyn explains in *Fumifugium,* "when the Wind blows Southern, [it] dilates it self all over...the opposite part of *London,* especially about *St. Paul's,* poysoning the *Aer* with so dark and thick a Fog, as I have been hardly been able to pass through it" (8). Although not identifying it as St. Paul's, in 1659 Evelyn writes of a "spacious *Church* where I could not discern the *Minister* for the *Smoak;* nor hear him from the peoples barking," the smoke "so fatally seizing on the *Lungs*...that the *Cough* and *Consumption* spare no man."[59] This problem was further exacerbated by the particular meteorological inversion characteristic of the Thames Valley, which causes London's distinctive fog. Because both fog and smoke tend not to readily dissipate over London, it sets up moist conditions that are near perfect at enabling caustic interaction between sulfur dioxide and building materials. (Although not coined until centuries later, the word *smog* enters the English language as a contraction specifically intended to describe the meteorological condition whereby an amalgam of "smoke-fog" hung over London.)[60] Hopeful that Charles II might show the same concern for buildings attacked by air pollution as had his father, Evelyn cleverly (and prescriptively) takes for granted in the opening of *Fumifugium* that "your Majesty who is a lover of noble Buildings, Gardens, Pictures, and all Royal Magnificences, must...desire to be freed from this prodigious annoyance...once it enters, there can nothing remain long in its native Splendor and Perfection," as "it is this horrid Smoake which obscures our Churches" ("The Epistle," 6).

In an intriguing turn of events, the damage that St. Paul's cathedral received from sea coal smoke played a role in one of the many scandals of the day. Although, as Dugdale noted, Charles's "princely heart was moved" to undertake St. Paul's restoration, initially he was able to raise only £5,500 for the purpose. However, when William Laud was made bishop of London in 1628, the situation changed dramatically. Laud quickly began levying a host of fines in order to finance the restoration—fines that, as they made him increasingly unpopular, helped lead to his impeachment by Parliament in 1640, confinement to the Tower in 1641, trial in 1644, and

---

59. Ibid., 30.
60. The word *smog* was coined in 1905 by H. A. Des Voeux while delivering a paper entitled "Smoke and Fog." See the OED, "smog," definition 1a.

beheading in 1645. Although it was one of the smaller fines he enforced, by April 1635 alone, Laud was able to obtain twice what Charles I originally raised for St. Paul's restoration (£11,000) by heavily fining sea coal burners.[61] As noted earlier, beginning in the fourteenth century, those burning sea coal faced being subject to "heavy forfeiture,"[62] but as seventeenth-century London was increasingly dependent on sea coal's cheap appeal, this was rarely enforced. While it helped to make Laud enormously unpopular, levying fines against polluters in order to remediate the damage that they caused was, as an environmental strategy, well ahead of its time. It also seems more than coincidental that Laud was tutor to Sir Kenelm Digby who, in putting forth the idea that sea coal was responsible for both "pyisicall and pulmonicall distempers,"[63] was one of Evelyn's acknowledged primary influences.

One of the unanswered questions concerning *Cooper's Hill* is that if London was so engulfed in a cloud of sea coal pollution, how was it possible to make out St. Paul's cathedral from such a distance? Denham could, of course, merely be taking poetic license here, but there were times when it may indeed have been possible. As mentioned earlier, Evelyn noted that "when *New-castle* was besieg'd and blocked up in our late Wars [there was a]…great Dearth and Scarcity of Coales" (7), which not only cleared the sky, but so diminished the pollution problem that certain species of plants endangered by the sea coal smoke returned to London. Similarly when, on a number of occasions, Charles I attempted to sell the rights to tax the sea coal trade on the Thames in the late 1630s, sea coal availability (and hence air pollution) was temporarily interrupted. It is possible that these occasions not only afforded Denham an opportunity to actually view St. Paul's from Cooper's Hill, but, in providing him with such a marked contrast to London's normally polluted state, may have helped inspire the section of the poem describing the city in a cloud of pollution. In the early drafts of the poem from the 1640s, there is no direct mention of air pollution surrounding St. Paul's, but in the 1655 draft, written when sea coal availability had not been interrupted for years, the cathedral appears rising

---

61. For Laud's fines on sea coal burning, see *Extraordinary Monyes paid into the Receipt of his Maiesties Exchequer, since the beginning of His Reigne, till Aprill 1635* (London, 1643), 4.

62. *Calendar of Close Rolls,* Edward (1302–7), 5.537.

63. Sir Kenelm Digby, *Of the Sympatheticƙ Powder,* (London, 1669), 23.

from the "mist" of the city: "Under his [the cathedral's] proud survey the City lies, / And like a mist beneath a hill doth rise" (25–26).

When issues like air pollution emerged into appearance in Renaissance texts, they created a major representational challenge. In spite of the treatment that London's air-pollution problem receives in *Paradise Lost, Cooper's Hill,* and other early modern texts, public opinion was not generally against sea coal use. While visitors to London seemed to have almost universally objected to the air-pollution problem,[64] the English themselves had mixed feelings about their sea coal use. As the anonymous author of the 1644 *Artificiall Fire, of Coale for Rich and Poore* made clear, there was a time in recent memory when

> some fine Nosed City Dames used to tell their husbands: O Husband! We shall never bee well, we nor our Children, whilst wee live in the smell of this Cities smoke; Pray, a Country house for our health, that we may get out of this stinking Seacole smell.[65]

However, because of the dearth of coal during the various blockades of Newcastle, "many of these fine Nosed Dames now cry, Would to God we had Seacoale, O the want of Fire undoes us! O the sweet Seacoale fire we use to have, how we want them now."[66]

While *Artificiall Fire* was obviously a political pamphlet produced by the sea coal industry, even its tongue-in-cheek parody of "fine Nosed City

---

64. John Nef notes,

> Foreigners who visited the rapidly growing city [London] were astonished at the filthy smoke from tens of thousands of domestic fires and from hundreds of workshops. There was no spectacle like it anywhere on earth. With its breweries, its soap- and starch-houses, its brick-kilns, sugar-refineries, earthenware-works, and glass furnaces, London seemed to some of these visitors to have been rendered unfit for human habitation.

"Coal Mining and Utilization," 77. Nor was the perception limited to London: during her seventeenth-century tour of the English countryside, Celia Fiennes noted of Newcastle that "this Country all about is full of this [sea] Coale, ye sulfur of it taints ye aire and it smells strongly to strangers." *Through England on a Side Saddle,* 175 Similarly, in his diary of 1698 Henri Misson noted that "the smell of sulfur caused by this [burning sea coal] is somewhat offensive to those that are just come from abroad, but one is soon used to it," *Memoirs and Observations in His Travels over England,* quoted from Maureen Waller's *1700: Scenes from London Life* (London: Hodder & Stoughton, 2000), 140.

65. Cited by John Neff in *Rise of the British Coal Industry,* 198.

66. Ibid.

Dames" makes clear that Evelyn's concerns over sea coal use and human health were widespread at the time. On the other hand, *Artificiall Fire* makes equally clear that, because early modern London was indeed dependent on inexpensive sea coal, it was sorely missed when supplies were short—even wistfully lamented. Henry Glapthorne has a character give voice to the idea in his 1635 play *The Lady Mother,* "Would I were in my native City [London] ayre agen, within the wholesome smell of seacole."[67] Because cold, damp winters were believed (correctly, given statistics from London's mortality rolls) to be associated with a variety of very serious illnesses, heat from sea coal was to many not only a universal cure, but perhaps the difference between life and death. This was not only the case in London, but increasingly in outlying areas as well.[68]

Although sea coal use had been known to be dangerous for centuries, its burners had at times been fined and jailed; John Graunt, Margaret Cavendish, Sir Kenelm Digby, and others had theorized that sea coal smoke was especially noxious; Tundale, Shakespeare, Milton and many other writers had imagined Hell as engulfed in coal-smoke pollution; and John Evelyn had penned the first tract to take as its subject modern air pollution, England—like many countries today—simply could not walk away from the cheap appeal of fossil fuel. This presented a major representational challenge.

At a time when nationalistic pride often centered on London (usually contrasted directly to Paris and Rome), scores of writers produced works praising the city: John Coke (1550), William Camden (1586), Thomas Platter (1599), Michael Drayton (1619), Sir William Davenport (1648), to name but a few.[69] As Platter concisely stated it on the eve of the seventeenth century, England's capital

> is so superior to other English towns that London is not said to be in England, but rather England to be in London, for England's most resplendent objects may be seen in and around London: so that he who sightsees London...may assert without impertinence that he is properly acquainted with England.[70]

67. Henry Glapthorne, *The Lady Mother* (Oxford: Oxford University Press, 1958), 9.
68. See *John Taylor's Last Voyage,* in *Travels through Stuart Britain,* 198.
69. For early modern works praising London, see Lawrence Manley's *London in the Age of Shakespeare,* 49ff.
70. Platter is quoted from Ibid., 37–38.

While not all such depictions were positive, even those writers who make mention of London's coal use, such as Thomas Gainsford in 1618, often intentionally misrepresented (in direct contrast to Denham, Evelyn, and others) the city's air pollution problem: "Instead of foggy mists and clouds, ill air, flat situation, miry springs, and a kind of staining clay, you have in London a sun-shining and serene element for the most part."[71]

Furthermore, there were powerful political and economic forces that benefited from misrepresenting London's air-pollution problem. A 1649 pamphlet drew attention—as do many modern works produced by industries heavily invested in the exploitation of natural resources—to the profound economic advantages of such enterprises:

> many thousand people are employed in this trade of coals; many live by working of them in the pits; many live by conveying them in wagons to the river Tyne; many men are employed in conveying coals...aboard ships: one coal merchant employeth five hundred, or a thousand, in his works of coal.[72]

Not only did the coal industry directly benefit thousands, but powerful interests, such as those of Charles I and Parliament, had much to gain from its trade. As noted earlier, the revenue that Charles received during the 1630s from taxing sea coal transported on the Thames was so appealing to investors that he tried on a number of occasions to make a quick profit by selling the rights of the tax. Moreover, after the Great Fire (through the Rebuilding Act of 1667), Parliament imposed such a hefty tax on sea coal brought into the port of London that it is thought by some historians to have crippled the city's economy.[73]

Nor were sea coal's profits reaped only by the central government: as Jonathan Barry notes, "Coal traders...or 'lords of coal,' as they were dubbed at the time, were already in a dominating position [in Newcastle] by the mid-Elizabethan period...each of the major coal traders served a

---

71. Ibid., 44.

72. Reprinted in Joan Thirsk's and J. P. Cooper's *Seventeenth-Century Economic Documents* (Oxford: Clarendon Press, 1972), 363–64.

73. For more on these fines, see T. F. Reddaway's *The Rebuilding of London after the Great Fire,* (London: Edward Arnold, 1951), 181 ff., as well as Eric S. Wood's *Historical Britain: A Comprehensive Account of the Development of Rural and Urban Life and Landscape from Prehistory to the Present Day* (London: Harvill Press, 1995), 518.

term as mayor of the town."[74] The anonymous *Artificiall Fire,* for example, was likely produced by or for the "lords of coal." Consequently, these coal traders (like modern interests that have a monopoly on fossil fuel) acknowledged the often-heard argument that "we shall never bee well, we nor our Children, whilst wee live in the smell of this Cities smoke," but brought attention to the fact that as soon as the supply of fossil fuels was cut, such as during the Newcastle blockades, the cry would be that "the want of Fire undoes us!"[75] In short, *Artificiall Fire* attempted to make clear to the citizens of London the deep, unresolved contradiction in their stance toward coal—which was, not surprisingly, at the crux of the problem in representing air pollution at the time—namely that Londoners, hating what they could not do without, were unable to reconcile their need for coal with the dangers it wrought both on their health and on their glorious city/nation.

Consequently, early modern Londoners, at once knowing the risks involved with sea coal's use and fearing what life would be like without it (especially during winter, the flu and pneumonia season), found themselves in much the same position that much of the planet occupies today. In fact, although a preindustrial city, London was likely the first place on the planet to experience on a large scale what is now a global dilemma: How can we live without burning the fossil fuels that we know are wreaking havoc with the environment (in particular the atmosphere), as well as our very health, when the energy that they supply is paradoxically essential for our life and health? This is certainly a question that I am in no position to answer. However, as noted above, it does reveal an important representational challenge faced by Renaissance writers: How do we speak about that which we can live neither with nor without?

Of course, it is possible to speak or write about something as both a solution to one problem and the cause of another, but how exactly does one justify the seemingly irrational behavior of trying to protect one's health by knowingly doing oneself harm—perhaps far greater harm—in the process? It would be easy enough for someone outside of the situation to draw attention to such paradoxical behavior (as noted earlier, visitors to early modern London, almost universally appalled by the air-pollution problem, were

74. Jonathan Barry, *The Tudor and Stuart Town: A Reader in English Urban History, 1530–1688.* (London: Longman, 1990), 276.

75. *Artificiall Fire* (London), 198.

quick to give their opinions of it), but from the point of view of someone caught on the horns of the dilemma, desperately maintaining a life grip on the very practices threatening life, it might be difficult to confront, let alone explain, such actions. From a writer's point of view, the challenge is once removed but no less difficult: How does one go about drawing attention to such seemingly irrational behavior on the part of one's readers? This is, of course, not to say that it would be impossible to write about such behavior (and actually expect the intended audience to read it), but it would be far easier if there was a way to avoid the horns of the dilemma altogether.

One solution would be to suggest, though obviously counter to the facts, that consumers themselves are not the cause of the problem. Instead, it could be argued that other individuals, through selfish and insensitive acts, are bringing it about. Even if this were not true, a clever and effective writer might be able to make it seem as if this was indeed the case. This, as we have seen, was Evelyn's answer.

Regardless of the practical merits of Evelyn's protective hedge surrounding London, his approach to the aforementioned representational problem was a masterstroke. Moreover, it presages a broad swath of modern environmental writing that similarly focuses on the actions of industry, or government, rather than consumers. Let me be clear in saying that in many cases this approach is certainly justified (works such as Rachel Carson's *Silent Spring* come to mind). There is, however, something to be learned from *Fumifugium*. Since we know that industry could not have been the principal cause of the air-pollution problem in early modern London, Evelyn was obviously not representing the facts accurately, but rather deploying a highly effective rhetorical strategy. Because there is an obvious genealogical (if not causal, given that Evelyn's text is not well known today among environmentalists) connection between *Fumifugium* and some modern environmental literature, it does raise a question regarding the extent to which this rhetorical strategy is also deployed in these modern works. This is not to say that the individuals involved are misrepresenting the facts intentionally. To the contrary, as the representational problem is related to the paradoxical behavior of maintaining a life grip on the very practices threatening life, which is even more common today than it was in early modern London, it is certainly possible that the individuals generating these works, being themselves guilty of the same environmental actions in their personal lives, would have difficulty confronting their own questionable behavior. Consequently, such individuals would not necessarily be misrepresenting anything intentionally, but rather explaining what they believe to be true—perhaps desperately need to believe to be true—in order to justify to themselves their own environmental actions.

In short, perhaps the most important lesson to be learned from *Fumifugium* may be that, when confronted with the challenge of representing what neither writer nor reader may wish to acknowledge about their own actions, the causes of environmental problems may be misrepresented unintentionally. Again, this need not always be the case, but it is a real danger brought about by the challenge of representing a problem that nearly everyone is causing, but, unable to stop, is likewise hesitant to confront. And, of course, the danger is even greater today. *Fumifugium* is important and fascinating to consider because, dating from a time when we clearly know that industry could not have been the principle cause of the environmental problem, it shows that casting blame on industry may have as much, or even more, to do with our inability to face the issue—and our role in contributing to the problem—than it does with the actions of industry.

Let me be very clear here: I am not marshaling this argument in defense of twenty-first-century industries that pollute the atmosphere and contribute to global warming. However, it is an important phenomenon about which we should be aware. With respect to our present global warming crisis, while it is true that coal-burning power plants are the primary source of atmospheric carbon dioxide released by human beings in the United States (such power plants currently produce 2.5 billion tons of CO_2 annually), the second largest source, directly releasing nearly 1.5 billion tons of the gas into the atmosphere each year, comes from consumers' automobiles. Although it may be as difficult for us to confront our immediate and personal role in altering the atmosphere as it was for early modern Londoners, it is nonetheless important that we do not let a rhetorical strategy—which ironically is tailor-made to draw our attention to the problem—obfuscate our role in contributing to the crisis, especially regarding our automobile use (as well as, for that matter, our consumption of electricity produced by coal-burning power plants).

In contrast to the ecological and representational challenges that came with early modern London's air-pollution problem, in the next chapter I want to consider the extraordinary efforts taken in Renaissance England to stop an altogether different environmental crisis.

6

ENVIRONMENTAL PROTEST LITERATURE
OF THE RENAISSANCE

The *Oxford English Dictionary* (OED) suggests that, prior to 1644, the word *leveller* had only two rather obscure meanings, describing either someone who took soundings or one who took aim at something. But that was to change dramatically in the 1640s when the term began to be applied to an emerging political group.[1] "The Levellers," as Thomas Corns notes, were "named by their enemies, to suggest that they sought to level all the social distinctions and rights of property on which society in early modern England was perceived to be founded. It was a term they disliked and disputed."[2] There are, however, a number of problems here. First, although ignored by the *OED,* the word *leveller* was in fact used as early as 1607, by both the individuals themselves and their enemies, to describe certain radical political protesters. Second, although in 1607, the word was

---

1. See "leveller," definitions 1 and 2 in the *OED*.
2. Thomas N. Corns, "Radical Pamphleteering," in *The Cambridge Companion to Writing of the English Revolution,* ed. N. H. Keeble (Cambridge: Cambridge University Press, 2001), 76.

already beginning to take on the notion of leveling social distinctions, it had an entirely different meaning at the time. Third, although the *OED* further suggests that the related term *digger* was not applied to a political group until 1649,[3] it was likewise similarly used in 1607. Understanding who these early Levellers and Diggers were, as well as the identity of similar protesters from the 1620s, 1630s, and 1640s, will make clear not only the often-ignored environmental component of these related movements, but also how, in the seventeenth century, England's countryside began appearing as if for the first time in places all across the island.

While I have hereto considered how the encroachment of London into its surroundings facilitated the emergence into appearance of the threatened environs to its citizens and artists, the countryside not only similarly appeared elsewhere in England when other environs were threatened but led to efforts to preserve the unique ecosystems under threat (like the Moorfields discussed in chapter 3). What was at stake was the question of land use. Whenever land is radically changed in order to serve a new use, such as the conversion of London's rural surroundings into suburbs, these places are ideally situated to make their belated emergence into appearance, not only to people entering the changing locales, but also to those exiled from the places as a result. The latter group is wonderfully given voice by Meliboeus in Vergil's first Eclogue. In the present chapter, I would like to consider how thousands of Meliboeuslike individuals rose up across England in the seventeenth century to defend the newly emerging, endangered countryside, as well as draw attention to issues of environmental justice.

Before embarking on a consideration of these early seventeenth-century environmental protesters, it is important to differentiate them from the mid-century Levellers and Diggers that have so interested critics in recent decades. The issue centers on land use. The early protesters were violently opposed to changes in land use, rioting, as we shall see, in order to protest proposed agricultural changes to England's countryside. When this happened, unique ecosystems, which had supported local communities for generations, emerged into appearance as if for the first time at the moment of their endangerment. This appearance (the moment when human beings became more thematically aware of their surrounding environs: what we

---

3. See "digger" definition 1d in the *OED*.

call environmental consciousness) was chronicled by the people inhabiting these places, as they undertook to systematically describe, inventory, and champion their local habitats as places worthy of being saved.

The midcentury Levellers and Diggers, on the other hand, were concerned (as critics such as Corns and Nigel Smith have compellingly argued) principally with issues relating to rights of property. When Gerald Winstanley and other Diggers attempted to farm St. George's Hill in April 1649, they questioned just who had legal right to that property. As he held that the wealth of the Commonwealth should be common to all, Winstanley felt that he and his companions had certain rights to land that had traditionally been held in common. As the privatization of England's commons, in the form of the enclosure movement, had been debated for centuries, Winstanley attempted to leverage to his advantage an issue that seemingly would pit the mass of England's disenfranchised poor against wealthy landowners. However, because Winstanley in some sense had misunderstood the enclosure debate, believing that it centered principally on the issue of property rights, he not only failed to gain the support of the disenfranchised poor, but to his surprise, found that the poor were at times violently opposed to his Digger movement.

In his 1649 *Appeal to the House of Commons,* Winstanley made clear that the Diggers had "plowed and dig'd upon *Georges-Hill* in *Surrey,* to sow corn for the succor of man [and to]...mprove the Commons and waste Lands to our best advantage."[4] "And not only this Common, or Heath shall be taken in and Manured by the People," suggested Winstanley in his *True Levellers Standard,* "but all the Commons and waste Ground in England, and the whole World" (260). As is clear from these and other such passages,[5] Winstanley (like Francis Bacon, Samuel Hartlib, and many

---

4. Winstanley's *Appeal to the House of Commons* is cited from *The Works of Gerrard Winstanley,* ed. George E. Sabine (New York: Russell and Russell, 1965), 301. All additional references to Winstanley are to this collection and will be cited parenthetically.

5. See also Winstanley's *Declaration from the Poor Oppressed People of England,* in which he notes that he intends "to Dig and Plough up the Commons, and waste Lands through England" (270). Moreover, when called to Whitehall to present his case regarding St. George's Hill to Thomas Fairfax, Winstanley's argument, as recorded at the time by Bulstrode Whitelocke, was that his "intent is to restore the Creation to its former condition...that they [the Diggers] intend not to meddle with any man's property nor to break down any pales or enclosures, but only to meddle with what was common and untilled, and to make it fruitful for the use of man." Whitelocke is cited in Lewis H. Berens's *The Digger Movement in the Days of the Commonwealth As*

other agricultural reformers in the seventeenth century) wanted to change the way that England used its natural resources by developing vast tracks of untilled land for new agricultural purposes. What made Winstanley's approach unique was that he held that such changes in land use should be undertaken by, and for the principal benefit of, England's poor, rather than its wealthy landowners. Nonetheless, Winstanley suggested particularly radical land reforms, not only advocating the conversion of pasture to arable land, but making clear, in his *Declaration from the Poor Oppressed People of England,* that

> the main thing we aym at, and to which we declare our Resolutions to go forth, and act, is this, To lay hold upon, and as we stand in need, to Cut and Fell, and make the best advantage we can of the Woods and Trees, that grow upon the Commons, To be a stock for our selves and our poor Brethren....For we say our purpose is, to take those Common Woods to Sell them, now at first a stock for our selves, and our children after us, to plant and manure the Common land. (272–74)

Because Winstanley proposed and began to enact sweeping changes in land use, which included deforesting tracts of land in order to finance his projects, it is not surprising that recorded in his writings is a counterprotest made by the local people of St. George's Hill, which he was intent on developing. Noting in a 1649 "Letter to the Lord Fairfax" that "many of the Countrey-people [of St. George's Hill]...were offended at first" by his acts of land reform, Winstanley optimistically writes that "we expect, that these angry neighbors, whom we never wronged, nor will not wrong, will see their furious rashness to be folly, and become moderate" (282).[6] Having traditionally used the nearby common for the grazing of their cattle and other uses, these people violently rejected Winstanley's plans for changes in land use, asserting their rights to use the land as they traditionally had by letting their cattle graze on, and hence destroy, the young crops planted by Winstanley and his companions. While few records survive to record what

---

Revealed in the Writings of Gerrard Winstanley, the Digger, Mystic and Rationalist, Communist and Social Reformer (London: Simpkin, Marshall, Hamilton, Kent, 1906), 37.

6. See also Winstanley's *A Declaration of the Bloudie and Unchristian Acting of William Star and John Taylor of Walton* (295–98) for the counterprotest made by the inhabitants of St. George's Hill.

the people living in the area surrounding St. George's Hill thought of the Diggers, it would hardly be surprising if, in spite of his many protestations regarding his concern for the earth, Winstanley was thought by these people to be just another projector who wanted to radically alter their common for a new use. As we shall see directly, the 1607 Levellers and Diggers were far more like these local people of St. George's Hill than their mid-century namesakes.

In early May 1607 England's so-called "Midland Revolts" broke out in parishes across Northamptonshire, then quickly spread to Warwickshire and Leicestershire by the end of the month. As historian John Martin succinctly notes, "The reasons for the selection of sites of protest are clear. These parishes almost without exception had experienced almost total enclosure, considerable depopulation and the conversion of land from arable to pasture within the previous ten years."[7] Equally clear was the reason informing the method of protest. As Edmund Howes reflected back on the riots in 1615, he noted that the participants "violently cut and broke downe hedges, filed up ditches, and laid up all such inclosures of Commons."[8] As Howes made clear, the protesters, who often included women and children, were not intent on attacking individuals or goods, but rather only wanted to "leavell" the ditches that both marked and drained recently enclosed land: these "tumultuous persons in Northamptonshire, Warwicke, and Leicestershire...being in some places of men, women, and children, a thousand together...these riotous persons bent all their strengths to leavell and lay open inclosures, without exercising any manner of theft, or violence upon any mans person, goods, or cattell."[9]

Given that the common goal of these protesters was to level ditches, it is perhaps not surprising that they quickly took on the name of "Levellers." As Howes noted, on the May 27, 1607, the king sent various officials "to doe justice upon the leavellers, according to the nature of their offenses."[10] Not only were the protesters named Levellers by their enemies, but as the Earl of Shrewsbury made clear in a letter of June 11, 1607, describing to

7. John Martin, *An Atlas of Rural Protest in Britain, 1548–1900,* ed. Andrew Charlesworth (Philadelphia: University of Pennsylvania Press, 1983), 34.

8. John Stow and Edmund Howes, *Annales,* 890.

9. Ibid.

10. Ibid.

Sir John Manners how the rebellion was put down, it was a term they applied to themselves as well: "1000 of thease fellowes who term themselves levellers were busily digging. . . . [At first they] fought desperatelie; but at the second charge they ran away, in which there were slain som 40 or 50 of them, and a very great number hurt."[11] Although ignored by the *OED,* this may not only be the first time that the word *leveller* signaled a political group, but also the first time the word was used to describe the activity of literally leveling ground. The name was still in use decades later. In 1618, Lord Chief Justice Montague noted how recent protesters were like the earlier "levellers in Northamptonshire." The word kept this meaning into the 1620s and 1630s.[12] Given that the main objective of the Levellers was (as another 1607 account described it) the literal "casting in of the ditches,"[13] it is perhaps also not surprising that these protesters also called themselves "Diggers." In fact, their principal manifesto was the 1607 "The Diggers of Warwickshire to all other Diggers." (This has also been ignored by *OED.*)[14]

The 1607 Levellers and Diggers were therefore so named because they were literally intent, through digging, on leveling the ditches that both marked and drained recently enclosed land. However, even at the time it was realized that this literal leveling of land might also lead to the leveling of, as Corns noted, "social distinctions." Divining the far-reaching social

11. Reprinted in Edmund Lodge's *Illustrations of British History, Biography, and Manners, in the Reigns of Henry VIII, Edward VI, Mary, Elizabeth, & James I...* (London, 1838), vol. 3, 196.

12. Lord Chief Justice Montague from *Calendar of State Papers, Domestic Series,* James I, vol. 10 (1620), 532. Similarly, in 1620, the Justices of Northamptonshire argued that cheap corn should be made available to the people to "prevent their discontent and tumultuous leveling" (*Calendar of State Papers, Domestic Series,* 130). The word *leveller* also appears in the sense of both political protester and leveler of ground in the 1631 revision of Stow's *Annales,* which this time was undertaken by George Buck. John Stow, Edmund Howes, and George Buck, *The Annales, or, Generall Chronicle of England* (London, 1631), 890.

13. From a June 1, 1607, account mentioned in the *Records of the Borough of Leicester; Being a Series of Extracts from the Archives of the Corporation of Leicester,* ed. Mary Bateson, et al. (London: C. J. Clay, 1899), 59.

14. The *OED* suggests that the word *digger,* as applied to a political group, is first used to describe "a section of the Levellers in 1649, who adopted communistic principles as to the land, in accordance with which they began to dig and plant the commons" ("digger," definition 2d). However, as I argue in this chapter, it seems clear that a similar meaning was intended in the 1607 "The Diggers of Warwickshire to all other Diggers," recently reprinted in *The Writing of Rural England, 1500–1800,* eds. Stephen Bending and Andrew Mcrae (New York: Palgrave Macmillan, 2003), 146–47.

implications of the movement, Robert Wilkinson argued in a sermon of June 21, 1607, that the Levellers "accompt [account] with clergy men, and counsell is given to kill up Gentlemen, and they will levell all states as they levell bankes and ditches."[15]

While it is important to consider the political implications of what these early Levellers were attempting, to focus exclusively on this would be to ignore the environmental component of the protests. The 1607 Levellers and Diggers were less concerned with shifting ownership of property (as Howe noted, they did not exercise "any manner of theft, or violence upon any mans person, goods, or cattell")[16] than they were with changing patterns of land use. For centuries the disputed arable Midlands had produced a variety of goods that supported local economies. With enclosure, however, these economies would be destroyed: not because ownership of the property would be transferred to wealthy landowners, but because these landowners were completely eradicating existing ways of life by converting arable land to pasture. As the protesters succinctly explained the situation in 1607 in "The Diggers of Warwickshire to all other Diggers," wealthy landowners had "depopulated and overthrown whole townes, and made therof sheep pastures."[17] If the much-needed, grain-producing fields were replaced by pasture, the only equivalent cataclysm would be, as the Diggers argued, the worst crop failures in recent memory: "If it should please God to withdraw his blessing in not prospering ye fruits of the ye Earth but for one yeare (God forbid) there would be a worse, and more fearfull dearth happen then did in K. Ed. ye seconds tyme, when people were forced to eat Catts and dogs flesh, and women to eate theye owne children."[18] Fear that food shortages would result if arable fields were converted into pasture was widespread at the time. The concern behind the Midland Revolts is echoed in Shakespeare's *Coriolanus,* likely written in Warwickshire at Stratford-on-Avon in 1608, which took as one of its principal themes the

---

15. Robert Wilkinson, *A Sermon Preached at North-Hampton the 21. Of June Last Past, before the Lord Lieutenant of the County, and the Rest of the Commissioners There Assembled Vpon Occasion of the Late Rebellion and Riot in Those Parts Committed* (London, 1607), F2-F3. See the *OED* for "accompt," which is an archaic form of "account."

16. Edmund Howes, *The Annales,* 890.

17. *The Writing of Rural England, 1500–1800,* 146. The original is the British Library: MSS 787, art. 11.

18. Ibid.

political fallout resulting from grain shortages.[19] But more than simply arguing that the existing grain-producing economy met the subsistence needs of its people, the Diggers suggested that the "comon fields being layd open, would yield as much comodity" for "our Comonwealth" as would the new pasture-based economy.[20]

What is at first paradoxical about the example of the 1607 Leveller and Diggers is that, while the agricultural change they resisted was the conversion of arable land to pasture, the local people of St. George's Hill opposed Winstanley and his Diggers in their efforts to convert pasture (and forests) to arable land. However, as noted in chapter 2, because what is "natural" for each of us is often the backdrop into which we are born, regardless of in what state we find those natural environs, it should come as no great surprise that, when those environs emerge into appearance as the result of a perceived environmental crisis, they can appear as a "nature" worth fighting for. Consequently, the countryside emerging into appearance (which can signal the birth of an ecological consciousness) need not be "wilderness," but can emerge from a variety of different, and indeed even extensively developed, environs.

While the 1607 Levellers and Diggers provide a fascinating example of early seventeenth-century environmental protests, a slightly later, and much larger and more widespread group, the fenland protesters of the 1620s through the 1640s, are in many respects even more remarkable. Because the fens, which were vast areas of England's wetlands, were generally far less developed than most other areas in the early seventeenth century, the discourse that emerged out of these protests strikingly presages certain modern environmental arguments for the preservation of wilderness and "nature." This is not to say that the 1607 Levellers and Diggers, protesting the conversion of previously developed ecosystems such as arable land into pasture, did not also develop environmental positions. But as the fenlanders' arguments in defense of the largely undeveloped fens are closely related to modern arguments for the protection of wilderness, they make it particularly easy for us, from our present perspective, to see in them the emergence of an environmental consciousness.

---

19. For the role that the 1607 Midland insurrections play in Shakespeare's *Coriolanus*, see E. C. Pettet's "*Coriolanus* and the Midlands Insurrection of 1607," in *Shakespeare Survey*, vol. 3 (1950).
20. Ibid.

Nonetheless, such a consciousness can and did emerge elsewhere throughout early modern England, often over arable and otherwise previously developed land. The overarching environmental importance of such an emerging consciousness is that, arising as it does alongside of a countryside emerging into awareness, it often prompts the inhabitants of a place to pause and consider not only the newly appearing countryside but the manner in which they inhabit that place. Any understanding of environmental "consciousness" that focuses exclusively on wilderness and "nature" to the exclusion of the central dynamic whereby we become conscious of the countryside and the earth (regardless of what state they are in at the time of the emergence) is simply misguided.

Like the 1607 Levellers and Diggers, the fenland protesters of the first half of the seventeenth century fiercely rejected the sweeping changes the English countryside was undergoing. As the following fenlander song from the period (published by Sir William Dugdale in 1662) reveals, the people of the fens also violently rejected the enclosure of land for pasture:

> Come Brethren of the water, and let us assemble,
> To treat upon this matter, which makes us quake and tremble;
> For we shall rue it, if 't be true, that fens be undertaken,
> And where we feed in Fen and Reed, they'll feed both Beef and bacon.
>
>   * * *
>
> Behold the great design, which they do now determine,
> Will make our bodies pine, a prey to crows and vermine:
> For they mean all Fens to drain, and waters to overmaster,
> And will be dry, and we must die, 'cause Essex cows want pasture.
> Away with boats and rudder, farewell both boots and skatches,
> No need of one or th' other, men now make better matches;
> Stilt-makers all and tanners, shall complain of this disaster,
> For they will make each muddy lake for Essex calves a pasture.
> The feather'd fowls have wings, to fly to other nations;
> But we have no such things, to help our transportations;
> We must give place (oh grievous case) to horned beasts and cattle,
> Except that we can all agree to drive them out by battle.[21]

---

21. Sir William Dugdale, *History of Imbanking and Drayning of divers fens and marshes*... (London, 1662), 391–92.

As this song (which is literally a call to arms) suggests, environmental justice was a central issue for these early protesters, as they were concerned
that sweeping changes in land use would have disastrous effects for the
already economically disadvantaged individuals living in these regions.
What made this argument significantly different (as well as of special interest to the environmental justice movement) than the hotly debated enclosure issue, was that concern was not principally over ownership of newly
enclosed property being shifted to wealthy landowners (which would simply be an economic issue, rather than also an environmental one), but
rather, that sweeping environmental changes were being brought about by
these landowners in order to greatly benefit themselves, while also bringing significant hardships to a group that was already economically disadvantaged. Simply put (as it was by these protesters), both the environment
and the poor were suffering in the service of the wealthy.

This song further suggests what outsiders increasingly characterized as
marginal and waste—whether in the Midlands, fens (such as in Lincoln-
shire, Norfolk, Cambridgeshire, and Somerset), or elsewhere—actually
provided a bounty of goods for nearby populations. Historian Barry Reay
nicely lays out an inventory of the threatened lands throughout England,
as well as specifically in the fens:

> Common or manorial wastes, woods, and meadows provided pasture for
> cattle, horses, pigs, sheep, and geese. Woods and heaths yielded a range
> of building material and fuel. The product varied with the locality: sand,
> stone, coal, wood, peat, turf, gorse of furze, fern, rushes. The commons sup-
> plied food too: nuts, fungi, herbs (used in healing as well as eating), berries,
> fish, birds, game. All had considerable value for consumption or sale. The
> marshland, peat, and silt areas of the fens, for example, supplied turf for
> fuel; reeds for thatching; rushes for baskets, mats, and lighting; alders and
> willows for basket making; hemp and flax for spinning and weaving; fish
> and wildfowl for food and feathers; and fertile common pasture for feeding
> cattle, horses, and sheep.[22]

If major changes in land use were allowed to occur in any of these unique
ecosystems, all this might be lost—along with the distinctive ways of
human life adapted to these places.

---

22. Barry Reay, *Popular Cultures in England 1550–1750* (London: Longman, 1998), 173–74.

To some modern environmentists, arguing for the preservation of a local ecosystem largely based on its value to human beings may seem hopelessly anthropocentric and misguided. However, it is important to distinguish between a culture intent on destroying a unique ecosystem so that it might be remade entirely to serve human needs and another fighting for its preservation, its people having adapted themselves over the centuries to the unique character of the place. Consequently, what is important about these environmental protests of the seventeenth century is that they raised a debate over just how human beings should dwell in environs that were already inhabited by human beings.

By the seventeenth century the manner in which England was managing its vast areas of marshes and fens had already been an issue for centuries, with the first Commission of the Sewers set up in order to mediate over wetlands in 1258. (Fens, incidentally, are the sometimes-flooded lowlands, which occur throughout England, while marshes are generally coastal areas into which the sea sometimes encroaches.)[23] In dealing with the fens prior to the end of the sixteenth century, as fen historian H. C. Darby notes, the "regional custom, the *consuetudo loci,* was of paramount importance in the development of an individual economy, and in the maintenance of a local habit of life quite different from that found in the normal community. . . . Variously called *consuetudo marisci,* the *consuetudo patrie,* or the *forma et custuma marisci*" (*mariscus* being Medieval Latin for "marsh"), the numerous examples of local culture that Darby cites "bear witness to a whole body of local right and custom that had been evolved through the ages to meet the exigencies of fen life."[24]

Accepting these "exigencies of fen life," the perception of the fenlands in the medieval period was often positive, drawing attention to the immense fecundity and fertility of the regions. For example, the monk Hugo Candidus noted of fenland in 1150 that it "is very useful for men; for in it are found wood and twigs for fires, hay for the fodder of cattle, thatch for covering houses, and many other useful things. It is, moreover, productive of birds and fishes. For there are various rivers, and very many

---

23. For a concise overview of the early modern distinction between marshes and fens, see "Marshes" by Ann Reeves and Tom Williamson, as well as "Fenlands" by Christopher Taylor in *The English Rural Landscape,* ed. Joan Thirsk (Oxford: Oxford University Press, 2000), 150 and 167, respectively.

24. H. C. Darby, *The Medieval Fenland* (London: David and Charles Limited, 1974), 22, 148–49.

waters and ponds abounding in fish. In all these things the district is most productive."[25] Similarly, a 1381 account suggests that a local fen provided "profit of turfs...cattle...fishing and fowling" and other resources.[26] Even as late as 1587, William Harrison argues that "it should not be amiss to speak of our fens...which are not only endued with excellent rivers and great store of corn and fine fodder [but at]...Ely the...inhabitants...take wood, sedge, turf, etc., to burn, likewise hay for their cattle and thatch for their houses."[27] Because, prior to 1600, efforts to drain the fens were for the most part rather ineffective, small-scale private initiatives, early seventeenth-century accounts of the regions were often quite similar to that offered by Candidus—but they were also often very different. Before considering how an emerging English discourse attempted to reshape the common perception of the fens in the seventeenth century, it is interesting to note how visitors to the island, who were largely unaffected by this rhetoric, viewed its wetlands.

In July 1603, Germany's Baron Waldstein, while visiting England, noted in his journal that "we pushed on...to Huntington, the country town, which is 12 miles from Cambridge. It is nobly—and at the same time attractively—situated; it lies in a piece of country which is surrounded by Fens, it is alive with game and fish, and is far superior to any of the other towns in the neighborhood."[28] Similarly Frederick, Duke of Wirtemberg, in describing his trip to London in 1592, noted that "between London and Oxford the country is in some places very fertile, in others very boggy and mossy; and such immense numbers of sheep are breed on it...that it is astonishing. There is besides a superabundance of fine oxen and other good cattle."[29] As Waldstein made clear, having a choice view of wetlands was once considered advantageous for even the most exclusive of properties: at

---

25. Candidus is cited and translated by Darby in *The Medieval Fenland,* 21.

26. Quoted in W. H. Wheeler, *A History of the Fens of South Lincolnshire, Being a Description of the Rivers Witham and Welland and Their Estuary, and an Account of the Reclamation, Drainage, and Enclosure of the Fens Adjacent Thereto* (London: J. M. Newcomb, 1897), 314–15.

27. William Harrison, *The Description of England: The Classic Contemporary Account of Tudor Social Life,* ed. Georges Edelen (Washington, DC: Folger Shakespeare Library and Dover, 1994), 439–40.

28. Baron Waldstein, *The Diary of Baron Waldstein: A Traveller in Elizabethan London,* trans. and annotated by G. W. Groos (London: Thames and Hudson, 1981), 109.

29. *England as Seen by Foreigners in the Days of Elizabeth and James the First...,* trans. William Brenchley Rye (London: J. R. Smith, 1865), 30.

Hampton Court, the palace "is situated by the Thames on a very long and wide alluvial plain; it is larger than any other in England so it is commonly—and deservedly—known as 'England's Wateringplace.' This is considered to be the most splendid of the palaces."[30]

It is certainly true that even writers like Harrison, who looked favorably on the fens, drew attention to their drawbacks, noting that "the wholesomeness of the air there is not a little corrupted"; nonetheless, Harrison immediately counters such statements by making clear that the fens are "excellently well served with all kinds of provisions, but especially of fresh-water fish and wild fowl."[31] Yet many seventeenth-century descriptions find no such beauty in the fenlands. In a 1629 pamphlet the fens are depicted as a place where the "Aer [is] Nebulous...the Water putred and muddy, yea full of loathsome vermine; the Earth spuing, unsaif and boggie." Some of the fens most celebrated resources, "reed" and "sedge," are described as "ranke trash."[32] By 1653 Samuel Hartlib boldly declares that "too much of England [is] being left as waste ground in Commons, Mores, Heaths, Fens, Marshes, and the like, which are all Waste Ground," but Hartlib quickly adds, are "all capable of very great Improvement."[33] Why were the fens described so differently in the seventeenth century? It is to Hartlib's promise of improvement that the changing representation of fens can be traced.

It has long been noted by historians that, in response to a rising population and a variety of cultural shifts, a large-scale movement to "improve" what was considered either unproductive or underproductive land swept through England in the sixteenth and seventeenth centuries. Prior to the Royal Society, the work of Hartlib and his circle represents some of the most complete articulations of this mindset. While fenland reclamation was generally motivated by this movement, for more than twenty-five years agricultural historian Joan Thirsk has been advancing a theory to account for the urgent desire to develop the fens, which emerged during the second half

---

30. Baron Waldstein, *Diary of Baron Waldstein,* 147.

31. Ibid., 67.

32. H. C., *A Discourse Concerning the Drayning of the Fennes and Surrounding Grounds...* (London, 1629), 4. Reprinted in 1647 as *The Drayner Confirmed.*

33. Samuel Hartlib, *A Discoverie for Division or Setting out of Land, as to the best Form. Published by Samuel Hartlib Esquire for Direction and more Advantage and Profit of the Adventurers and Planters in the Fens...* (London, 1653), 3.

of the sixteenth century. The issue centered on oil. Not the fossil fuels at the center of modern environmental debates, but the vegetable oils crucial for a variety of protoindustrial practices, such as rope and textile manufacture. Prior to 1550 most of these oils were imported into England. But when the 1549 *Discourse on the Commonweal* noted that such imported "oil cost a third more in 1549 than it did in 1542," the issue was taken quite seriously, and, as Thirsk observes, was soon linked to national security: "In 1553, when Spain stopped the sale of alum abroad... William Cholmely put the obvious next question, 'What if Spain did the same with oil? How should we have oils to work our wool withal?'"[34] Considering how vital cloth sails and rope riggings were to the country's security, it is hardly surprising that the last quarter of the sixteenth century saw England feverishly attempting to develop a domestic oil production program (the first bill promoting such manufacture was introduced into Parliament in 1572).

The question, however, was where to grow the much-needed coleseed and hemp from which the oils were extracted. As Thirsk notes, the oil projectors did not have to look far, as "coleseed and hemp, as everyone knew, were excellent crops on newly drained fen. Thus the plan to produce oil at home was linked with drainage projects."[35] Similarly, "rapeseed...first envisaged as a substitute for oil imports... was found to be ideally suited to land newly made available for arable cultivation through drainage of the fens."[36] Not surprisingly, then, "as the oil project gathered momentum so did the projects for fen drainage. With increasing regularity the flooding of the fens had engaged the Privy Council...a general drainage bill was drawn up in 1585."[37] Finally, a sweeping mandate in the form of the General Draining Act was passed in 1600 for, as H. C. Darby notes, "the recovery of many hundred thousand Acres of Marshes" and fens.[38] Because there was no funding for the projects, a call went out to individuals with sufficient capital to undertake such projects, who were, for this reason,

---

34. Joan Thirsk, *Economic Policy and Projects: The Development of Consumer Society in Early-modern England* (Oxford: Clarendon, 1978), 67. The 1649 *Discourse on the Commonweal* is also quoted from Thirsk.

35. Ibid., 69–70.

36. Joan Thirsk, *Alternative Agriculture: A History, From the Black Death to the Present* (Oxford: Oxford University Press, 1997), 78.

37. Joan Thirsk, *Economic Policy and Projects,* 70.

38. Quoted in H. C. Darby, *The Draining of the Fens* (Cambridge: Cambridge University Press, 1956), 29.

known as "undertakers." The importance of coleseed, hemp, and rapeseed grown on reclaimed fenland, especially for national security, would be restated throughout the seventeenth century; by 1685, the point is celebrated in verse by Sir Jonas Moore in his epic poem, written to commemorate the work of the fen-drainers:

> Here thrives the lufty Hemp, of Strength untam'd
> Whereof vast Sails, and mighty Cables fram'd,
> Serve our Royal Fleets, Flax soft and fine
> To the East Countrey's envy, could we joyn
> To England's Blessings, Holland's industry,
> We all the World in wealth should outvie.

* * *

> Here grows proud Rape, whose price and plenty foyls
> The Greenland Trade, and checks the Spanish Oyls.[39]

As the seventeenth century opened, England prepared to go into large-scale domestic oil production as a variety of patents were issued for oil extraction from seed, while at the same time various schemes for draining the fens were put forth. But while the technical difficulties may have been overcome, the undertakers met fierce resistance from local people in and near the fens. Because fen reclamation projects under James never quite gained momentum, it was not until the work stepped up during the reign of Charles I that the first of the major seventeenth-century fenland riots took place over the Hatfield Level in 1627.[40] Not long after, in August 1628, the much larger Isle of Axholme riots broke out. Such riots became increasingly common (and bloody) up until the Civil War.[41] The

---

39. Sir Jonas Moore, *The History or Narrative of the Great Level of the Fenns, Called Bedford Level*... (London, 1685), 78.

40. There were minor fenland riots in the fifteenth and early seventeenth centuries. Quoting from original sources, Dorothy Summers notes, for example, how at Littleport work was interrupted in 1618 by "quarellous, and contentious and refractory persons, making question of the power of the Commissioners" to allow the fens to be drained, *The Great Level: A History of Drainage and Land Reclamation in the Fens* (London: Newton Abbot, 1976), 60. Nonetheless, in comparison to the fenland uprisings of the second quarter of the seventeenth century, these were relatively small in scale.

41. For a history of fenland riots in the first half of the seventeenth century, see Keith Lindley's *Fenland Riots and the English Revolution* (London: Heinemann, 1982), 57–107 and elsewhere.

ferocity of the riots is more understandable when the unprecedented scope of the reclamation projects is put into perspective. For example, one of the cannels created to drain the fens, the so-called Bedford "River" (which was completed in 1637), was, as historian Christopher Taylor notes, "over 60 feet wide and nearly 21 miles long.... This was probably the greatest engineering achievement in England since Roman times, yet it is poorly documented."[42] Although now largely forgotten, the significance of this achievement was not lost on Moore, who, in his seventeenth-century epic, compared the Bedford River to both the Straights of Magellan and the Pillars of Hercules:

> When to your Glory, all your Banks shall stand,
> Like the immortal Pyramide.
>
> * * *
>
> When Bedford's stately bank, and noble Drain,
> Shall Parallel the Straights of Magellane,
> Or Hercules his Pillars in due Fame,
> Because they wear your Livery in their Name.[43]

In order to sway public opinion against the increasingly vocal and violent fenlanders, one of the first major seventeenth-century prodrainage tracts, *A Discourse Concerning the Drayning of the Fennes and Surrounding Grounds,* was published in 1629 by H. C. Reprinted in 1647 as *The Drayner Confirmed,* this is an important document, not only for its questionable environmental stance and attempts to consolidate a negative image of the existing fens (in direct contrast to the aforementioned favorable representations of the time), but also because it records the environmental arguments of the fenlanders. Because these early fenland rioters did not produce a great deal of their own literature, insofar as H. C. and others responded to their arguments on a point-by-point basis, we can get some sense of the fenlander approach. In addition, since small-scale attempts to drain the fens had been met with resistance for centuries, there also exist earlier accounts of the fenlander position. For example, although Thomas Fuller's

---

42. Christopher Taylor, "Fenlands," 181.
43. *History of the Great Level of the Fenns,* 74.

History of the University of Cambridge was published in 1655, he lays out in detail the "Arguments pro and con Fen-draining. A. D. 1436" as they had been handed down to him.[44] While it is questionable whether Fuller's account is truly representative of the fifteenth-century fenland debate, it nonetheless provides an insight into how the discussion was framed prior to the middle of the seventeenth century.

Presaging the protests of modern environmentalists, the fenlanders' call for the maintenance of diversity in the wetlands, both in plant and animal life, may be the single most important argument that they advanced. Although registering this need for diversity in a variety of ways, one of the most common centered on local birds and fish. As H. C. noted, "the drayning some say will decay Fishing and Fowling."[45] In laying out the discussion in the form of answers made to the arguments of the protesters, Fuller unfolds the fenlander case: "The Fens, preserved in their present property, afford great plenty and a variety of fish and fowl, which here have their seminaries and nurseries; which will be destroyed on the drainage thereof."[46] This fenlander argument obviously had implications for areas well beyond the fens; these wetlands were the "seminaries and nurseries" of both migratory waterfowl, which ranged throughout England, and the species of fish that filled the many streams with headwaters in the fens.

Such an argument is important for two reasons. First, it shows an understanding that loss of local wildlife habitat can have regional, even countrywide, ecological ramifications. Much has been made of Ernst Haeckel's 1866 coining of the word *ecology*, which signals an awareness that isolated ecosystems are often deeply enmeshed not only with nearby wildlife habitats, but also with the larger environment in which they exist.[47] It is clear from the early modern fenland debates, however, that this awareness existed long before Haeckel. It is also a noteworthy example of how environmental consciousness can appear in a very modern way while having little to do with "wilderness." Because the local countryside emerged into appearance to the people of the fens at the moment it was endangered, it

---

44. Thomas Fuller, *The History of the University of Cambridge* (London, 1840). I quote from the 1840 edition. Fuller's original text is from 1655.

45. H. C., *A Discourse*, 6.

46. Thomas Fuller, *History of the University of Cambridge*, 106–7.

47. See, for example, Jonathan Bate's *Romantic Ecology: Wordsworth and the Environmental Tradition* (London: Rutledge, 1991), 36–39.

need not have been wilderness. What mattered was that, in surveying the countryside that had recently appeared, the fenlanders found it to have great environmental value. The fenlander argument for the protection of the "seminaries and nurseries" of fish and fowl was also important politically because it raised the debate over wetland preservation to a national level. As we shall see, both sides soon argued directly to Parliament that the humble fens were of national importance.

Perceptively realizing the significance of the fens' wildlife resources, H. C. concedes to the fenlanders that "it is neither possible nor profitable to drayne [certain fens]...which be the chiefe places for Fish and Fowl."[48] However, he quickly moves to characterize other fenland as flooding so unpredictably as to make fowling at times altogether impractical: for "the water overflowing all, the Fowles are so dispersed, that men cannot come at them."[49] This last point provides an early example of a rhetoric that will come to dominate English land-use policy by century's end: that the vagaries of certain local ecosystems are so great that destruction of these otherwise fertile places is justified. As H. C. passionately pleads in order to sell the idea, if the fens

> be drowned perpetually and become of no use at all....What then will become of the fishing and fowling (their principall comodities) when the game is dispersed so wide that it will not be worth the labour and charge to goe about to take them? What will become also of the multitude of poore people, who now live (though very meanly) in those Fennes by taking Fish and Fowle, by gathering Hassocke, Reede, & c. and by transporting by their Boates passengers and commodities too and fro?[50]

H. C. is, of course, ignoring (recent floods not withstanding) the fact that for centuries fishing and fowling had been possible in the fens in spite of frequent flooding. Furthermore, it had long been realized that periodic inundation, which often meant that the fens were of use as pasture only in the summer, nonetheless greatly increased the fertility of the land.[51] As

---

48. H. C., *A Discourse*, 6.
49. Ibid.
50. Ibid., 2.
51. As John Leland noted during his mid-sixteenth-century travels through England: "Below Ivington the ground is low lying, and although there is much good meadowland it is so often inundated that scarcely once in six years can the grass be saved." *John Leland's Itinerary: Travels in Tudor England*, ed. John Chandler (Phoenix Mill, UK: Alan Sutton, 1993), 223. Similarly, in his

William Elstobb reflects back from the eighteenth century on the situation of the Isle of Ely fens, "when any floods happened they...continued not long, so that they [the meadows] were not damaged, but made better by such overflowings."[52] Although writing after the Civil War, when fen draining took on a somewhat different political import, Andrew Marvell in his "Upon Appleton House" makes a similar point as we learn that the celebrated, immensely fertile meadow of stanzas 47–58 is, like fenland, subject to postharvest flooding.[53]

Further rebuking the fenlander call for wildlife diversity, Fuller suggests that once the fens were destroyed, domestic animals raised on the reclaimed land would be superior to the wild: "A large first makes shorter recompense for the shorter second course at any man's table. And who will not prefer a tame sheep before a wild duck, a fat ox before a well-grown eel?"[54] Not only was this argument in favor of domestic species over wild applied to animal life, but given the pressing need to drain the fens in order to introduce hemp and coleseed, it is hardly surprising that the undertakers' arguments extended to plants as well. The fenlander position, as stated by Fuller, was that "the Fens afford plenty of sedge, turf, and reed."[55] The undertakers countered that these "commodities are inconsiderable to balance the profit of good grass and grain, which those grounds, if drained, would produce."[56] H. C.'s answer is stronger still: "Reed or Sedge" is merely "ranke trash," while "so great a quantitie therefore of rich Land being gayned, would meruailously increase & support the multitude of his Maiesties subjects, wherein consisteth the glorie and strength of a Kingdom."[57]

1587 *Description of England,* William Harrison observed that "fenny bogs we have many in England...they are very profitable in the summer half of the year." *The Description of England,* 283.

52. William Elstobb, *An Historical Account of the Great Level of the Fenns Called Bedford Level, and Other Fens, Marshes, and Low-Lands in This Kingdom...* (London, 1793), 200–201.

53. Andrew Marvell, "Upon Appleton House," stanza 59. As we shall see, writing at a time when the debate over the feasibility of draining fens for winter pasture raged both in and out of Parliament, Marvell clearly sided with the fenlanders.

54. Thomas Fuller, *The History of the University of Cambridge,* 106–7.

55. Ibid., 107.

56. Ibid.

57. H. C., *A Discourse,* 5, 6. Conceding that it is the very moistness of the fens that provides excellent conditions for certain plants (the fenlanders "find less" reed and sedge "upon the ground in dry yeares then in wet"), H. C. counters that "it must be confessed that ground which beareth Reed and Sedge will not be fruitful if it be dry, because such ranke trash requireth a great deal of moisture."

Throughout the seventeenth century this same point will be repeatedly put forth: that many indigenous plants are far inferior to introduced species, which in addition to coleseed, hemp, and rapeseed, also included clover, trefoil, carrots, turnips, and sainfoin.[58] Such arguments, however, did not go unchallenged. Although not in reference to the fens, in his "The Mower against the Gardens," Marvell wonders why "the world was searched, through oceans new" for exotic plants, while, in his poem "Man," George Herbert considers the far-reaching implications of losing indigenous species: "More servants wait on man / Than he'll take notice of; in ev'ry path / He treads down that which doth befriend him, / When sickness makes him pale and wan."[59] Herbert's point is that even the seemingly insignificant plants we marginalize might well be the "herbs [that] gladly cure our flesh" in time of sickness.[60]

In spite of the fact that the early fenland protesters fiercely argued in defense of plant and animal diversity, by the middle of the seventeenth century it became clear how influential the drainers' rhetoric had become, as at least some fenlanders largely dispensed with arguments for diversity, claiming instead that the undrained fens could support a variety of introduced species. "The undertakers have always vilified the Fens," noted an anonymous 1646 pamphlet, "and have mis-informed many Parliament men, that all the Fens is a mere quagmire...and of little or no value: but those of us which live in the Fens, and are neighbors to it, know the contrary."[61] While we might expect a traditional catalog of indigenous fen resources to follow, instead the author provides a list composed almost exclusively of introduced species:

For first the Fens breed infinite number of serviceable horse, mares, and colts....

Secondly we breed and feed great store of young cattle, and keep great dayeries....

---

58. On the replacement of indigenous plants with new monocultures in the seventeenth century, see L. A. Clarkson's *The Pre-Industrial Economy in England, 1500–1750* (London: Batsford, 1972), 57–59.

59. Marvell's "The Mower against Gardens" is cited from *The Poems of Andrew Marvell,* line 17. Herbert's' "Man" is from *The Works of George Herbert,* ed. F. E. Hutchinson (Oxford: Clarendon Press, 1941), lines 43–46.

60. Herbert, "Man," 23.

61. *The Anti-projector, or, The History of the Fen Project* (n.p., 1646?), 8.

> Thirdly, we mow off our Fens fodder, which feeds our cowes in win-
> ter... we have the richest and certainest corn land in England, especially for
> wheat and barley....
>
> Fourthly, we keep great flocks of sheep upon the fens.
>
> Fifthly, our Fens are of great relief, not onley to our neighbors the up-
> landers, but to remote Countries, which otherwise som years thousands of
> cattle would want of food.
>
> Sixtly, we have great store of Osier [willows], Reed, and Sedge,
> which... sets many poor on work.
>
> Lastly, we have many thousand Cottagers, which live on our Fens, which
> otherwise must go a begging.[62]

True, reed and sedge are listed, and the tract concludes by calling the
much-hated "Cole-seed and Rape...but trash and trumpery...in respect
to the fore-recited commodities, which are the rich Oare of the Commonwealth,"[63] but here (as well as in a similarly worded 1650 pamphlet by Sir
John Maynard)[64] there is no mention of fish, fowl, peat, turf, rushes, alders,
or other previously prized resources of the fens.

H. C.'s argument that drained land would "would meruailously increase
& support the multitude of his Maiesties subjects"[65] introduces another important feature of the fenland debates. As noted earlier, prior to the seventeenth century the fens were often depicted as remarkably fertile places
that adequately sustained local populations. The fenlanders contended that
"many thousands of poor people are maintained by the fishing and fowling
of the Fens, who will be at a loss of livelihood...if the Fens be drained."[66]

---

62. Ibid.

63. Ibid.

64. Maynard provides a very similar catalog, no doubt taken directly from *The Anti-projector*:

Our Fens as they are, produce great stores of Wooll and Lambe, and large fat Mutton, besides infinite quantities of Butter and Cheese, and do breed great store of Cattell, and are
stockt with Horses, Mares, and Colts, and we send fat Beefe to Markets, which affords
hides and Tallow, and for Corne, the Fodder we mow off the Fens in summer, feeds our
Cattell in winter: By which means we gather such quantities of Dung, that it inriches our
upland, and Corne-ground.... Besides, our Fennes relieve our neighbours, the Uplanders,
in a dry summer, and many adjacent Counties: so thousand of Cattell besides our own are
preserved, which otherwise would perish.

Sir John Maynard, *The Picklock of the Old Fenne Project* (London, 1650), 12.

65. H. C., *A Discourse*, 6.

66. Fuller, *History of the University of Cambridge*, 107.

As it turns out, they were correct. "Recent research has largely confirmed," notes historian Keith Lindley, "the view that the fens, far from being barren waste prior to the drainage, supported a large population of small farmers who exploited its valuable natural resources in a way that enabled them to live tolerably well compared with the peasantry of other agricultural regions."[67] In general terms, we could say that the people of the fens, thanks to their time-honored *consuetudo loci* and *consuetudo marisci,* had successfully adapted their culture and customs to the place. However, in order to justify the drainage, a wholesale effort was undertaken to depict the fenlanders as being little more than beggars in order to make the reclamation not just socially important, but indeed an act of charity.

While such rhetoric was common and effective, it did not go unchallenged. Michael Drayton, for example, depicts the fenlanders as uniquely industrious in his 1622 *Polyolbion:*

> The toyling *Fisher* here is tewing of his Net:
> The *Fowler* is imployed his lymed twigs to set.
> One underneath his Horse, to get a shoot doth stalk;
> Another over Dykes upon his Stilts doth walke:
> There other with their Spades, the Peats are squaring out,
> And others from their Carres, are busily about,
> To draw out Sedge and Reed, for Thatch and Stover fit.[68]

Nonetheless, insofar as the prodrainage faction was formulating an approach that is still used today to justify the development of the countryside (that the benefit to disadvantaged human beings far outweighs any environmental fallout), it was crucial to portray the fenlanders as being greatly in need of help. In his 1662 *History of Imbanking and Drayning of Divers Fenns and Marshes,* Sir William Dugdale noted that in Lincolnshire "before this drayning, the Country thereabouts was full of wandering Beggars; but very few afterwards; being set on work in weeding Corn, burning of ground, thrashing, ditching, Harvest work, and other Husbandry."[69] Similarly, in 1647, William Killigrew asked "how can it be thought that

---

67. Lindley, *Fenland Riots and the English Revolution,* 6.
68. Michael Drayton, *The Second Part, or a Continuance of Polyolbion* (London: 1622), 108.
69. Dugdale, *History of Imbanking and Drayning of Divers Fenns and Marshes,* 145.

the Commoners should oppose the draining by which they have so great benefit, and which was first so pleasing to them, that many thousands of Commoners did works two years in the drains, and thousands of them did since gaine very well by helping in the Drainers first Harvest?"[70] In Fuller's words, "Many whose hands are becramped with laziness, live (and only live, as never gaining any estates) by that employment. But such, if the Fens were drained, would quit their idleness, and betake themselves to more lucrative manufactures."[71]

The fenlanders, however, suggested that all the benefits would go to the undertakers: "It will again be objected, that although the drayning will be beneficiall to the Lords and Owners, yet the poore Commoner shall be in danger to loose his common."[72] To this, H. C. responds with an argument in defense of development that bears a strong resemblance to what we might call "trickle-down economics":

> The Commoner who dwelleth upon, or neere the Common will make good
> shift if the rich man dwell but a mile off, as in the fen it will often be. But
> if the Land which is set out for the recompence of the drayning be let, part
> to the poorer sort at reasonable rents, then the poore man having several
> grounds (adioyning to the Commons) wherein to succuour hs Cattell at
> need and whereupon to get Foather for them, he may shift with his Neigh-
> bour so much the better.[73]

"Grant them drained," the fenlanders answered, but "as now great fishes prey on the less, so then will wealthy men devour the poorer sort of people."[74] Fuller responds (somewhat hopefully) that "oppression is not essential either to draining or enclosure."[75] In 1652 Walter Blith similarly suggests that "as to the Drayning or laying dry of the Fenns...through a corrupt selfish Spirit may monopolize to his private advantage particu-

70. William Killigrew, *An Answer to such Objections as were made by some Commoners of Lincoln-shire...Concerning the Draining of those Fenns which lye between Lincoln, Berne, & Boston* (London, 1647), 15.

71. Fuller, *History of the University of Cambridge,* 107.

72. H. C., *A Discourse,* 6.

73. Ibid., B1.

74. Fuller, *History of the University of Cambridge,* 107–8.

75. Ibid., 108.

lar mens Interests, and in, and under pretense of doing a Common Goode, may utterly ruine a thousand souls. Corrupt self, or Corruption it self will endeavor this; but an Ingenious Spirit scorns perfidiousness."[76]

These debates over fenland draining were not obscure issues at the time; indeed, they caught the attention of such popular writers as William Camden. In his *Britannia,* Camden offers a rather mixed impression of the fen: first maligning its inhabitants (as often was done with rural populations), then drawing attention to the disadvantages of the annual flooding, but nonetheless ending with a traditional praise of its bounty of indigenous plants. Residents of the fenlands of Cambridgeshire, he asserts, are

> a kind of people according to the nature of the place where they dwell rude, uncivill, and envious to all others whom they call Upland-men: who stalking on high upon stilts, apply their mindes, to grasing, fishing and fowling. The whole Region it selfe…in winter season and sometimes most part of the yeere is overflowed by the spreading waters of the rivers Ouse, Grant, Nen, Welland, Gelene, and Witham, having not loades and sewers large enough to voide away….[yet] Great plenty it hath…of reed also to thatch their Houses, yea and of Alders, besides other watery Shrubs. But chiefly it bringeth forth exceeding stores of willowes.[77]

If Camden had stopped here, his observations would not be of particularly great interest, but he went further, siding with two principal parts of the fenlander position: that the reclamation would ultimately fail (like the sixteenth-century efforts to drain Italy's Pontine Marshes) and that such large-scale attempts to alter the landscape would go against what God had ordained:

> As touching the drying up of this Fenny country, what discourse and arguing oftentimes there hath beene either by way of sound and wholesome counsell, or of a goodly pretence and shew of a common good, even in the High Court of Parliament, I list not to relate. But it is to be feared least (that which hath often happened to the Pontine Marshes of Italy) it would come againe to the former state so that many think it the wisest and best course according to the sage admonition in like case of Apollo his Oracle, *Not to intermeddle at all with that which God hath ordained.* [Camden's emphasis][78]

---

76. Walter Blith, *The English Improver Improved, or, the Survey of Husbandry Surveye: Discovering the Improveableness of All Lands…* (London, 1652), 52.

77. William Camden, *Britannia* (London, 1607), 491.

78. Ibid., 492.

The failed attempts to drain Italy's Pontine Marshes were repeatedly offered by the fenlanders as an argument against making the same folly in England. "Grant the Fens drained with great difficulty, they will quickly revert to their old condition, like the Pontaine Marshes in Italy."[79] Although Fuller optimistically replied that "moderate cost, with constant care, will easily preserve what is drained," the fenlander admonition proved to be correct, with many of the drainage efforts of the first half of the seventeenth century ending in ruin.

Moreover, not only were the drainage efforts often unsuccessful, but a horrific downside quickly became apparent: the flooding continued, but in different areas. As Sir John Maynard noted in 1650: "The cheats of the undertakers...made many thousands of Acres, that were never drowned, and the most part of the Land which was better by overflowing in the nature of river Meadows, to be hurtfully surrounded," for "the undertaker is like the Tinker...he draynes one Acre for himself, and drownes two of his neighbours."[80] This idea appears in Sir John Denham's midcentury poem *Cooper's Hill*. Although, in 1655, the image is meant to be an allegory for mob rule, Denham is also describing what literally happens when "The Husbandmen with...Their greedy hopes" attempt to keep their land from flooding:

> When a calm River rais'd with sudden rains,
> Or Snows dissolv'd, oreflows th'adjoyning Plains,
> The Husbandmen with high-rais'd banks secure
> Their greedy hopes, and this he can endure.
> But if with Bays and Dams they strive to force
> His channel to a new, or narrow course;
> No longer then within his banks he dwells,
> First to a Torrent, then a Deluge swells:
> Stronger, and fiercer by restraint he roars,
> And knows no bound, but makes his power his shores.[81]

Although, for Denham, this is in part an allegory, Camden deals with a similar, entirely literal situation in which the residents of Lincolnshire are always on guard against "a mighty confluence of waters out of the higher

---

79. Fuller, *History of the University of Cambridge,* 107.
80. Maynard, *Picklock of the Old Fenne Project,* 8.
81. Denham, *Cooper's Hill,* 1655 text, 349–58.

countries…and hardly with all the bankes and dammes that they make against the waters, are able to defend themselves from great violence and outrage thereof."[82] The concluding image of *Cooper's Hill* could only have been an effective allegory for Denham if many of his readers already believed that meddling (in the form of drainage projects) with divine design was both ineffective and in fact morally wrong—as, suggested Denham, was tampering with a king's rule.[83]

This point (as Camden succinctly states it, *"Not to intermeddle at all with that which God hath ordained"*) was a common sentiment at the time with respect to the fens. While certain modern environmentalists warn us not to interfere with "nature's plan," in the seventeenth century, the counsel as Camden and others gave it was not to meddle with God's. Perhaps not surprisingly, advocates of fen drainage put forth counterarguments. As Sir William Dugdale opens his prodrainage treatise:

> That works of Drayning are most ancient and of divine institution, we have the testimony of holy Scripture. *In the beginning God said, let the waters be gathered together, and let the dry land appear; and it was so: And the Earth brought forth grass, and herb yielding seed, & the fruit-tree yielding fruit after his kind, and God saw that it was good.* [Dugdale is paraphrasing Gen. 1:9–11]
>
> Again, after the Deluge, it was through the divine goodness that *the waters were dryed up from the earth, and the face of the ground was dry.* [Gen. 8:3][84]

Biblical floods, for obvious reasons, proved a popular theme, with the fenlanders noting that "God saith to the water, 'Hitherto shalt come, and no further,' Job xxxviii.11. It is therefore a trespass on Divine prerogative for man to give other bounds to the water." To which the undertakers replied,

---

82. Camden, *Britannia,* 529.

83. Given that (1) Charles had much to gain from the draining, (2) the controversy soon caught the attention of Oliver Cromwell and others, and (3) the drainage projects themselves were proving to be as ineffective as they were unpopular, Denham wisely directs the blame away from the King to the "greedy hopes" of the "Husbandmen" (*Cooper's Hill* 1655, 351–52). Although the argument would have received sympathy primarily from royalists, Denham is correct in noting that, as the Undertakers received the lion's share of the reclaimed fenland, these greedy husbandmen should perhaps also receive most of the blame. Moreover, if the projects went too far, "if with Bays and Dams they strive to force" the river into a new course and, as a result, "No longer then within his banks he dwells" (353–55), it is the Undertakers who should be blamed for their greedy mismanagement of the responsibility conferred upon them by the king, not Charles himself.

84. Dugdale, *History of Imbanking and Drayning,* 1.

"The argument holdeth in application to the ocean.... But it is a false and lazy principle, if applied to fresh waters."[85]

In order to sidestep such dubious arguments, as well as to defend themselves against the claim that they were tampering with God's creation, supporters of the undertakers, such as Sir Jonas Moore, brought attention to the fact that buried in the fens was "an abundance of Timber Trees." Because it was "well known, that in [certain]...ground and water, timber trees will not thrive or grow,"[86] Moore, Dugdale, and others concluded that the fens were "apparently a woody country at first"; indeed, "this vast [Bedford] levell was, at first, a firm land."[87] Moreover, H. C. noted of "the historic William of Malmesburie...who lived about 1200 yeares since, that in his time it [the fenland] represented a very Paradise, for that in pleasure and delight it resembleth Heaven it self; in the very Marshes bearing trees that for their straight talness, and same without knots, strive to touch the Starres."[88] Because it was so argued that the fens were created dry and paradiselike, and likely only flooded (as Dugdale speculated) "by some great Earthquake,"[89] it was suggested that draining these wetlands was a way of repairing the damage of the Fall. Moore, for example, imagines the reclaimed fenland as becoming an Eden-like place

> Where Cities shall be built, and Houses tall,
> As the proud Oak, which your Founders call,
> Fair Orchards Planted, and the Myrtle Grove,
> Adorn'd, as it were the Scene of Love,
> Gardens with Flowers of such auspicious hew,
> You'd swear, that Eden in the Desert grew.
> When with the change of elements, suddenly
> There shall a change of Men and Manners be;
> Hearts, thick and tough as Hydes, shall feel remorse,
> And Souls of Sedge shall understand Discourse,
> New hands shall learn to Work, forget to steal,
> New leggs shall go to Church, new knees shall kneel.[90]

---

85. Ibid.
86. Moore, *History of the Great Level of the Fenns,* 2.
87. Dugdale, *History of Imbanking and Drayning,* 172, 171.
88. H. C., *A Discourse,* 5.
89. Ibid., 172.
90. Moore, *History of the Great Level of the Fenns,* 74.

Although often ignored by critics, the debate raging over fenland reclamation contributed to the causes that brought about England's Civil War.
Part of the issue centered on the king's role in the drainage projects. In
some areas, such as in the Hatfield Level (the first of the seventeenth century's major drainage projects, which contained seventy thousand acres),
Charles I actually became an undertaker himself. In other cases the job fell
to well-capitalized undertakers who were to give the king a portion of the
reclaimed land. Although Charles I ultimately received less, in 1621, when
the Great Level project began, James was to take delivery of 120,000 acres
of the reclaimed land. Similarly, the king was to receive 21,500 acres of the
Lindsey Level. In short, the king had much to gain from the draining of
the fens. As the chief engineer in charge of a number of the projects, Sir
Cornelius Vermuyden suggested to Charles I in 1638 regarding undrained
fenland, "these Lands being a continent of about 400,000 Acres, which
being made Winter ground would be an unexpected benefit to the Com-
mon-wealth of Six hundred thousand pounds *per Annum* and upwards."[91]

Not surprisingly, the political fallout of these projects was soon felt. As
Keith Lindley explains:

> The urgent fiscal needs of early Stuart governments gave birth to a number
> of money-making expedients which directly challenged established prop-
> erty rights and ultimately raised wider constitutional issues. A series of
> ambitious drainage schemes initiated or encouraged by the King, which im-
> pinged upon the livelihood of the inhabitants of approximately 1430 square
> miles of fenland in eastern England, exposed an entire region of the king-
> dom to such a challenge. The large-scale enclosure of previously common-
> able fens, which accompanied these schemes, falls into the same category as
> ship money and other expedients which undermined property rights and
> demonstrated absolutist tendencies in central government.[92]

As Sir John Wray argued in the House of Commons in May 1640, England
faced three major problems: taxes on ship money, not maintaining an adequate army, and the situation whereby "we stand not ensured of our *Terra
Firma,* for the fen-drainers have entered our lands, and not only made

---

91. Sir Cornelius Vermuyden, *A Discourse Touching the Drayning of the Fennes…* (London,
1642), 2. Although not published until 1642, this tract was written in 1638.

92. Keith Lindley, *Fenland Riots and the English Revolution,* 1.

waste of them, but also have disseised us of part of our soil and freehold."[93] Although ship money is often cited as an issue leading up to the Civil War, as Lindley correctly suggests, the fen situation played its part. However, Lindley's contention that this issue centered principally on property rights is misleading, as land use needs to be taken into account.

While the fenland environmental protests continued throughout the 1630s, the people of the fens also took their case to court. As Sir Philip Warwick noted in 1701 in his *Memoirs of the Reign of King Charles I,* in a surprising turn of events, a figure who would come to play a singular role in the coming revolution emerged to defend the fenlanders in 1638:

> Principle Gentlemen, whose habitations confined upon the Fenns…whether it was publick spirit or private advantage…a stranger cannot determine; they made propositions unto the King to issue out commissions of Sewers to drayn those lands, and offer a proportion to be freely given the Crown for its countenance and authority therein….And now the King is declared the principall Undertaker for the drayning; and by this time the vulgar are grown clamorous against the popular Lords and Undertakers; tho' they had much better provisions for them than their interest ever was before: and the Commissioners must by multitudes and clamours be withstood; and as the head of this faction, Mr. Cromwell in the year 1638 at Huntington appears.[94]

We further know from a 1637 report that "Mr. Cromwell of Ely hath undertaken they [the fenlanders] paying him a groat for every cow they have upon the common to hold the drainers in suit of law for five years and that in the meantime they should enjoy every foot of their common."[95]

With Cromwell and others coming to their defense, the fenlanders' rebellion began to have far-reaching effects. As Lindley notes,

> As political tension mounted from the period of personal rule to the final outbreak of civil war, all the drainage schemes became targets of renewed offensives, with commoners combining appeals to Parliament with direct action. While the commoners looked to the House of Commons for a

---

93. From the Proceedings of the Short Parliament 1640, quoted in Ibid., 109.
94. Sir Philip Warwick, *Memoirs of the Reign of King Charles I* …(London, 1701), 250.
95. Quoted by Lindley in *Fenland Riots and the English Revolution,* 95.

sympathetic hearing and expected them to remedy their grievances, the undertakers sought the assistance of the House of Lords, which took over the
role...of protecting their interests and suppressing riots and disorders on
their land. These contrary appeals to Commons and Lords eventually resulted in a constitutional clash between the two Houses which helped to
heighten the political temperature.[96]

It would, of course, be misleading to suggest that the environmental protests and lawsuits of the fenlanders played too great a role in the events
leading up to the Civil War. Nor should it be inferred that Oliver Cromwell had any particular concern for the fenland. While opposing the king
on the issue of the fens proved a popular stance, once the king was dispensed with, the new Commonwealth administration began its own wave
of fen draining. Indeed, as Sir William Killigrew noted in 1653, "I am
tould that my Lord Generall Cromwell should saye the drayninge of the
fens was good worke, but that the drayners had too great a proportion of
the land for their hazard and charges."[97] Similarly, while the Leveller John
Lilburne came to the aid of the fenlanders in November of 1651 by suggesting that it was only through "Tyranny and injustice" that the fenland
"commoners endeavouring to defend their own possessions" were "condemned as rioters," his motivations, like Cromwell's, were likely largely
political rather than environmental.[98]

Nonetheless, as an anonymous pamphlet of 1655 argued, to some fenlanders, the Civil War was waged in part because the undertakers "took
away our Commons [and]...fought with the King against the Parliament,
to the utmost of their powers, to maintain those operations and arbitrary
proceedings; the King is condemned for that and such like Arbitrary and
tyrannical proceedings."[99] As a consequence, the fenlanders were outraged

---

96. Ibid., 108.
97. Sir William Killigrew is quoted from H. C. Darby's *Draining of the Fens,* 80.
98. John Lilburne, *The case of the tenants of the Mannor of Epworth in the isle of Axholm in the County of Lincoln...* (London, 1651), 3. Lilburne weighs in on the environmental debate, argu-
ing that the fens were "extraordinarily good for Milch, Kine, and feeding fat cattel, and breeding young cattel, though not for corn, and the greatest part of those grounds being much the better for grass, for the over-flowings of water, and the Winter, and worth more to remain for grass, then to be plowed for corn" (Ibid., 2).
99. *A breviate of the cause depending, and proofes made before the committee of the late Parliament for the Fens by the inhabitants between Borne and Kime Eae, in the county of Lincolne, being lords,*

that, having in part fought a war to regain their fens, the drainage efforts were renewed under Cromwell: "We the Owners and Commoners have lost and ventured our lives and considerable Estates in Parliaments service, and have received no recompence; and shall the conquered, who have put us to vast expense, enjoy what they have illegally taken, and we recovered by blood, purse, and Law?"[100] The fenlanders were, in fact, not exaggerating their role in the Civil War. As historian Brian Manning notes, "Cromwell recruited the regiment that contributed so much to parliament's victory in the civil war from the peasant farmers of Huntingdonshire and Cambridgeshire... helped no doubt by the fierce support that he had given to the fen commoners in their struggles against the drainage undertakers."[101] In terms of the early modern appearance of the countryside, the fenland debates (as well as the 1607 environmental protests) are essential because, through debates over threatened landscapes, the countryside was making its emergence into appearance all across England (and not just around London). Moreover, unlike London's day-trippers and prodigy-house builders, who threatened the newly appearing countryside, some groups desperately fought to protect their local environs. In the chapter that follows, I want to venture outside the island to consider how the countryside in England's colonies emerged into appearance through Edmund Spenser's views on Irish landscapes. In the process, it will unfortunately become clear that certain countrysides were imagined not as places worth saving, but rather, as ripe for exploitation. As we shall see, for this to have happened, a literary shift needed to occur: from the pastoral mode to the georgic.

---

owners and commoners of, and in the several Fens, where in Sir William Killigrew, &c. pretends a title as sharers with the late Earle of Lindsey (n.p., 1655), 10.

100. Ibid.

101. Brian Manning, *The English People and the English Revolution* (London: Bookmarks, 1991), 271.

EMPIRE, THE ENVIRONMENT, AND THE GROWTH OF GEORGIC

"Were the colonized to disappear," speculated Sartre while reading Albert Memmi, "so would colonization—with the colonizer." By this, Sartre simply meant that if the colonized were to disappear, "there would be no more subproletariat, no more over-exploitation."[1] While this is certainly true, many postcolonial theorists have further registered the original

---

1. Jean-Paul Sartre, Introduction to *The Colonizer and the Colonized,* by Albert Memmi, trans. Howard Greenfield (Boston: Orion Press, 1965), xxvii. Sartre is, in fact, paraphrasing Memmi who held that "if the colonized is eliminated.... Along with the colonized, colonization would disappear, and so would the colonizer" ("Si l'on supprime le colonisé... Avec le colonisé dispara- îtrait la colonisation, colonisateur compris"). I have chosen to cite Sartre here as opposed to Memmi because, at least as he expresses it in this introduction, Sartre's understanding of the col- onized/colonizer relationship is far less nuanced than Memmi's. Because Sartre understands the "colonized" only as human beings (and not also as a place, as Memmi seems to suggest at times) acting as economic subproletariats, and not also as subalterns used to consolidate the colonizer's selfhood, which Memmi goes a long way toward intimating, Sartre's passage provides a conve- nient counterpoint to two central ideas I explore in the present essay. Memmi is quoted in English from *The Colonizer and the Colonized,* 149, and in French from *Portrait du Colonisé précédé du Por- trait du Colonisateur* (Paris: Buchet/Chastel, 1957), 189.

Memmi-inspired statement to also mean that, in addition to the material, economic injury to the colonized is added the insult (and further injury) of the colonizer consolidating a sense of "self" by relegating the colonized to a realm of "otherness" as subaltern. In this view, if the colonized other were to disappear, the colonizer's very sense of self would risk disappearing as well.

There are, however, difficulties with this approach. Along with Sartre, many postcolonial theorists seem to conceive of the "colonized" exclusively as human beings. One of the more sobering insights of the twentieth century is that, as an unexpected by-product of material and technological modernity, we human beings, not unlike coal or a farmer's field, began to see ourselves and others as mere things to be used, what we all too casually call "human resources." Perhaps because of the dizzying, far-reaching implications of this epiphany, we often forget that the same sort of violence can, of course, be done to "natural resources." Human beings are colonized, but so are the places they inhabit. Indeed, the colonial enterprise itself often understood the "colonized" as both people and places. True, in some instances it would be the human resources that would appeal most to the colonizer, with the prospect of labor so inexpensive that literally thousands of hours of human labor could be lavished in the making of a single wool rug or bolt of silk fabric. On the other hand, the natural resources, which in this case supply the wool and silk, also had immense, often even greater, appeal to the colonizer.

"It has not been so long," Memmi reminds us, "since Europe abandoned the idea of a possible total extermination of a colonized group."[2] Part of the purpose of the present chapter is to consider the rationale behind this abandoned enterprise: some colonizers, willing to eradicate what they saw as largely irrelevant indigenous populations, conceived of the "colonized" exclusively as natural resources and place. Perhaps because of the horror of this genocidal situation, we sometimes forget that the indigenous people of the place were really just so much collateral damage, a case of being in the wrong place at the wrong time. Although under no circumstances was the colonization of place ever considered inessential to the colonial project, in extreme cases in which it was exclusively the project, we can most clearly

2. Memmi, *Colonizer and the Colonized,* 149.

see not only its importance, but also how colonization was able to consolidate a sense of self for the colonizer at the expense of indigenous people without, as Sartre and Memmi suggested, relegating them to the status of "colonized." This brings us to Edmund Spenser.

What Edward Said noted in 1993 is certainly no longer the case, "that literary historians who study the great sixteenth-century poet Edmund Spenser [generally]...do not connect his blood-thirsty plans for Ireland, where he imagined a British army virtually exterminating the native inhabitants, with his poetic achievements."[3] Indeed, in the years since Said penned this, it has sometimes seemed as if literary historians who study Spenser have done little but connect his "blood-thirsty plans for Ireland...with his poetic achievements." But was Spenser's thirst, as Said and so many others have argued, really for blood? In Spenser's writings, as Andrew Hadfield correctly argues, "land and people were firmly separated, Irish land forming part of the ancient English unity and Irish people cast in the role of intractable 'otherness' which must be removed."[4] Consequently, Spenser did not have a thirst for Irish blood—blood was the by-product, not the purpose, of his plans—but a hunger for its land. This served Spenser's personal as well as his national ambitions, as he was rewarded with thousands of acres of land on the estate of Kilcolman. This is not to deny what so many critics (including Hadfield) have recently argued, that Spenser helped consolidate a sense of English self at the expense of the Irish people,[5] but it is nonetheless the case that the bloody elimination of the Irish people, and the representation of them in a way that facilitated this goal, was by no means the poet's primary objective.

While I have hereto suggested that Renaissance pastoral helped facilitate the appearance of the countryside surrounding London and throughout the island, the pastoral mode was not generally all that useful a tool for the colonial project. After all, literature that emphasized *otium* as an

---

3. Edward Said, *Culture and Imperialism* (London: Vintage, 1993), 5.

4. Andrew Hadfield, *Edmund Spenser's Irish Experience: Wilde Fruit and Salvage Soyl* (Oxford: Clarendon, 1997), 108.

5. Andrew Murphy, who is one of the many scholars of the opinion that Spenser considered the "other" to only be human beings, argues that, "taken together, *A View of the Present State of Ireland* and *The Faerie Queene* present a diverse and complex meditation on the question of Otherness," but only as it "establish[es] points of discontinuity between the two peoples." *But the Irish Sea Betwixt Us: Ireland, Colonialism, and Renaissance Literature* (Lexington: University of Kentucky Press, 1999), 65–66.

ideal would be of little help in generating interest in the hard work that colonization required. True, conceiving of a prospective colony as a *locus amoenus* might capture the imagination of a potential colonizer, but once the colonial project was underway, a new ethic was needed to exploit the colonized place. Enter the georgic. In his *Georgics,* Virgil boldly and famously declared that agricultural "Labor omnia vicit" ("Labor conquers all").[6] As noted in my Introduction, in the sixteenth century, writers such as Julius Caesar Scaliger began to praise georgic labor while condemning pastoral *otium.* What we can call the "georgic ethic" also played a major role both in motivating the enormous fenland reclamation projects of the seventeenth century, as well as the even more massive efforts to colonize new lands. To understand why, it will be helpful briefly to consider shifts in early modern England's agricultural practices.

Although England's population had soared to nearly 5 million by the beginning of the fourteenth century, the English totaled perhaps less than half that number by the end of the century, in part because of the bubonic plague, and in part because of widespread famines resulting from the collapse of an enormously successful, grain-producing economy.[7] While it might seem paradoxical, given that the population was merely returning to its previous size, in the next three centuries, the English felt an urgent need to utilize undeveloped (or underdeveloped) places as a way of providing for a growing population. There are several reasons for this, but perhaps none more significant than changes in farming practices. Cereal farming, not only resented as the basis of a former economy in shambles, but of less actual importance given the reduced population, received a major challenge from wool production which, together with the desire to impark what had previously been farmland, led to a stepped-up enclosure movement in the fifteenth century, which as Christopher Taylor aptly notes, "caught the contemporary 'headlines.'"[8] But so too did a variety of other agriculturally dictated efforts to claim or reclaim land in the fifteenth through seventeenth

---

6. Virgil's *Georgics,* trans. H. Rushton Fairclough (London: W. Heinemann, 1916), 1.145, translation mine.

7. While exact numbers are still debated, with the preplague estimates anywhere from 4.5 to 6 million, it is generally held that England's population was at least halved in the fourteenth century. See for example John Hatcher's *Plague, Population, and the English Economy, 1348–1500* (London: Macmillan, 1977), 68–73.

8. Christopher Taylor, *Fields in the English Landscape* (London: J. M. Dent, 1975), 115.

centuries. Deforestation, although begun on a wholesale basis in England more than a thousand years before, had so captured the public imagination that by 1653 Sylvanus Taylor declared that "all men's eyes were upon the forests."[9] All of these efforts, including the fenland reclamation projects discussed in the previous chapter, were in a broad sense "colonial" in that the land in question was being appropriated for entirely new uses.

But even as England was looking inward for new land, it cast its gaze elsewhere. Ireland came into view first. Pastoral literature would come to play a role in this colonial enterprise. In order to understand how, it is first important to realize that the above-mentioned changes in agricultural practices were to some measure generated by (and generative of) pastoral and georgic literature. As Ordelle Hill notes, when the grain-based economy thrived "in the fourteenth century, [a]...plowman-type literature dominated" instead of the pastoral mode. Then, as Hill further explains,

> at the end of the fourteenth century and the beginning of the fifteenth, the plowman literature gave way to the writings about the new farmer, independent and for the most part thriving. By the middle of the fifteenth century, a strong "native" pastoral type of literature had developed and would, in the sixteenth century, contribute to the prominent pastoral literature of the Elizabethan age.[10]

Simply put, plowman literature was popular when England's economy was strongly rooted in grain production on tilled land. But with this economy in distress, a new pastoral literature took its place. This, however, needs to be further clarified. Sixteenth-century pastoral literature was in some cases actually inspired by real landscapes that strongly resembled the pastoral ideal, complete with shepherds and flocks of sheep. Spenser's cousins in Althorp, for example, who owned more than fourteen thousand sheep during Spenser's lifetime, lived against just such a backdrop.[11] The literal setting that pastoral purported to represent did not, however,

9. Sylvanus Taylor, *Common Good; Or, the Improvement of Commons, Forests, and Chases by Enclosure,* quoted by Thirsk in "Agricultural Policy," 310.

10. Ordelle G. Hill, *The Manor, the Plowman, and the Shepherd: Agrarian Themes and Imagery in Late Medieval and Early Renaissance Literature* (Selinsgrove, PA: Susquehanna University Press, 1993), 20.

11. For an account of Spenser's Althorp relatives, see M. E. Finch's *The Wealth of Five Northamptonshire Families, 1540–1640,* pref. by H. J. Habakkuk (Oxford: Northamptonshire Record Society at Oxford University Press, 1956), 38–65.

always look like the pastoral ideal. Because of the fourteenth-century collapse of the grain-based economy, large-scale demesne farming operations
largely disappeared as well. As a consequence, estates were increasingly
managed in the fifteenth century by letting the land to peasant farmers,
with the landlord becoming a *rentier,* thereby forcing renters to shoulder
the responsibility of making farming viable in economically very uncer-
tain times.[12] So, although the activity was in a sense more georgic (in that it
was distinguished by aggressive cultivation and working of the soil, rather
than merely letting sheep graze on enclosed land), as far as the landowner
was concerned, both enterprises were largely characterized by *otium,* with
the landlord free to collect rents while imagining himself as shepherd to a
flock of tenants; at peace with his surroundings.

However, it would be a mistake to imagine this landscape as the sort of
bucolic world portrayed in pastoral literature, as early modern sheep herd-
ing was big, cutting-edge business that was definitely positioned toward
the future. While, as early as the twelfth century, wool had been a major English export to the Flemish and then to the Italians and Germans, by the end
of the fourteenth century wool exports declined dramatically, as nearly all
production went to fuel England's own protoindustrial juggernaut.[13] As the
economy rebounded, farming became such a successful financial enterprise
during the sixteenth century that wealthy landowners, who were in many
respects the equivalent of twentieth-century oilfield owners, began giving
up their roles as *rentiers* by not renewing leases; instead, they began vertically
integrating their enterprises by taking on the role of farmer themselves.[14]
Not surprisingly, following the 1523 publication of John Fitzherbert's *Boke
of Husbondrye,* a century of works by Thomas Tusser, Barnabe Googe, Andrew Yarranton, and others helped teach these landowners how to cultivate
the soil.[15] Consequently, as both Alastair Fowler and Anthony Low have

---

12. E. M. Harcrow, "The Decline of Demesne Farming on the Estates of Durham Cathedral
Priory," *Economic History Review,* ser. 2, 7 (1955): 345–56.

13. See T. H. Llyod's *The English Wool Trade in the Middle Ages* (Cambridge: Cambridge University Press, 1977).

14. As Joyce Youings notes, in the sixteenth century "the energetic landowner sought whenever possible to take land, either to farm himself, or to create new tenancies for shorter terms."
"The Church," in *The Agrarian History of England and Wales,* ed. Joan Thirsk (Cambridge: Cambridge University Press, 1967) vol. 4, 311.

15. For a brief history of English-farm literature in the sixteenth century, see E. L. Ernle's
"Obstacles to Progress," in *Agriculture and Economic Growth in England, 1650–1815,* ed. E. L. Jones
(London: Methuen, 1967), 49–65.

persuasively argued, classical-georgic literature also became increasingly appealing to this new English farmer.[16] By the mid-to-late sixteenth century, this new agricultural model of active management quickly made fortunes for many. Spenser's cousins in Althorp, for example, had secured an annual income approaching eight thousand pounds by the opening years of the seventeenth century (most of it coming from the management of their herds) and had so dramatically married to advantage that, by 1618, the once-humble family of graziers was offered an earldom.[17]

The message here is clear: control of land meant power, wealth, and prestige. But two very different models of land control are here at work. The first, what we can call "pastoral," affords the landowner, as landlord, a position of relative *otium,* as he need not directly engage with the land. The second, emerging sixteenth- and seventeenth-century model, the "georgic," casts the landowner as active farmer. Of course, the particular activity in either case could be farming, herd management, or both. Nonetheless, from an environmental perspective, the move from the pastoral to the georgic approach has far-reaching implications, as it potentially positions human beings in an active, aggressive posture toward the earth. This is not to say that pastoral practices are environmentally benign; indeed, they were in many cases the same activities, although carried out by members of different social groups. However, as active, georgic approaches to the land began influencing writers (whether they themselves owned land or not), these practices had a role in generating georgic discourse.

In some sense the above distinction between pastoral and georgic was adopted by Anthony Low in his *Georgic Revolution.* However, Low largely fails to take into account the underlying agricultural component (and hence environmental implications) of these versions of pastoral and georgic. By his own admission, Low's understanding of georgic owes a large debt to William A. Sessions's 1980 article on "Spenser's Georgics," which argued that "Vergil discovered his essential strategy in the *Georgics.* The message of the Maecenas-commissioned *Georgics* was to reclaim the

---

16. For the resurgence of interest in the georgic mode in the sixteenth century, see Anthony Low, *The Georgic Revolution* (Princeton: Princeton University Press, 1985), as well as Alastair Fowler, "The Beginning of English Georgic," in *Renaissance Genres,* ed. Barbara Kiefer Lewalski (Cambridge, MA: Harvard University Press, 1986), 105–25.

17. M. E. Finchs, *The Wealth of Five Northamptonshire Families,* 38–65.

imperial homeland by a series of difficult labors in historical time: '*Labor omnia vicit.*'"[18] Sessions considers the essential component of Spenserian georgic to be labor, but labor having little to do with actual agriculture. "Spenser thought," argues Low,

> that Britain, like Vergil's Rome, was at a crux in history, a moment when, if men and women seized the opportunity, civil strife and sectarian violence might give way to a just and fruitful imperial unity, a new *pax Romana,* a third Troy...this georgic vision Vergil also incorporated into the *Aeneid,* with its heavy stress on labor.... The georgic mode descends to *The Faerie Queene* largely through the mediating influence of the *Aeneid.*[19]

In so doing, Low distances labor, which he argues was central to Spenser's understanding of georgic, from that with which we generally take georgic to be most concerned: agriculture.

Consequently, in the 1980s Sessions and Low interpreted georgic, as Alpers and Patterson did pastoral, as having much to do with politics and little to do with actual landscapes. In contrast to this approach, which regrettably privileges political interests over environmental, and further fails to consider how these interests are interrelated, in this chapter I consider how nondiscursive agriculture practices played a major role in generating early modern georgic discourse.[20]

This georgic ethic is written large throughout *The Faerie Queene.* As early as Book I, we learn that Redcross, England's foremost knight, although of noble Saxon blood, was raised as a plowman:

> Thence she brought into this Faery lond
> And in a heaped furrow did thee hyde,
> Where thee a Ploughman all vnweeting fond,

---

18. William Sessions, "Spenser's Georgics," *England Literary Renaissance* 10 (1980): 204.

19. Ibid., 39.

20. As Alastair Fowler notes, "the georgic revolution" does not emerge, as Low suggests, new and fully formed in Spenser's *Faerie Queene,* but had been taking shape in this particular incarnation throughout the sixteenth century (Fowler, "The Beginning of English Georgic," 105–25). This coincides with the shift in agricultural practices I have been chronicling. Furthermore, because Low fails to sufficiently consider shifts in these practices, he cannot adequately account for the late-medieval appearance of plowman figures, as in Langland and Chaucer, both of whom certainly played a part in an earlier georgic revolution. (For Low's attempt to accommodate Langland and Chaucer in his theory of georgic, see *Georgic Revolution,* 178–88.)

As he his toylesome teme that way did guyde,
And brought thee vp in ploughmans state to byde,
Whereof *Georgos* he thee gaue to name;
Till prickt with courage, and thy forces pryde,
To fairy court thou cam'st to seek for fame,
And proue thy puissaunt armes, as seemes thee best became.[21]

The message is clear: the truly virtuous man, even though of noble blood, begins life by taking an active georgic role as steward to the land. As Belphoebe further makes the point in Book II, "Ne can the man, that moulds in ydle cell, / Vnto happie mansions attaine" (II, iii, 41). Although Sessions and Low note that Spenser is here echoing both Genesis 3:19 and Hesiod's *Works and Days,* both critics take this as merely mandating human labor toward any worthy goal, rather than a specific injunction, as it is clearly in both Genesis and Hesiod, to work the land.[22] Nonetheless, Low's comment here is squarely on the mark: "God's injunction to Adam to go forth and earn his bread in the sweat of his face, which was traditionally taken to be a curse resulting from the fall, may instead be taken as an invitation, an opportunity to resist the consequences of the fall."[23] However, as Spenser was obviously aware, in Genesis 3:23 it is clear that this invitation is for Adam not merely to do generic labor, but literally "to till the ground from whence he was taken."[24]

Although the georgic ploughman is a recurring figure throughout *The Faerie Queene,* perhaps his most interesting appearance is not as Redcross, but as the poet himself. Whenever the narrator seems weary of his labor, or alternately ready to resume his work, the image of the ploughman is often

---

21. Edmund Spenser, *The Faerie Queene,* ed. A. C. Hamilton, text edited by Hiroshi Yamashita and Toshiyuki Suzuki (Harlow, England: Longman, 2001), I. x.66. All references to *The Faerie Queene* are to this edition and are cited parenthetically.

22. William Sessions, "Spenser's Georgics," 224, 229. Low, *Georgic Revolution,* 42.

23. Low, *The Georgic Revolution,* 42. This notion that humanity cannot just "resist the consequences of the fall," but should actually repair them through our works would become very important to Francis Bacon. In the closing lines of the Second Book of *The New Organum* Bacon declares that "by the Fall man declined from the state of innocence [but this]...can be repaired...by the arts and sciences." Insofar as sixteenth-century artisanal and georgic agricultural practices became a major influence on Bacon, he generalized the attempt to remake the earth into a garden through both work and applied technology as a precept of the New Science. *The New Organon,* ed. Lisa Jardine and Michael Silverthorne (Cambridge: Cambridge University Press, 2000), 221.

24. All references to the Bible are to the Authorized Version.

invoked. When fatigued in Book IV, he declares as canto v ends "But here my wearie teeme nigh ouer spent / Shall breath it selfe awhile, after so long a went" (IV, v, 46). Similarly canto iii of Book V ends as "turne we here to this faire furrowes end / Oure wearie yokes, to gather fresher sprights" (V, iii, 40). And in Book VI, which is in some sense entirely devoted to the georgic mode, canto ix opens with the narrator realizing that his work is not yet finished:

> Now turn againe my teme thou jolly swayne,
>   Back to the furrow which I lately left;
>   I lately left a furrow, one or twayne
>   Unplough'd, the which my coulter hath no cleft:
>   You seem'd the soyle both fayre and frutefull eft,
>   As I it past, that were too great a shame,
>   That so rich frute should be from us bereft;
>   Besides the great honor and defame,
> Which should befall to Calidores immortall name.
>
> (VI, ix, 1)

Aside from the depictions of the poet as ploughman in Book VI, ploughmen and georgic labor are positively portrayed throughout this book at canto ix, 2; ix, 3; ix, 14; ix, 30; ix, 37; xi, 48; and elsewhere. From these many examples it is clear, as Low exhaustively argued, that the georgic ethic pervades the whole of Book VI.[25] This ethic is equally clear in Book VI's negative examples: those individuals who neglect the tending of the earth. The "Salvage Man" of canto iv, although in many respects admirable in his innocence, is ultimately found to be "a bad Stuard [who] neither plough'd nor sowed" (VI, iv, 14). And the "Salvage Nation," which possesses few of the Salvage Man's virtues, never gives itself to "drive / The painefull plough" (VI, viii, 35). Similarly, the Brigands who capture Pastorella are a "lawless people...That neuer vsde to liue by plough nor spade, / But fed on spoile and booty" (VI, x, 39). As has been often noted, these last two groups are clearly representative of the Irish.

From medieval depictions onward, Ireland seems to have had a split identity in English literature. In Ranulph Higden's *Polychronicon* (1327–52),

---

25. Although not on an ecocritical register, for a discussion of the infusion of Book VI of *The Faerie Queene* with the georgic ethic, see Low, *Georgic Revolution,* 35–70.

it was idealized as a pastoral land in which there was "plente of hony and of mylk and of wyn."[26] But, in Higden and many other depictions, as Elizabeth Rambo succinctly notes, "the people are characterized as generally despicable."[27] Along with these descriptions of the land as a pastoral *locus amoenus* (which date back to Giraldus, likely the first medieval chronicler to actually visit Ireland) is often the suggestion that only with proper (read: English and georgic) stewardship, can Ireland realize its potential to become an immensely fertile place.[28] This notion of Ireland's unrealized fecundity is perhaps clearest in Renaissance depictions, such as this often quoted passage by Luke Gernon, a contemporary of Spenser, and magistrate in the Munster province where the poet settled:

> This Nymph of Ireland is at all parts like a young wench that hath the green sickness for want of occupying. She is very fair of visage and hath a smooth skin of tender grass. Indeed, she is somewhat freckled (as the Irish are)—some parts darker than other. Her flesh is of a soft and delicate mold of earth and her blue veins trailing through every part of her like rivulets.... Her breasts are round hillocks of milk-yielding grass, and that so fertile that they contend with the valleys. And betwixt her legs (for Ireland is full of havens) she hath an open harbor, but not much frequented.... Of her complexion she is very temperate, never too hot nor too cold, and hath a sweet breath of favonian wind. She is of a gentle nature.[29]

While most postcolonial critics have focused on the early modern representation of the Irish people by the English, those that have looked to depictions of the land, such as Shirley Adawy Peart, have often done so by considering the role of gender.[30] Ireland was repeatedly seen by Gernon

---

26. Ranulph Higden, *Polychronicon Ranulphi Higden*...trans. John Trevisa (1387), ed. Churchill Babington (London, 1874), 35.

27. Elizabeth L. Rambo, *Colonial Ireland in Medieval English Literature* (Selinsgrove, PA: Susquehanna University Press, 1994), 36.

28. Indeed Giraldus equates the development of Ireland with the cultivation of his writing ability: "I have decided that my Muse, as yet untrained, should exercise itself by way of practice in this field, though it is confined and arid, rough and untilled, it may yet be cultivated with my pen." (*Hac igtur in area, arta licet et arida, hispida quoque et inculta, sed stili beneficio forsan excolenda, musam adhuc rudem se tanquam preludio quodam exercere constitui.*) Giraldus, *Expurgnatio Hibernica,* ed. T. W. Moody et al. (Kildare: Royal Irish Academy, 1978), 24–25.

29. Luke Gernon, *A Discourse on Ireland,* in *Elizabethan Ireland: A Selection of Writings by Elizabethan Writers on Ireland,* ed. James P. Myers (Hamden, CT: Archon Books, 1966), 242–43.

30. Shirley Adawy Peart, *English Images of the Irish, 1570–1620* (Lewiston, NY: Edwin Mellen, 2002).

and others as a virgin in "want of occupying." Spenser's depiction of the land in *A View of the Present State of Ireland* is, as Peart notes, "tender and loving in tone, as if invoking a much-loved woman":[31]

> And sure yt is yet a most bewtifull and sweete Countrie as any vnder heaven: seamed throughout with manie goodlie ryvers replenished with many sortes of fishe most aboundantlie: sprinckled with verie manie sweete Ilandes and goodlie lakes like little inland seas…adorned with goodlie woodes fitt for buildings of howses and shipps so commodiouslie.…Also very full of verie goode portes and havens opening vpon England, [and] Scotland, as inviting vs to come vnto them…besydes the soyle yt self is most fertile, fit to yield all kynde of fruite that shall be committed therinto.[32]

As Peart suggests, "the land's penetrability is foregrounded; it opens 'upon England and Scotland' and is 'inviting us to come unto them,' as Ireland is waiting for her English husbandman. Spenser stresses Ireland's wifely qualities—the fertility, fruitfulness, and mildness."[33]

The notion that colonial lands were prospective virgins in wait of a "husbandman" was common from at least the sixteenth century onward. For example, in a dedicatory letter to Sir Walter Raleigh, Richard Hakluyt describes the colony of Virginia as waiting for Raleigh's "embraces," and ready to "bring forth new and most abundant offspring" as "no one has yet probed the depths of her hidden resources."[34] When the word *husbandman* was used in the emerging sixteenth-century georgic period, it was often in opposition to those who took a leisurely approach to land stewardship— the very *otium* that had for generations been the pastoral ideal of the landed gentry. Not surprisingly, as the georgic husbandman ethic took hold in the sixteenth century, *otium* quickly became a vice.

The early modern English often portray the Irish living a life characterized by *otium,* with no discernible desire to work the land. In the early seventeenth century, Fynes Moryson noted that owing to "nothing

---

31. Ibid., 151.

32. Edmund Spenser, *A View of the Present State of Ireland,* ed. R. L. Renwick (London: Eric Partridge, 1934), 25–26. References to *A View* are to this edition and are cited parenthetically in the text.

33. Shirley Adawy Peart, *English Images of the Irish,* 151.

34. Richard Hakluyt, *The Original Writings and Correspondence of the Two Richard Hakluyts,* intro. by E.G.R. Taylor (London: Printed for the Hakluyt Society, 1935), 2:367.

more...then...the plenty of the land," the Irish had largely failed to till the soil actively, living either by "spoyles and Robberyes" or the "feeding of Cowes...in thick woods abounding with grasse."[35] As mentioned earlier, such a depiction of the Irish appears in Book VI of *The Faerie Queene* in the form of the "lawless people....That neuer vsde to liue by plough nor spade, / But fed on spoile and booty" (VI, x, 39).

But to Spenser's generation, it was not only the Irish who let the immense fertility of their land go to waste, but their own English colonizing forefathers who had not performed their husbandmanly, georgic duties. It has long been argued by historians such as John Jeudwine that, in the sixteenth century, while England "was leaping forward in agricultural wealth, in Ireland the perpetual raids, organized by the great nobles, made agriculture dangerous and discouraged any use of the land except for pastoral purposes" ("pastoral purposes" understood literally as cow or sheep raising).[36] When Sir John Davies set forth *A True Discovery of the True Causes Why Ireland Was Never Entirely Subdued* in 1612, from the first two "causes" onward, he repeatedly returns to the failure of generations of English to be good husbandmen—first (as in this opening example) metaphorically:

> The defects which hindered the perfection of the conquest of Ireland were of two kinds and consisted, first, in the faint prosecution of war, and next, in the looseness of the civil government. For the good husbandman must first break the land before it can be made capable of good seed; and when it is thoroughly broken and manured, if he will not forthwith cast good seed into it, it will grow wild again and bear nothing but weeds; so a barbarous country must first be broken by a war before it will be capable of good government; and when it is fully subdued and conquered, if it be not well planted and governed after the conquest, it will eftsons return to the former barbarism.[37]

---

35. Fynes Moryson, *Shakespeare's Europe,* ed. Charles Hughes (London: Skerratt and Hughes, 1903), 200.

36. John W. Jeudwine, *The Foundations of Society and the Land* (New York: Arno Press, 1975), 389.

37. Sir John Davies, *A True Discovery of the True Causes Why Ireland Was Never Entirely Subdued...,* ed. James P. Myers Jr. (Washington, DC: Catholic University of America Press, 1988), 71–72. Additional references to Davies in this paragraph are to this volume and are cited parenthetically in the text.

It is difficult to decide what is more disturbing here, the notion that it is necessary to "break" Ireland by war, or conceiving of the relationship that human beings have to the earth as a war in which the land needs to be "fully subdued and conquered." In any event, this is an example of the "georgic" approach to the earth being adapted as a metaphor for the colonial enterprise itself. In a literal sense, Davies believed that previous generations of English colonizers had failed because they were not, in a variety of ways, good husbandmen to the land: "The lands conquered from the Irish were not well distributed [and]... were too large" to be well-managed (144–45). These "English lords did not reduce the woods and wastes in forests and parks" in order to reclaim the land for tillage (161). In tolerating the "idleness in the Irish," the English lords had let "the land waste" (167). The idleness of the Irish was a major reason why Ireland was never entirely subdued, as the "soldier [Irish farmer laborer] in one night did consume the fruits of all his labor, *longique perit labor irritus anni*" ("and the useless labor of a long year has perished," 167). The "Irish...have chosen to be beggars in foreign countries [rather] than to manure their own fruitful land at home" (168).

Much has recently been made of the fact that Spenser and others of his generation were critical of the "Old English" landlords in Ireland because they had become too Irish themselves, especially in using the Irish language.[38] However, a major perceived failing of these Old English was that (according to this new generation) they were, like the Irish, simply poor husbandmen who had failed to work the soil. Early in *A View of the Present State of Ireland,* Spenser has the character Eudoxus naïvely ask what harm can come from not working the land:

> What faulte can ye fynde with this Custome, for though yt bee an ould Scythian vse yet it is verye behouefull in this countrie of Ireland where there are greate mountaines and waste desertes, full of grasse, that the same should bee eaten downe and nourrishe manye thousand of Cattle, for the goode of the whole realme. (64)

---

38. For a consideration of how the Old English allegedly became too Irish themselves, see Hadfield, *Edmund Spenser's Irish Experience,* 20–25 and elsewhere. For example, in a much-quoted passage from Spenser's *A View,* Irenius argues that "the Childe that suckethe the milk of the" Irish nurse, although "afterwardes he be taughte English yeat the smacke of the first will allwaies abide with him and not onelye of the speche but allsoe of the manners and Conditicions" (119).

Although his companion Irenius offers a provisional answer at this point in the text, near the end of the dialogue, when Eudoxus again innocently asks if we should "not counte in this trade of husbandrie pasturinge of Cattell and kepinge of theire Cowes" (203), Irenius launches into a tirade against those who do not practice what he considers to be conscientious and careful husbandry:

> I doe not meane to allowe any of those able bodies which are able to vse bodelie labour, to follow a fewe Cowes, grasinge....For this keping of Cowes ys of yt self a verie Idle lyfe and a fytt nurserie for a thief.... And to saye truth through Ireland bee by nature counted a greate soyle of pasture, yett had I rather haue fewer Cowes kept and men better mannred, than to haue such huge increase of Cattell, and noe increase of good Condycions, I would therefore wishe that there were some ordynance made amongst them, that whatsoeuer kepeth 20 kien should kepe a plough goinge, for otherwise all men would fall to pasturaige, and none to husbandrie, which is a great cause of all this dearth, now in England, and a cause of the vsuall stealthes nowe in Ireland, for looke into all Countries that lyve in such sorte by kepinge of Cattle, and yow shall fynde that they are verie barbarous and vncyvill.... And therefore since now wee purpose to drawe the Irish, from desyre of warrs and tumultes to the loue of peace and Civillitie, It is expedient to abridge, theire Custome of heardinge and augment theire more trade of tillinge and husbandrie. (203–4)

It is clear here that the failure to adopt a georgic ethic is found to be responsible for a surprising number of society's problems. But what is truly shocking is just what punishment is deemed fit for such an offense.

In what may now be the most cited passage from Spenser's canon, the character Irenius makes clear the horrific result of neglecting the responsibilities of the husbandman:

> Out of eurie Corner of the woodes and glinnes they Came Crepinge forthe uppone their handes for theire Leggs Coulde not beare them, they loked like Anotomies of deathe, they spake like ghosts Cryinge out of theire graues, they did eate at the dead Carrions, happie wheare they Coulde finde them, Yea and one another soon after, in so muche as the verye carkasses they spared not to scrape out of theire graves. And if they founde a potte of water Cresses or Shamarocks theare they flocked as to a feaste for the time, yeat not able longe to Continue thearewithall, that in short space theare weare

non allmoste lefte and a moste populous and plentifull Countrye sodenlye lefte voide of man or beaste...yeat sure in all that warr theare perished not mainie by the sworde but all by the extreamitye of famine *which they themselves had wroughte.* (emphasis added, 135)

This passage is often interpreted as Spenser suggesting that famine is the horrible consequence of Irish disobedience to lawful authority. As Andrew Hadfield suggests, "They have threatened the power of the prince, the very basis of any legal and social order, and so have to pay the price."[39] However, the nature of what the Irish are portrayed as rebelling against needs to be taken into account.

This passage was likely based on an actual scene Spenser witnessed on an English-controlled Munster plantation. Returned to its sixteenth-century georgic context, it is clear that first and foremost Spenser believes the famine to be the result of the failure of both the Irish and the Old English to adopt a georgic ethic and act as proper husbandmen. In a sense, the Old English are doubly implicated; had they gained control of the land, in both of Davies's senses (the "land" as the entire country as well the actual soil), this famine would never have happened. Furthermore, in *A View* Irenius goes to great lengths to make clear that, in their failure to import English landlord-tenant laws and practices to Ireland, the Old English themselves discouraged proper husbandman behavior in the Irish (64–65, 105–8, 203). But the Irish, insofar as they were for centuries perceived as having never been adequate husbandmen, are found to be deserving of what "they themselves had wroughte."

Immediately prior to the above-cited passage describing the Irish famine, Irenius makes clear that this will only be the fate of those "stout and obstinate Rebells, such as will never bee made duetifull and obedient, nor brought to labor...having once tasted the lycensius lyfe, and being acquainted with spoyl" (134). Indeed, even Irenius is surprised by what few georgic skills these rebels have, for in such a "ritch and plentifull Countrye, full of Corne and Cattell...you would have thought they would haue bene hable to stande longe, yet err one yeare and a half, they were brought to such wretchednes" (135). Insofar as their lack of georgic ethic, as Spenser's

---

39. Hadfield, *Edmund Spenser's Irish Experience,* 67.

Irenius attempts to convince his companion Eudoxus (and with him, of
course, the English reader), inevitably lead to the demise of the Irish people, sending a massive English army into Ireland will merely accelerate
the inevitable. Any lawful Irish surviving the planned assault will have to
prove that "by his further travell and labor of the earth he shalbe able to
provide him self better," or die as well (161).

According to Spenser, the one hope the Irish had of survival, namely,
becoming successful husbandmen—which would have saved them from
destruction from either nature or England—they had largely refused for
centuries. Indeed, the poet does not propose to wage war directly on the
Irish in a conventional sense, but instead merely to set up the conditions
for their own self-destruction. Spenser, wielding poetic justice, formulated
a plan that allowed the Irish to be undone by what he argues is their own
tragic flaw. In some sense, Spenser had reason to believe the plan would
actually succeed. In 1580, Lord Justice William Pelham suggested that the
colonization of Munster required the complete elimination of the local
Irish people, which the Queen categorically refused to allow. But then, in
less than a year came the great Munster famine (which Spenser witnessed),
with the result that, in the words of historian Michael Maccarthy-Morrogh,
"by 1582 the situation had changed, in Munster at least, and human destruction was no longer a prerequisite for colonization. Since there were so
few left in Munster, repopulation [it was argued] would have to come from
England."[40] Spenser wanted to set up conditions that would allow history
to repeat itself. Of course, the poet did not consider the notion that English
colonial practices had in large measure caused the Munster famine, instead
laying the blame entirely at the feet of the Irish, who allegedly lacked an
adequate georgic ethic with respect to the earth.

As became increasingly clear to many in the generations immediately
before Spenser, georgic had supplanted pastoral as the guiding ethic of
the age. Consequently, Spenser and others began to portray negatively the
otium of both Irish herdsman and Old English landlords who leisurely
left the management of their lands to others. What is astonishing is that,
by the close of the sixteenth century, this georgic project was so successful, both agriculturally and rhetorically, that Spenser was able to use its

---

40. Michael Maccarthy-Morrogh, *The Munster Plantation: English Migration to Southern Ireland, 1583–1641* (Oxford: Clarendon, 1986), 28.

ethic to justify the genocide of a people. Because the natural resources of Ireland were so appealing, and the Irish were perceived as unwilling to be conscripted into assisting in their exploitation, it was necessary to intensify the centuries-old project of representing the Irish negatively. Returning to the terms in which I framed this discussion, this was not done in order to fashion the Irish people into the "colonized." On Sartre's economic register, Spenser and others had represented to England (and quite possibly actually believed themselves) that, unusable as "human resources," the Irish could never be colonized as subproletariats. This did not mean, however, that the Irish people were useless to the colonial enterprise. Indeed, the colonizer's sense of georgic "self" was in part consolidated by negative representations of the outmoded pastoral ethic of the Irish "other," which gave the English a clear idea of what they themselves must never become. However, as I noted in my Introduction, this is not to implicate the georgic ethic environmentally. True, with respect to both fenland and Ireland we see the horrific downside of such an ethic, but in "To Penshurst" and other similar works, careful georgic stewardship of a place is prescribed as a force to counter its exploitation.

SELECT BIBLIOGRAPHY

Adorno, Theodor. *Aesthetic Theory*. Eds. Gretel Adorno and Rolf Adorno. London: Athlone, 1997.

Alpers, Paul J. *The Singer of the Eclogues: A Study of Vergilian Pastoral*. Berkeley: University of California Press, 1979.

——. *What is Pastoral?* Chicago: University of Chicago Press, 1996.

The Anti-projector, or, The History of the Fen Project. n.p., 1646?

Arendt, Hannah. *The Human Condition*. Chicago: Bantam, 1958.

Bacon, Francis. *The New Organon*. Eds. Lisa Jardine and Michael Silverthorne. Cambridge: Cambridge University Press, 2000.

Barclay, Alexander. *The Eclogues of Alexander*. Oxford: Oxford University Press, 1928.

Barry, Jonathan. *The Tudor and Stuart Town: A Reader in English Urban History, 1530–1688*. London: Longman, 1990.

Bate, Jonathan. *Romantic Ecology: Wordsworth and the Environmental Tradition*. London: Routledge, 1991.

Bateson, Mary. *Records of the Borough of Leicester; Being a Series of Extracts from the Archives of the Corporation of Leicester*. Ed. Mary Bateson et al. London: C. J. Clay, 1899.

Beaumont, Sir John. *Bosworth-field*. London, 1629.

Berens, Lewis H. *The Digger Movement in the Days of the Commonwealth As Revealed in the Writings of Gerrard Winstanley, the Digger, Mystic and Rationalist, Communist and Social Reformer*. London: Simpkin, Marshall, Hamilton, and Kent, 1906.

Bilson, Thomas. *The Survey of Christ's Sufferings for Mans Redemption.* London, 1604.

Blith, Walter. *The English Improver Improved; or the Survey of Husbandry...* London, 1652.

Boeckel, Bruce. "Landscaping the Field of Discourse: Political Slant and Poetic Slope in Sir John Denham's *Cooper's Hill.*" *Papers on Language and Literature* 34.1 (1998).

Brautigam, Dwight D. "The Court and the Country Revisited." In *Court, Country, and Culture: Essays on Early-modern British History in Honor of Perez Zagorin.* Eds. Bonnelyn Young Kunze and Dwight D. Brautigam. Rochester, NY: University of Rochester Press, 1992.

Brayshay, Mark. *Topographical Writers in South-West England, Exeter Studies in History.* Exeter: University of Exeter Press, 1996.

Brett-James, Norman G. *The Growth of Stuart England.* London: George Allen & Unwin, 1935.

A breviate of the cause depending, and proofes made before the committee of the late Parliament for the Fens by the inhabitants between Borne and Kime Eae, in the county of Lincolne, being lords, owners and commoners of, and in the several Fens, where in Sir William Killigrew, &c. pretends a title as sharers with the late Earle of Lindsey. n.p., 1655.

Brink, J. R. *Michael Drayton Revisited.* Boston: Twayne, 1990.

Burton, Robert. *The Anatomy of Melancholy: What It Is with All the Kinds, Causes, Symptoms, Prognostics, and Several Cures of It in Three Partitions: With Their Several Sections, Members, and Subsections, Philosophically, Medicinally.* London: Chatto and Windus Piccadilly, 1883.

Calendar of Close Rolls. Edward I (1302–7).

Calendar of State Papers, Domestic Series. Elizabeth I (1578).

———. James I. (1620).

———. Charles I. (1627–28).

Camden, William. *Britain: Or, a Chorographicall Description of the Most Flourishing Kingdomes, England...* London, 1610.

Cantor, Leonard Martin. *The Changing English Countryside, 1400–1700.* London, New York: Routledge & Kegan Paul, 1987.

Carew, Richard. *The Survey of Cornwall.* London, 1602.

Carew, Thomas. "To Saxham." In *The Works of Thomas Carew.* London, 1640.

Carus-Wilson, E. M. *Essays in Economic History.* London: E. Arnold, 1954.

Cato, Marcus Porcius. *Libri de re rustica, M. Catonis, Marci Terentii Varronis, L. Iunii Moderati Columellae, Palladii Rutilii, quorum pagina seque[n]ti reperies.* Paris, 1533.

———. *On Agriculture.* Loeb Classical Library. Cambridge, MA: Harvard University Press, 1934.

Cavendish, Margaret. *Poems and Fancies.* London, 1655.

Chalklin, Christopher W. *The Provincial Towns of Georgian England: A Study of the Building Process, 1740–1820.* London: Edward Arnold, 1974.

Chapman, George, trans. *The Georgics of Hesiod.* In *George Chapman's Minor Translations: A Critical Edition of His Renderings of Musaeus, Hesiod and Juvenal.* Ed. Richard Corballis. Salzburg: Salzburg University Press, 1984.

Chaudhuri, Sukanta. *Renaissance Pastoral and Its English Developments.* Oxford: Oxford University Press, 1989.

Clarkson, L. A. *The Pre-Industrial Economy in England 1500–1750.* London: Batsford, 1972.

Cohen, Jeremy. *Be Fertile and Increase, Fill the Earth and Master It: The Ancient and Medieval Career of a Biblical Text.* Ithaca: Cornell University Press, 1989.

Coleman, D. C. *Industry in Tudor and Stuart England: Studies in Economic and Social History.* London: Macmillan, 1975.

Collinson, Patrick. "John Stow and Nostalgic Antiquarianism." In *Imagining Early-modern London: Perceptions and Portrayals of the City from Stow to Stype, 1598–1720.* Ed. J. F Merritt. Cambridge: Cambridge University Press, 2001.

Corns, Thomas N. "Radical Pamphleteering." In Th*e Cambridge Companion to Writing of the English Revolution.* Ed. N. H. Keeble. Cambridge: Cambridge University Press, 2001.

Cowley, Abraham. *Plays and Sundry Verses.* Ed. A. R. Waller. Cambridge: Cambridge University Press, 1906.

Crashaw, Richard. "A Hymn of the Nativity, Sung by the Shepherds." In *The Complete Works of Richard Crashaw.* Ed. A. B. Grosart. London: Robson and Sons, 1872.

Crosby, A. W. *Ecological Imperialism: the Biological Expansion of Europe, 900–1900.* Cambridge: Cambridge University Press, 1993.

Crowe, William. *Lewesdon Hill.* Oxford, 1788.

Cunningham, William and Peter. *The Poems of William Drummond of Hawthornden: With Life.* London: Cochrane and M'Crone, 1833.

Darby, H. C. *The Draining of the Fens.* Cambridge: Cambridge University Press, 1968.

———. *The Medieval Fenland.* London: David and Charles, 1974.

Davies, Sir John. *A True Discovery of the True Causes Why Ireland Was Never Entirely Subdued...* Ed. James P. Myers, Jr. Washington, DC: Catholic University of America Press, 1988.

Denham, Sir John. *Cooper's Hill.* London, 1642, 1655.

Dickens, Charles. *Dombey and Son.* New York: Penguin, 1970.

Digby, Sir Kenelm. *Of the Sympathetick Powder.* London, 1669.

The Diggers of Warwickshire to all other Diggers. London, 1607.

Dix, Frank. *Royal River Highway: A History of the Passenger Boats and Services on the River Thames.* London: David and Charles Press, 1985.

Doelman, James. *Early Stuart Pastoral.* Toronto: Centre for Reformation and Renaissance Studies, 1999.

Drayton, Michael. *Poly-Olbion.* London, 1612.

———. *The Shepheardes Garland.* In *The Works of Michael Drayton.* Eds. J. W. Hebel et al. Oxford: Blackwell Press, 1931.

Du Bartas, Guillaume de Salluste, Josuah Sylvester et al., *Du Bartas His Deuine Weekes and Workes...* London: By Humfrey Lownes, 1613.

Dudley, Dud. *Dud Dudley's Metallum Martis, or, Iron Made with Pit-Coale, Sea-Coale...* London, 1665.

Dugdale, Sir William. *The History of St. Paul's Cathedral in London...* London, 1658.

———. *History of Imbanking and Drayning of Divers Fens...* London, 1662.

Durling, Robert M. *Petrarch's Lyric Poems: The Rime Sparse and Other Lyrics.* Cambridge, Mass.: Harvard University Press, 1976.

DuRocher, Richard J. "The Wounded Earth in *Paradise Lost.*" *Studies in Philology* 93 (1996).

Edwards, Karen. *Milton and the Natural World.* Cambridge: Cambridge University Press, 1999.

Elstobb, William. *An Historical Account of the Great Level of the Fenns Called Bedford Level, and Other Fens, Marshes and Low-Lands in This Kingdom...* London, 1793.

Empson, William. *Some Versions of Pastoral.* London: Chatto & Windus, 1935.

Engels, Friedrich. *The Condition of the English Working Class in England in 1844.* New York: Macmillan, 1958.

Ernle, E. L. "Obstacles to Progress." In *Agriculture and Economic Growth in England, 1650–1815.* Ed. E. L. Jones. London: Methuen, 1967.

Evelyn, John. *A Character of London...* London, 1659.

——. *Fumifugium...* London, 1661.

——. *Silva.* London, 1706.

——. *Elysium Britannicum, or the Royal Gardens.* Ed. John E. Ingram. Philadelphia: University of Pennsylvania Press, 2001.

Extraordinary Monyes paid into the Receipt of his Maiesties Exchequer, since the beginning of His Reigne, till Aprill 1635. London, 1643.

Fairchild, Thomas. *The City Gardener: Containing the Most Experienced Method of Cultivating and Ordering Such Ever-Greens, Fruit-Tress, Flowering Shrubs, Flowers, Exotick Plants, &C., as Will Be Ornamental, and Thrive Best in the London Gardens.* London, 1722.

Fiennes, Celia. *Through England on a Side Saddle in the Time of William and Mary.* London: Field and Tuer, 1888.

Finch, M. E. *The Wealth of Five Northamptonshire Families, 1540–1640.* Oxford: Printed for the Northamptonshire Record Society at Oxford University Press, 1956.

Fitter, Christopher. "'Native Soil': The Rhetoric of Exile Lament and Exile Consolation in *Paradise Lost.*" *Milton Studies* 20 (1984).

Flinn, Michael W. "The Growth of the English Iron Industry: 1660–1760." *Economic History Review* 11.1 (1958).

——. "Timber and the Advance of Technology: A Reconsideration." *Annals of Science* 15.2 (1959).

Fowler, Alastair. "The Beginning of English Georgic." In *Renaissance Genres.* Ed. Barbara Kiefer Lewalski. Cambridge, MA: Harvard University Press, 1986.

——. *The Country House Poem: A Cabinet of Seventeenth-Century Estate Poems and Related Items.* Edinburgh: Edinburgh Press, 1994.

Frederick, Duke of Wirtemberg. *England as Seen by Foreigners in the Days of Elizabeth and James the First...* Intro. and trans. by William Brenchley Rye. London: J. R. Smith, 1865.

Friedman, Donald. *Marvell's Pastoral Art.* London: Routledge, 1970.

Fuller, Thomas. *The History of the University of Cambridge.* London, 1840.

Gardener, Eileen. *Visions of Heaven and Hell before Dante.* New York: Italica Press, 1989.

Gaskell, Elizabeth. *Mary Barton.* London: John Lehmann, 1947.

Geller, L. D. *Pilgrims in Eden: Conservation Policies at New Plymouth, New England.* Wakefield, MA: Pride Publications, 1974.

Gernon, Luke. *A Discourse on Ireland.* In *Elizabethan Ireland: A Selection of Writings by Elizabethan Writers on Ireland.* Ed. James P. Myers. Hamden, Connecticut: Archon Books, 1966.

Giamatti, A. Bartlett. *The Earthly Paradise and the Renaissance Epic.* Princeton: Princeton, 1966.

Gifford, Terry. *Pastoral, The New Critical Idiom.* London: Routledge, 1999.

Giraldus. *Expurgnatio Hibernica.* Ed. T. W. Moody et al. Kildare: Royal Irish Academy, 1978.

Glapthorne, Henry. *The Lady Mother.* Oxford: Oxford University Press, 1958.

Gomme, Sir Laurence. *The Making of London.* London: 1912.

Graunt, John. *Natural and Political Observations ... with reference to the Government, Religion, Trade, Growth, Air, Diseases, and the several Changes of the said City.* In *The Economic Writings of Sir William Petty.* Ed. Charles Henry Hull Cambridge, 1899.

Guiney, Louise Imogen, Geoffrey Bliss, and Edward O'Brien. *Recusant Poets.* New York: Sheed and Ward, 1939.

H. C. *A Discourse Concerning the Drayning of the Fennes ...* London, 1629.

Hadfield, Andrew. *Edmund Spenser's Irish Experience: Wilde Fruit and Salvage Soyle.* Oxford: Clarendon, 1997.

Hakluyt, Richard. *The Original Writings and Correspondence of the Two Richard Hakluyts.* Intro. E.G.R. Taylor. London: Printed for the Hakluyt Society, 1935.

Halliwell-Phillipps, James Orchard. *The Marriage of Wit and Wisdom: An Ancient Interlude.* London, 1853.

Harcrow, E. M. "The Decline of Demesne Farming on the Estates of Durham Cathedral Priority." *Economic History Review,* ser. 2, 7 (1955).

Hardie, Philip R. *Vergil, Critical Assessments of Classical Authors.* In *Routledge Critical Assessments of Classical Authors.* London: Routledge, 1999.

Hardin, Richard F. *Michael Drayton and the Passing of Elizabethan England.* Lawrence: University Press of Kansas, 1973.

Harrison, Robert Pogue. *Forests: The Shadow of Civilization.* Chicago: University of Chicago Press, 1992.

Harrison, William. *The Description of England.* London, 1577.

Hartlib, Samuel. *A Discoverie for Division or Setting Out of Land.* London, 1653.

Hatcher, John. *Plague, Population, and the English Economy, 1348–1500.* London: Macmillan, 1977.

——. *The History of the British Coal Industry.* Oxford: Clarendon Press, 1993.

Havens, Raymond Dexter. *The Influence of Milton on English Poetry.* New York: Russell and Russell, 1961.

Heidegger, Martin. "Building Dwelling Thinking." In *Poetry, Language, Thought.* Trans. Albert Hofstadter. New York: Harper and Row, 1971.

——. "The Origin of the Work of Art." In *Poetry, Language, Thought.* Trans. Albert Hofstadter. New York: Harper and Row, 1971.

——. *The Question Concerning Technology.* Trans. William Lovitt New York: Harper and Row, 1977.

Helgerson, Richard. *Forms of Nationhood: The Elizabethan Writing of England.* Chicago: University of Chicago Press, 1992.

Herrick, Robert. *The Poetical Works of Robert Herrick.* Ed. F. W. Moorman. London: Oxford University Press, 1951.

Hesiod. *Hesiod, the Homeric Hymns, and Homerica.* Loeb Classical Library. Trans. H. G. Evelyn-White. Cambridge, MA: Harvard University Press, 1914.

Higden, Ranulph. *Polychronicon Ranulphi Higden...* Trans. John Trevisa. Ed. Churchill Babington. London, 1874.

Hill, Christopher. *The Collected Essays of Christopher Hill.* Brighton, Sussex: Harvester Press, 1985.

Hiltner, Ken. "A Defense of Milton's Environmentalism." *English Language Notes* 40.3 (March 2003).

———. *Milton and Ecology.* Cambridge: Cambridge University Press, 2003.

———. "Ripeness: Thoreau's Critique of Technological Modernity." In *The Concord Saunterer.* Special *Walden* Sesquicentennial Issue, Ed. Richard J. Schneider and Laura Dassow Walls. Concord: Walden Society, 2004.

———. "'Belch'd fire and rowling smoke': Air Pollution in *Paradise Lost.*" In *Milton, Rights and Liberties.* Essays from the Eighth International Milton Conference. Eds. Christophe Tournu and Neil Forsyth. New York: Peter Lang, 2006.

———. "Renaissance Literature and Our Contemporary Attitude toward Global Warming." *Interdisciplinary Studies in Literature and the Environment* 16.3 (summer 2009).

———. "Early Modern Ecology." In *A Companion to English Renaissance Literature and Culture.* Oxford: Blackwell, 2010.

———. "Nature." In *The Princeton Encyclopedia of Poetry and Poetics.* Princeton: Princeton, University Press, 2011.

Homer. *Odyssey.* Loeb Classical Library. Trans. A. T. Murray. Cambridge, MA: Harvard University Press, 1919.

Horace. *Horace. The Odes and Epodes, with an English Translation.* Loeb Classical Library. Trans. Charles E. Bennett. London: W. Heinemann, 1929.

Hubbard, Thomas K. *The Pipes of Pan: Intertextuality and Literary Filiation in the Pastoral Tradition from Theocritus to Milton.* Ann Arbor: University of Michigan Press, 1998.

Hughes, Ann. *Conflict in Early Stuart England: Studies in Religion and Politics, 1603–1642.* London: Longman, 1989.

Huhn, Tom. Introduction to *The Cambridge Companion to Adorno.* Ed. Tom Huhn. Cambridge: Cambridge University Press, 2004.

Jeudwine, John W. *The Foundations of Society and the Land.* New York: Arno Press, 1975.

Johnson, Samuel. *Lives of the Poets.* New York: Scribner, 1896.

Jonson, Ben. *Ben Jonson.* Ed. C. H. Herford and Percy Simpson. Oxford: Clarendon Press, 1925–.

Kegel-Brinkgreve, E. *The Echoing Woods: Bucolic and Pastoral from Theocritus to Wordsworth.* Amsterdam: J. C. Gieben, 1990.

Kemp, Anne. *A Contemplation on Basset's Hill.* London, 1658?

Kermode, Frank. *English Pastoral Poetry: From the Beginnings to Marvell* London: G. G. Harrap, 1952.

Kerridge, Richard. "Environmentalism and Ecocriticism." *Literary Theory and Criticism: An Oxford Guide.* Oxford: Oxford University Press, 2006.

Killigrew, William. *An Answer to such Objections as were made by some Commoners of Lincoln-shire...Concerning the Draining of those Fenns which lye between Lincoln, Berne, & Boston.* London, 1647.

Landers, John. *The Field and the Forge: Population, Production, and Power in the Pre-Industrial West.* Oxford: Oxford University Press, 2003.

Lanyer, Amelia. *The Poems of Aemilia Lanyer: Salve Deus Rex Judaeorum.* Ed. Susanne Woods. Oxford: Oxford University Press, 1993.

Leland, John. *John Leland's Itinerary: Travels in Tudor England.* Ed. John Chandler. Phoenix Mill, England: Alan Sutton, 1993.

Lewalski, Barbara K. *Paradise Lost and the Rhetoric of Literary Forms.* Princeton: Princeton University Press, 1985.

———. *Writing Women in Jacobean England.* Cambridge, MA: Harvard University Press, 1993.

Lilburne, John. *The Case of the Tenants of the Mannor of Epworth in the Isle of Axholm in the County of Lincoln...* London, 1651.

Lindheim, Nancy. "Spenser's Vergilian Pastoral: The Case for September." *Spenser Studies* 11 (1994).

Lindley, Keith. *Fenland Riots and the English Revolution.* London: Heinemann, 1982.

Lipsius, Justus, John Stradling, Rudolf Kirk, and Clayton Morris Hall. *Tvvo Bookes of Constancie.* New Brunswick, NJ: Rutgers University Press, 1939.

Lloyd, T. H. *The English Wool Trade in the Middle Ages.* Cambridge: Cambridge University Press, 1977.

Lodge, Edmund. *Illustrations of British History, Biography, and Manners, in the Reigns of Henry VIII. Edward VI, Mary, Elizabeth, & James I...* Vol. 3. London, 1838.

Low, Anthony. *The Georgic Revolution.* Princeton: Princeton University Press, 1985.

Maccarthy-Morrogh, Michael. *The Munster Plantation: English Migration to Southern Ireland, 1583–1641.* Oxford, Clarendon, 1986.

Manley, Lawrence. *London in the Age of Shakespeare: An Anthology.* London: Croom Helm, 1986.

Manning, Brian. *The English People and the English Revolution.* London: Bookmarks, 1991.

Marinelli, Peter. V. *Pastoral: The Critical Idiom.* London: Methuen, 1971.

Martin, John. *An Atlas of Rural Protest in Britain, 1548–1900.* Ed. Andrew Charlesworth. Philadelphia: University of Pennsylvania Press, 1983.

Marvel, Andrew. *The Poems of Andrew Marvell.* Ed. Nigel Smith. London: Pearson Longman, 2003.

The Works of Andrew Marvell. Eds. T. Cooke and T. Hollis. London, 1726.

Maynard, Sir John. *The Picklock of the Old Fenne Project.* London, 1650.

McColley, Diane. *Milton's Eve.* Urbana: University of Illinois Press, 1983.

———. "Beneficent Hierarchies: Reading Milton Greenly." In *Spokesperson Milton: Voices in Contemporary Criticism.* Eds. C. W. Durham and K. P. McColgan. Selinsgrove, PA: Susquehanna University Press, 1994.

———. "Milton and Ecology." In *A Companion to Milton: Blackwell Companions to Literature and Culture.* Ed. T. N. Corns. Oxford: Blackwell, 2001.

———. *Poetry and Ecology in the Age of Milton and Marvell.* Surrey, UK: Ashgate, 2008.

McRae, Andrew. *God Speed the Plough: The Representation of Agrarian England, 1500–1660*. Cambridge: Cambridge University Press, 1996.

——. *The Writing of Rural England, 1500–1800*. New York: Macmillan, 2003.

Memmi, Albert. *Portrait du Colonisé précédé du Portrait du Colonisateur.* Paris: Buchet/Chastel, 1957.

——. *The Colonizer and the Colonized*. Trans. Howard Greenfield. Boston: Orion Press, 1965.

Merchant, Carolyn. *The Death of Nature: Women, Ecology, and the Scientific Revolution.* San Francisco: Harper & Row, 1980.

Milton, John. *The Riverside Milton*. Ed. R. Flannagan. Boston: Houghton Mifflin, 1998.

Misson, Henri. *Misson's Memoirs and Observations in His Travels over England*. In *1700: Scenes from London Life*. Ed. Maureen Waller. London: Hodder & Stoughton, 2000.

Moore, Sir Jonas. *The History or Narrative of the Great Level of the Fenns, Called Bedford Level...* London, 1685.

Moryson, Fynes. *Shakespeare's Europe*. Ed. Charles Hughes. London: Skerratt and Hughes, 1903.

Murphy, Andrew. *But the Irish Sea Betwixt Us: Ireland, Colonialism, and Renaissance Literature*. Lexington: University of Kentucky Press, 1999.

Nef, John. *The Rise of the British Coal Industry*. London: G. Routledge, 1932.

——. "Coal Mining and Utilization," *A History of Technology*. Ed. Charles Joseph Singer. Oxford: Clarendon Press, 1956.

O'Hehir, Brendan. *Harmony from Discord: A Life of Sir John Denham*. Berkeley: University of California Press, 1968.

——. *Expans'd Hieroglyphicks: A Critical Edition of Sir John Denham's* Cooper's Hill. Berkeley: University of California Press, 1969.

Ovid. *Metamorphoses I*. Loeb Classical Library. Ed. F. J. Miller Cambridge, MA: Harvard University Press, 1960.

Owen, George. *The Description of Pembrokeshire*. Ed. Dillwyn Miles. Llandysul, Wales: Gomer Press, 1994.

Patterson, Annabel. *Pastoral and Ideology: Vergil to Valery*. Berkeley: University of California Press, 1987.

Peart, Shirley Adawy. *English Images of the Irish, 1570–1620*. Lewiston, NY: Edwin Mellen Press, 2002.

Perlin, John. *A Forest Journey: The Role of Wood in the Development of Civilization*. New York: W. W. Norton, 1989.

Petrarch, Franciscus. *De Vita Solitaria (The Life of Solitude)*. Trans. Jacob Zeitlin. Urbana: University of Illinois Press, 1924.

——. *Petrarch's Bucolicum Carmen*. Trans. Thomas Goddard Bergin. New Haven, CT: Yale University Press, 1974.

——. *Rerum Familiarium Libri, I–Viii*. Trans. Aldo S. Bernardo. Albany, NY: State University of New York Press, 1975.

——. *Letters on Familiar Matters: Rerum familiarium libri IX-XVI*. Trans. Aldo S. Bernardo Baltimore: Johns Hopkins University Press, 1982.

Pettet, E. C. "*Coriolanus* and the Midlands Insurrection of 1607." *Shakespeare Survey* 3 (1950).

Platter, Thomas. *Travels in England.* London, 1599.

Poggioli, R. *The Oaten Flute: Essays on Pastoral Poetry and the Pastoral Ideal.* Cambridge, MA: Harvard University Press, 1975.

Pope, Alexander. *Selected Poetry and Prose.* Ed. Robin Sowerby. London, New York: Routledge, 1988.

Prest, John. *The Garden of Eden: The Botanic Garden and the Re-Creation of Paradise.* New Haven, CT: Yale University Press: 1981.

Putnam, Michael C. J. *Vergil's Pastoral Art: Studies in the Eclogues.* Princeton: Princeton University Press, 1970.

Puttenham, Richard. *The Arte of English Poesie.* London, 1589.

Raleigh, Sir Walter. *The Discovery of the Large, Rich, and Beautiful...* New York: Franklin, 1970.

———. *The Poems of Sir Walter Raleigh: A Historical Edition.* Ed. M. Rudick. Tempe: Arizona Center for Medieval and Renaissance Studies, 1999.

Rambo, Elizabeth L. *Colonial Ireland in Medieval English Literature.* Selinsgrove, PA: Susquehanna University Press, 1994.

Randall, Thomas. *Poems.* Oxford, 1638.

Reay, Barry. *Popular Cultures in England, 1550–1750.* London: Longman, 1998.

Reddaway, T. F. *The Rebuilding of London after the Great Fire.* London: Edward Arnold, 1951.

Rees, William. *Industry before the Industrial Revolution: Incorporating a Study of the Chartered Companies of the Society of Mines Royal and of Mineral and Battery Works.* Cardiff: University of Wales Press, 1968.

Riggs, David. *Ben Jonson: A Life.* Cambridge, MA: Harvard University Press, 1989.

Ross, Alexander. *Three Decades of Diuine Meditations... With a Commendation of the Priuate Countery Life.* London, 1630.

Røstvig, Maren-Sofie. *The Happy Man: Studies in the Metamorphoses of a Classical Ideal.* Oslo: Akademisk forlag, 1954.

Rudrum, Alan. *The Broadview Anthology of Seventeenth-Century Verse and Prose.* Ed. Alan Rudrum et al. Ontario: Broadview, 2000.

Rural Recreations. London, 1688.

Russell, Conrad. *Parliaments and English Politics, 1621–1629.* Oxford: Oxford University Press, 1979.

S [mith], J [ohn]. *The Lyric Poet, Odes, and Satyres Translated out of Horace into English Verse.* London, 1649.

Said. Edward. *Culture and Imperialism.* London: Vintage, 1993.

Sartre, Jean-Paul. Introduction to *The Colonizer and the Colonized.* By Albert Memmi. Trans. Howard Greenfield. Boston: Orion Press, 1965.

Savage, John Joseph Hannan. *The Manuscripts of Servius's Commentary on Vergil.* S.l.: s.n., 1934.

Scaliger, Giulio Cesare, and Frederick Morgan Padelford. *Select Translations from Scaliger's Poetics.* New York: H. Holt, 1905.

Schiller, Friedrich. "On Naïve and Sentimental Poetry." In *German Aesthetic and Literary Criticism: Winckelmann, Lessing, Hamann, Herder, Schiller, Goethe.* Ed. Hugh Barr Nisbet. Cambridge: Cambridge University Press, 1985.

Schubert, John Rudolph Theodore. *History of the British Iron and Steel Industry from C. 450 B.C. to A.D. 1775.* London: Routledge, 1957.

Sessions, George. "Ecocentrism and the Anthropocentric Detour." In *Deep Ecology for the Twenty-First Century.* Ed. George Sessions. Boston: Shambhala Press, 1995.

Sessions, William. "Spenser's Georgics." *England Literary Renaissance* 10 (1980).

Shepard, Paul. "Ecology and Man—A Viewpoint." In *Deep Ecology for the Twenty-First Century.* Ed. George Sessions. Boston: Shambhala Press, 1995.

Sidney, Philip. *An Apology for Poetry; or, the Defence of Poesy.* Ed. Geoffrey Shepherd. London: T. Nelson, 1965.

——. *The Countess of Pembroke's Arcadia.* Ed. K. Duncan-Jones. Oxford: Oxford University Press, 1985.

Snell, Bruno. *The Discovery of the Mind: The Greek Origins of European Thought.* Oxford: Blackwell, 1953.

Spenser, Edmund. *A View of the Present State of Ireland.* Ed. W. L. Renwick. London: E. Partridge, 1934.

——. *The Yale Edition of the Shorter Poems of Edmund Spenser.* Ed. W. A. Oram. New Haven, CT: Yale University Press, 1989.

——. *Fairie Queen.* Ed. A. C. Hamilton et al. Harlow, UK: Pearson Education, 2001.

Standish, Arthur. *The Commons' Complaint.* London, 1611.

Stopes, C. C. *The Life of Henry, Third Earl of Southampton: Shakespeare's Patron.* Cambridge: Cambridge University Press, 1922.

Stow, John. *The Annales, or, Generall Chronicle of England.* London, 1598, 1615, 1631.

Summers, Dorothy. *The Great Level: A History of Drainage and Land Reclamation in the Fens.* London: Newton Abbot, 1976.

Taylor, Christopher. *Fields in the English Landscape.* London: J. M. Dent, 1975.

Taylor, John. *Taylor on the Thames.* London, 1632.

——. *Travels through Stuart Britain: The Adventures of John Taylor, the Water Poet.* Stroud, UK: Sutton, 1999.

Taylor, Sylvanus. *Common Good; or the Improvement of Commons, Forests, and Chases by Enclosure.* London, 1653.

Theis, Jeffery S. "The Environmental Ethics of *Paradise Lost:* Milton's Exegesis of Genesis I–III." *Milton Studies* 34 (1996).

Theocritus. *Idylls* in *The Greek Bucolic Poets.* Loeb Classical Library. Eds. J. M. Edmonds et al. Cambridge, MA: Harvard University Press, 1950.

Thirsk, Joan. *Economic Policy and Projects: The Development of Consumer Society in Early-modern England.* Oxford: Clarendon, 1978.

——. *Alternative Agriculture: A History from the Black Death to the Present Day.* Oxford: Oxford University Press, 1997.

——. *The English Rural Landscape.* Ed. Joan Thirsk. Oxford: Oxford University Press, 2000.

Thirsk, Joan, and J. P. Cooper. *Seventeenth-Century Economic Documents.* Oxford: Clarendon Press, 1972.

Thomas, Keith. *Man and the Natural World: Changing Attitudes in England, 1500–1800.* London: Allen Lane, 1983.

Thompson, E. P. *The Making of the English Working Class.* London: Camelot, 1963.

Thomson, James, and J. Logie Robertson. *The Complete Poetical Works of James Thom-son*. London: Oxford University Press, 1908.

Thoreau, Henry David. *Walden*. Ed. J. Lyndon Shanley. Princeton: Princeton University Press, 1971.

Turner, James. *The Politics of Landscape: Rural Scenery and Society in English Poetry, 1630–1660*. Oxford: Blackwell, 1979.

Tusser, Thomas. *Five Hundred Points of Good Husbandry*. London, 1580.

Varro, Marcus Terentius. *Libri de re rustica, M. Catonis, Marci Terentii Varronis, L. Iunii Moderati Columellae, Palladii Rutilii, quorum pagina seque[n]ti reperies*. Paris, 1533.

———. *On Agriculture*. Loeb Classical Library. Cambridge, MA: Harvard University Press, 1934.

Vaughan, Henry. *The Complete Poems of Henry Vaughan*. Penguin English Poets. Ed. Alan Rudrum. Harmondsworth: Baltimore: Penguin, 1976.

Vermuyden, Sir Cornelius. *A Discourse Touching the Drayning of the Fennes*. London, 1642.

Virgil. *Eclogues* and *Georgics*. Loeb Classical Library. Eds. H. R. Fairclough and G. P. Goold. Cambridge, MA: Harvard University Press, 1999.

Waldstein, Baron. *The Diary of Baron Waldstein: A Traveller in Elizabethan London*. Trans. and annotated by G. W. Groos. London: Thames and Hudson, 1981.

Walton, John K. "Proto-Industrialization and the First Industrial Revolution: The Case of Lancashire." in *Regions and Industries*. Ed. Pat Hudson. Cambridge: Cambridge University Press, 1989.

Warwick, Sir Philip. *Memoirs of the Reign of King Charles I . . .* London, 1701.

Watson, Robert. *Back to Nature: The Green and the Real in the Late Renaissance*. Philadelphia: University of Pennsylvania Press, 2006.

Wheeler, W. H. *A History of the Fens of South Lincolnshire, Being a Description of the Rivers Witham and Welland and Their Estuary, and an Account of the Reclamation, Drainage, and Enclosure of the Fens Adjacent Thereto*. London: J. M. Newcomb, 1897.

White, Lynn Jr. "The Historical Roots of Our Ecological Crisis." In *The Ecocriticism Reader: Landmarks in Literary Ecology*. Eds. C. Glotfelty and H. Fromm. Athens: University of Georgia Press, 1996.

Whitman, Walt. "Song of Myself," from *Leaves of Grass*. Brooklyn, N.Y. [s.n.], 1855.

Wilkinson, Robert. *A Sermon Preached at North-Hampton the 21. Of June Last Past, before the Lord Lieutenant of the County, and the Rest of the Commissioners There Assembled Vpon Occasion of the Late Rebellion and Riot in Those Parts Committed*. London, 1607.

Williams, Laura. "To recreate and refresh their dulled spirits in the sweete and wholesome ayre: Green Space and the Growth of the City." In *Imagining Early-modern London: Perceptions and Portrayals of the City from Stow to Stype, 1598–1720*. Ed. J. F. Merritt. Cambridge: Cambridge University Press, 2001.

Williams, Raymond. *The Country and the City*. London: Chatto and Windus, 1973.

———. *Keywords: A Vocabulary of Culture and Society*. Rev. ed. New York: Oxford University Press, 1983.

Wilson, Arthur. *The History of Great Britain . . .* London, 1653.

Winstanley, Gerrard. *The Works of Gerrard Winstanley*. Ed. George E. Sabine. New York: Russell and Russell, 1965.

Wood, Eric S. *Historical Britain: A Comprehensive Account of the Development of Rural and Urban Life and Landscape from Prehistory to the Present Day.* London: Harvill Press, 1995.

Youings, Joyce. "The Church." In *The Agrarian History of England and Wales.* Ed. Joan Thirsk. Cambridge: Cambridge University Press, 1967.

Zacour, Norman P. *Petrarch's Book without a Name: A Translation of the Liber Sine Nomine.* Toronto: The Pontifical Institute of Mediaeval Studies, 1973.

Zagorin, Perez. *The Court and the Country: The Beginning of the English Revolution.* London: Routledge & K. Paul, 1969.

Zagorin, Perez, et al. *Court, Country, and Culture: Essays on Early-modern British History in Honor of Perez Zagorin.* Rochester: University of Rochester Press, 1992.

Zell, Michael. *Industry in the Countryside: Wealden Society in the Sixteenth Century.* Cambridge: Cambridge University Press, 1994.

Index